THE AMERICAN REVOLUTION:
MIRROR OF A PEOPLE

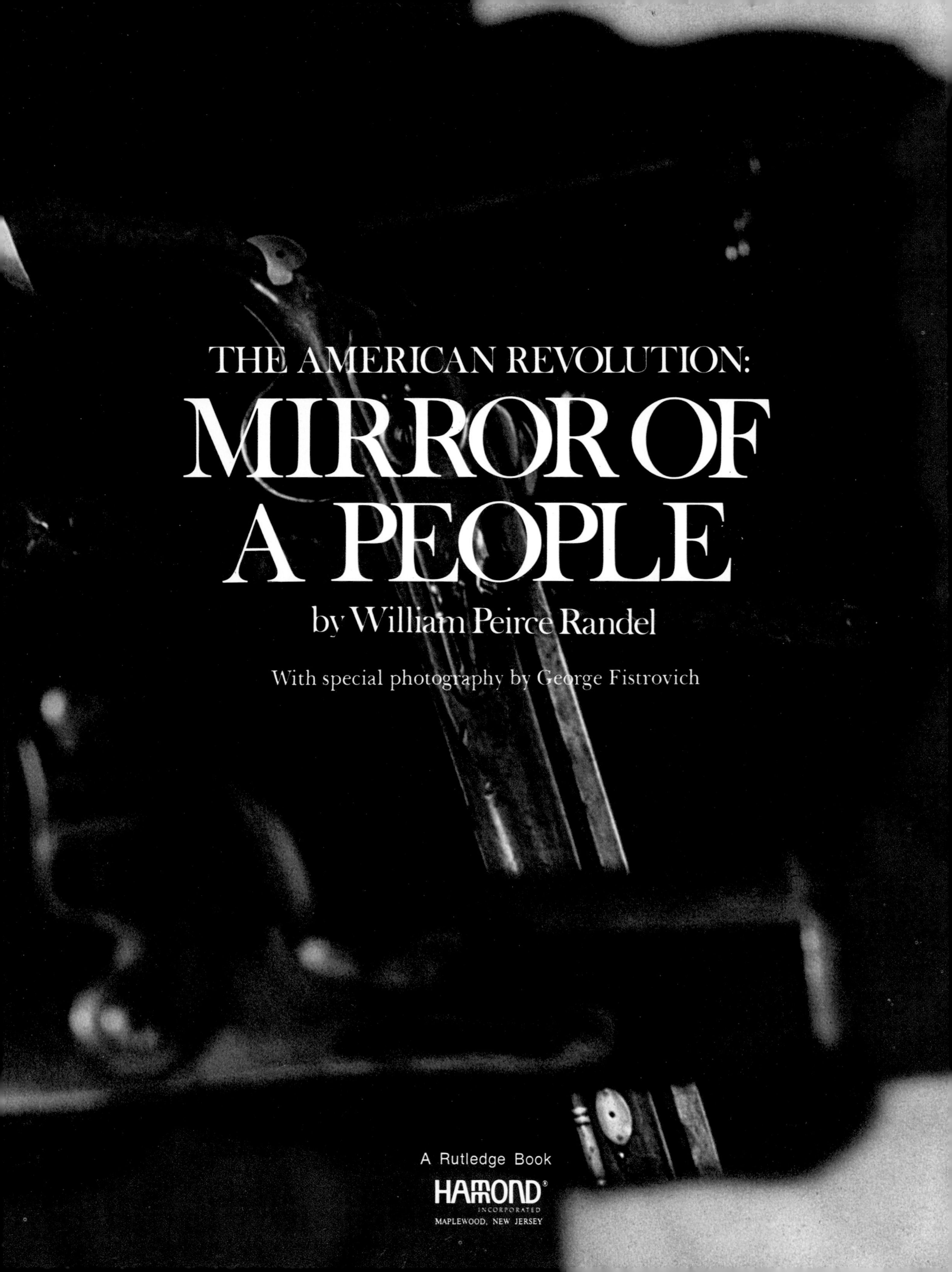

THE AMERICAN REVOLUTION:

MIRROR OF A PEOPLE

by William Peirce Randel

With special photography by George Fistrovich

A Rutledge Book

HAMMOND®
INCORPORATED
MAPLEWOOD, NEW JERSEY

Fred R. Sammis: *Publisher*
John T. Sammis: *Associate Publisher*
Doris Townsend: *Editor-in-Chief*
George Riemer: *Consulting Editor*
Allan Mogel: *Art Director*
Jeanne McClow: *Managing Editor*
Jeremy Friedlander: *Associate Editor*
Gwen Evrard: *Associate Art Director*
Joan Scafarello: *Art Editor*
Arthur Gubernick: *Production Consultant*
Penny Post: *Production Manager*
Margaret Riemer: *Editorial Assistant*
Sally Andrews: *Editorial Assistant*

Library of Congress Catalog Card Number 72-82982
ISBN: 0-8437-3729-8
Prepared and produced by Rutledge Books, 17 East 45th
Street, New York, N.Y. 10017
Published in 1973 by Hammond Incorporated, Maplewood, N. J.

Printed in Italy by Mondadori, Verona

For the descendants of Rebecca Jane Hosmer Belknap, 1846–1936

Contents

Preface 9

1. **Trouble in a Land of Plenty** 11
   "Very unfit for and very impatient for
     war"
   The American image

2. **"What Is the American, This New Man?"** 19
   Where they lived
   Where they came from
   Americans by force
   Americans in bondage
   "Doers, planners, achievers"

3. **The American Life—Cradle to Grave** 39
   "The 'borning-room' "
   Colonial schooling
   "Good boys at their books"
   Schooling in the South
   College—for the few
   Love and marriage
   Food in abundance

"To ward off chills and malarial fevers"
Diversions and entertainments
Holidays and festivals
"An acquisitive age"
"Living—and staying alive"
"Watering places"
"The universal gamble"
Crime—and punishment
Last rites

4. **Rural Americans** 107
   A self-sufficient people
   Farmers—competent and not?
   To market, to market
   "Worse ploughing is no where to be
     seen"
   "Tobacco was the villain"
   "Factories in the field"
   "A country industry"
   Wealth from the sea
   Spinners and weavers

5. **Urban Americans** 143
Wealth in the cities
"Country work, country pay"
Women's work
The colonial Big Five
Problems in the cities
The oldest, the smallest
Ben Franklin's city
Cities in the South
Writers and their readers
Master builders
"Everyday objects of grace and beauty"
Painters and their patrons
The stage, the players
The moral opera
Music everywhere
The learned professions

6. **Spreading the Word** 203
Getting from here to there
"Six days, Boston to New York"
"Their appointed rounds"

Freedom of the press
The printer as educator
By word of mouth

7. **The Sizzling Fuse** 219
The price of loyalty
Massacre and Tea Party
On the alert
Twilight of the governors
Government in transition

8. **The People's War** 231
Militia and Minute Men
Two ways of waging war
Weapons and defenses
"Don't one of you fire . . ."
The quality of generalship
Call to arms
Life in time of crisis
"When peace yielded to war"

Index 249
Credits 256

Preface

Until about 1900, history as it was found in books pretty much ignored the ordinary facts about life in the past. Wars and politics and Great Men got most of the attention; how the people lived didn't seem to count. One reason was the notion, begun by the Puritans and holding on well into the nineteenth century, that our history is no more and no less than the unfolding of a great divine plan. Not to emphasize the major events in this unfolding, and the men chosen to direct those events, smacked vaguely of heresy.

In 1826, for example, John Adams and Thomas Jefferson died on the Fourth of July, a few hours apart. Instead of viewing this as an astonishing coincidence, as we would today, a great many Americans took it as a heavenly sign of continuing divine interest. For these two men, besides serving as our second and third presidents, had been principal authors of the Declaration of Independence. By the centennial year of 1876, when there were no living former presidents to die off at auspicious moments, all the leaders in the struggle for independence had been promoted to demigods. Hero worship was at its peak. Interest in the ordinary life of 1776 took the form of contempt for its limitations and pity for the unfortunates who had endured such conditions.

The next fifty years produced a radical change in attitude. The mood of the 1920s, blasé and irreverent, made a fiasco of the sesquicentennial in 1926 and encouraged the debunking biographies that cut down to size one national hero after another: Who could go on revering a famous man after reading about his badly fitting false teeth, his hair-trigger profanity or his shady dealings in real estate? This debunking impulse, which barely survived the decade, was an odd offshoot of the social history movement. It was not really necessary to drag great men from their pedestals and point out their frailties in order to turn attention to their humble contemporaries, but perhaps it gave the common man of the past the first real chance for recognition.

A balanced perspective, suitable to the spirit of the bicentennial, gives the great figures of 1776 all the credit they deserve and at the same time examines the common life of the time. What people did for a living, with what tools and what sources of energy, in what surroundings and for what personal goals, has a special appeal to men and women much less confident today that what they do has integrity. The uncrowded simplicity of two centuries ago, on this continent, may rouse more envy than pity or condescension; those Americans had something that has become rare. They lacked, of course, the modern gadgets we take for granted, but they had no sense of being deprived; most of them enjoyed a rich, full life within the limits that current technology permitted anywhere on earth. If their horizons were rather limited, their feeling of community was strong. If their drive to get ahead made them indifferent to intellectual and cultural values, they were spared much of what most disturbs us today. They had their own special problems, such as how to keep their children alive beyond age eight or ten. On balance, however, though it may not have been the best time in all history to be alive, it was far from being the worst.

Cold logic might give some other year more importance—1789, for example, when the Constitution took effect and the new nation began to function. But in American thinking, 1776 has a more electrifying significance, symbolizing as it does the ultimate expression of freedom. The intention of this book is not to make readers sorry they were not born two centuries earlier but simply to offer a sampling, in text and graphics, of what life was like in America in the period that produced the Declaration and established our independence.

Waterboro Old Corner
January 7, 1973

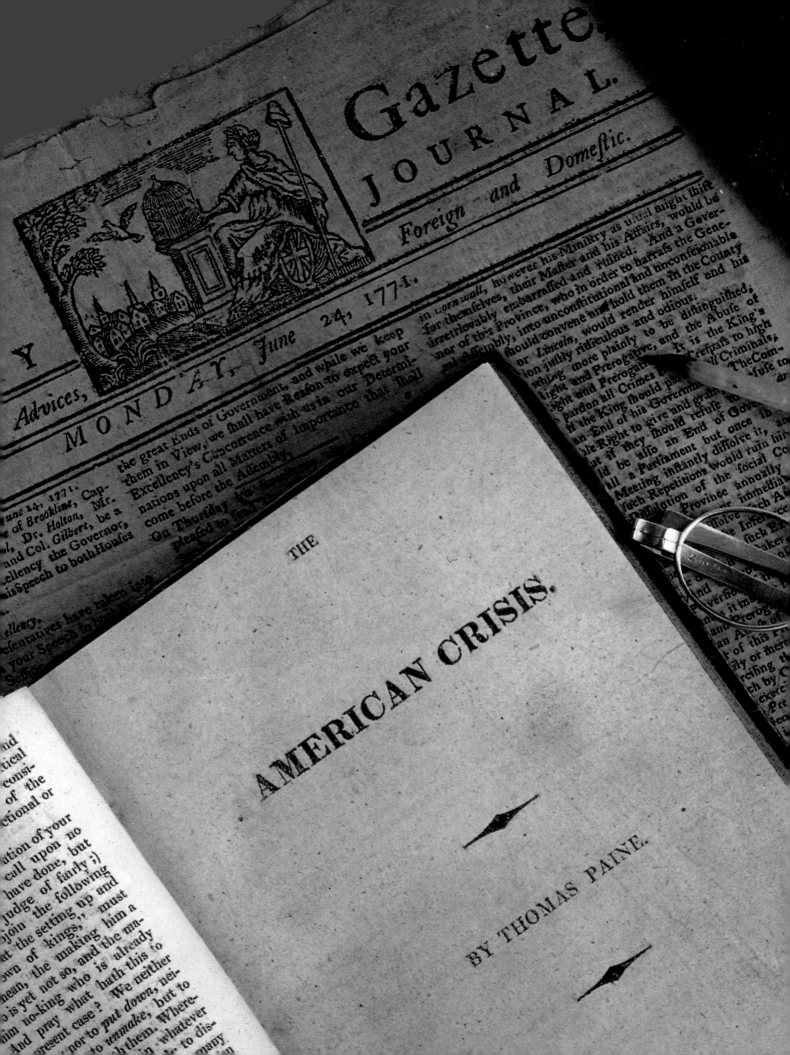

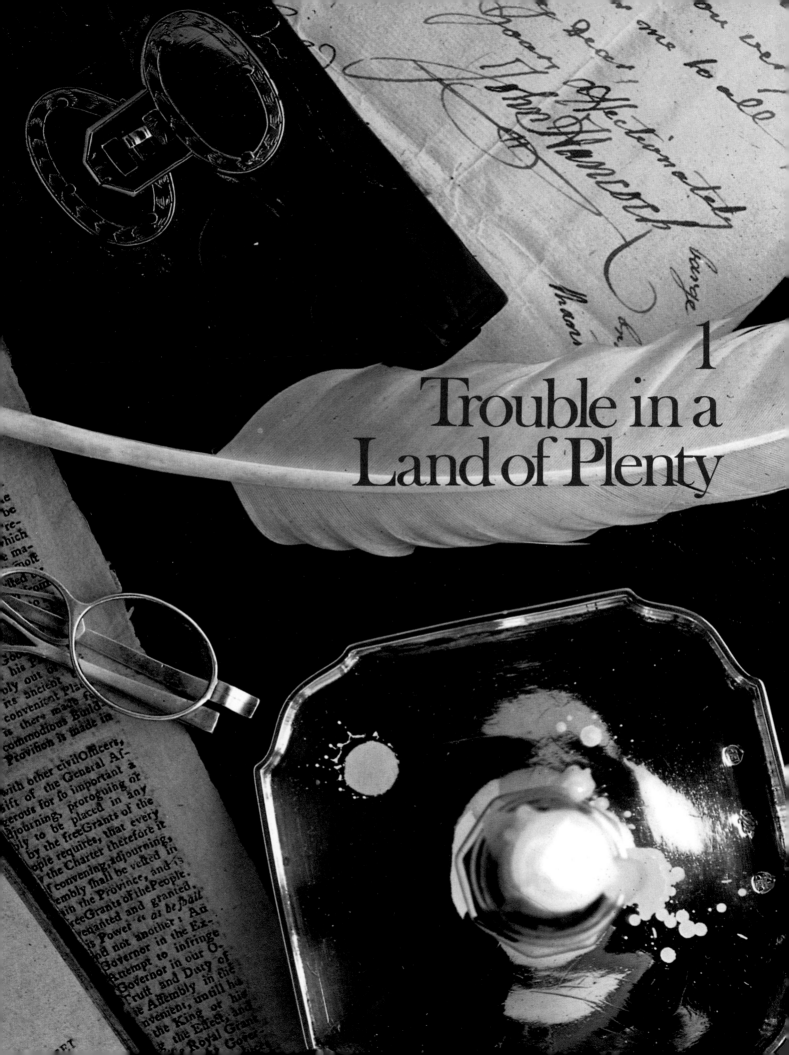

1
Trouble in a Land of Plenty

Men were riding hard that April night, all over Middlesex County, reining up at house after house to shout their grim warning and galloping off again into the darkness. A few of the riders were unlucky; one was Paul Revere, stopped by a British patrol just west of Lexington. But most got through, spurring their horses and spurred by the urgency. One who knew his way through Acton, the town beyond Concord, rode directly to the farm of Joseph Robbins, captain of a militia company. With a club he beat on the wall of the house, punctuating his message: "Up! Up! The Regulars have come to Concord. Rendezvous at Old North Bridge! Quick as possible. Alarm Acton!" These, at least, are the words as they were remembered later and as they were chiseled into a boulder, still standing, across the road from the Robbins farmhouse.

Nobody, however sound a sleeper, could have failed to hear; even the baby woke up and began to cry. Within minutes the captain was mounted and away, to round up his men, and John, his ten-year-old son, was astride the mare and headed for the Davis farm and others beyond. One stop was at Deacon Hosmer's, where there were three members of the new Minute Man company—Abner Hosmer and the two Blanchard boys, Calvin and Luther, who were learning the mason's trade from the deacon. Their father had been killed at Quebec, in the battle of 1759, and Johnny knew that they would not want to miss out on any action now.

At the Davis farm, a short walk by wood lanes and through an orchard, Abner and the Blanchards found the kitchen already crowded. Wives and sisters mingled with the men, urging them to eat and packing lunches of bread and meat and cheese for them. Isaac Davis—"Ike" to his friends but "Captain" to the recruits—was the calmest person there, moving from man to man inspecting muskets, filling

powder horns, doling out balls, shushing the excited talk of "getting a hit at old Gage." When thirty men had assembled, he said, the march would begin; but he hoped that fifty would turn out.

The sun was up when the Acton Minute Men formed ranks and marched to Acton Center and on toward the bridge at Concord; its rays caught the shock of red hair that made Abner conspicuous wherever he went. At one house or another along the route, latecomers fell into line, raising the number to forty. The fifer, Luther Blanchard, and Francis Barker, the drummer, set the pace with "The White Cockade."

At the crest of a hill they halted; they could look down on a British search party going through the buildings of Colonel Barrett's farm. Hidden there were cannon and gunpowder; would the Regulars think of looking in the great manure pile, just below the barn windows? Prudence dictating a detour, Davis chose a back road leading to the high ground north of the bridge, with a good view of Concord beyond the river. Men from

other towns kept arriving, by units and individually. Most of them knew the spot, for they had mustered there a few weeks before, on March 13.

Colonel Barrett had not been at home to greet the British search party. At the first alarm he had gone to the rendezvous site, where, as highest-ranking officer in the vicinity, he assigned positions to arriving companies and gathered their commanders around him in a council of war. Next to him in rank were Lieutenant Colonel Robinson of the Westford militia and Major Buttrick of the Concord Minute Men. The officers, if not the privates, hoped to avoid a collision. The munitions collected in recent weeks were all so cleverly hidden, they hoped, that the British were unlikely to find them and would, if left alone, abandon the search and return to Boston. The only cause for uneasiness was the presence of a small body of redcoats, three companies at most, on the causeway below the muster hill and on the same side of the river; but they gave no sign of wanting an engagement.

Nothing at all might have happened at the

bridge that clear spring morning had not the provincials noticed smoke rising from the village. The British, apparently, were burning Concord! It was enough to galvanize the provincial officers; they could not stand there idly and let the village burn. Captain Davis said to Major Buttrick in a bold voice, "I haven't a man that's afraid to go." Thereupon, led by Buttrick, Robinson and Davis, the several companies began their march down the hill toward the bridge, with the Acton Minute Men first in line. Colonel Barrett, on his horse, almost as if reviewing the troops, said to each company as it passed, "Don't fire first."

The Regulars hastily drew back across the bridge to a position they could better hold. To slow the rebel advance, they began taking up planks, only to draw from Major Buttrick an angry order to leave the bridge alone. This prompted a scattering of British shots, one of which wounded the fifer, and then a volley. In their nervousness, the Regulars for the most part fired too high, but some shots were very well aimed. Abner Hosmer died instantly, shot through the left cheek, and Captain Davis, hit in the heart, leaped involuntarily and fell across the causeway. (Acton legend has it that even in death he clutched his gun so tightly that his fingers had to be pried loose from it.) Major Buttrick now gave the order to fire and, at the range of fifty to seventy-five yards, the rebel volley felled several of the Regulars, including four of the eight officers. One soldier was dead and another dying as the British withdrew, in some confusion. Luckily a colonel arrived with reinforcements, discouraging close pursuit that might have meant a pitched battle on the village green, where, it turned out, the burning of Concord was a bonfire of papers and furniture taken from the townhouse.

The bodies of Davis and Hosmer and that of a third Acton man killed later in the day were carried to the Davis home, where their funeral a few days later attracted a great crowd. The third man, James Hayward, had gotten as far as Lexington in the pursuit of the retreating British. The day was unusually warm for April and at Fiske's Hill, pausing to get a drink at a well, Hayward almost collided with a redcoat who lifted his gun and cried out, "You are a dead man!"

"So are you," Hayward answered, and the two men fired at the same moment. The English soldier died at once, the American several hours later, with his father at his side.

"Are you sorry you turned out?" Deacon Hayward asked.

For answer the son called for his powder horn and bullet pouch. "I started," he said, "with one pound of powder and forty balls. You see what is left. . . . I never did such a forenoon's work before. I am not sorry."

The sentiment was general among the Americans who took part in that first battle of the Revolution; not one of them ever had reason to regret it. Ten years earlier, firing at the British would have been unthinkable, the act of a madman, perhaps, or of an outlaw. It was still unthinkable to tens of thousands in the colonies who remained loyal to the Crown.

In those few years what had divided the population so sharply, making rebels of so many who had once been as loyal as the Loyalists now were? Defiance was recent, in reaction to harsh British measures; were the Americans really ready in 1775 to go it alone? And if they were, what can explain that readiness?

John Adams, late in life, insisted that the Revolution was complete, "in the minds of the people," before the fighting began. His statement forces us to distinguish between the Revolution as a social movement and the revolutionary war that followed

or completed it. Both are facts of history, or parts of the same fact. By 1775, the rebels must have sensed that they had the wealth, the technology and the administrative ability not only to govern themselves but to force the British out. The British government, clearly, did not share the rebel belief and in any event was not ready to abandon its right to rule or to lose its American possessions. The big question in 1775 was therefore which side had the greater strength, in this clash of wills.

News of the Concord fight, spreading slowly down through the colonies, set off a whole battery of responses. Hotheaded rebels were exhilarated, impatient for a piece of the action. Loyalists were jolted; for them the prospect was ominous, for they had much to lose if rebellion spread. Tradesmen straining for greater income were also worried, for a general war might throw all into chaos. Scheming entrepreneurs had sudden dreams of military contracts and fat profits. Men with little property, barred from voting or running for office, were encouraged: The dislocation of spreading war might topple the privileged classes and lead to a broader sharing of political power. Thoughtful men, like Deacon Hosmer, cautious by principle but firm in opposing arbitrary government, could not avoid weighing the situation. A man facing death sees life in new perspective; a country on the verge of open violence has a new vision of reality. The action at Concord became a challenge to the bold and the apprehensive alike.

"Very Unfit for and Very Impatient for War"

General Gage, in his dual capacity of Massachusetts governor and commander of His Majesty's forces in North America, was more aware of colonial actualities than his superiors in London, who rejected his urgent pleas for more troops. But he took many of

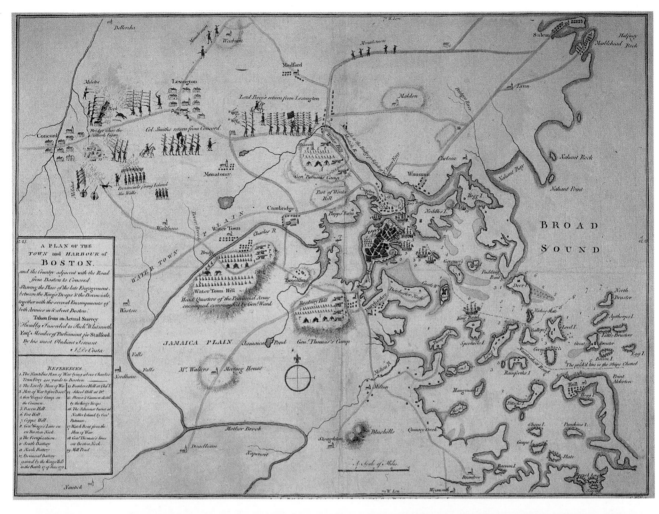

his cues from the Loyalists in Boston, who viewed the hinterland as a cultural desert without the resources for organized resistance. Other generals, in other port cities the British occupied in the course of the war, maintained this image of the rebels as being yokels, in an extension of the common European attitude toward peasants or innocuous rustics. Without control of the cities, the British were confident, the rebels would be unable to sustain their resistance and the rebellion would falter and die.

Edmund Burke and a few other Englishmen disagreed; in Parliament and in the press, they argued hard and long for conciliation. George III was adamant; rebellion was a crime, to be stamped out with no mercy. The majority of Parliament agreed, and the English public applauded every public expression of contempt for the colonials: Yahoos right out of *Gulliver's Travels*; the sweepings of English prisons; people so lacking in spirit and enterprise that they willingly sold themselves into bondage, hardly better than African slavery. One Englishman told Josiah Quincy that he thought all Americans were black. Others saw them as criminals. Samuel Johnson, who always spoke his mind frankly, once said of the American population, "Sir, they are a race of convicts, and ought to be content with anything we allow them short of hanging."

The most insulting English jibes disparaged the essential manhood of the colonials. The earl of Sandwich sneered that rebels would run at first sight of a redcoat or at the mere sound of a British cannon. Officers in the Boston garrison, before the march to Concord, gleefully reported rebel flight during British parades, as evidence that the earl was right. Two years later, in 1777, that opinion was still held among British generals; one remarked after the easy victory at Ticonderoga, "The American is an effeminate thing, very unfit for and very

impatient for war." The crowning insult came from another general who boasted that with a few Regulars, he could "geld all the American males, some by force and the rest with a little coaxing."

On a more responsible level, the British government could base its projections on undeniable facts. The colonies were separate administrative entities with no experience in political cooperation. No two were organized in exactly the same way. What was more, they often quarreled, especially over boundaries. The long and bitter dispute between New York and New Hampshire as to which owned Vermont had had to be settled by action of the Board of Trade in London. The great diversity of the colonies, moreover, cast in doubt their willingness and ability to unite, and so did the obvious antagonisms between coastal cities and rural interior, not to mention long-standing religious quarrels and marked differences in national origin and even in language.

These same thoughts were in the minds of American moderates, who hoped until the very end for some kind of compromise. By April, 1775, however, it was too late; the battle on the nineteenth need not have made war inevitable, but it so inflamed rebels everywhere that the hope of peace shrank virtually to zero. The rebel element in the Second Continental Congress, which convened the next month, was too strong and had the support of too much popular sentiment for conciliation to remain as a possibility.

The American Image

For ten years the antagonism had been growing. Neither side could accept the reasoning of the other. In the British view, the obvious prosperity of the colonies was the result of great generosity— mild laws, leniently enforced, and an expensive war waged to eliminate the French threat to the western frontier. The royal treasury had been depleted by that long struggle, and it was only just that the colonies, as the immediate beneficiaries, should bear part of the cost. Hence the series of tax measures beginning in 1763, the year the French and Indian War ended.

The American interpretation was quite different. The war to dislodge the French was fought not to protect the colonies but to increase British territory in America, and asking the colonies to share the cost was unwarranted if not insulting. As for laws and their enforcement, mildness was a matter of opinion. The best-known regulations adopted by Parliament were those intended to protect specific English industries to the disadvantage of colonial development.

On both sides the reasoning was faulty. English help had once been important but was hardly needed now. Colonial wealth and progress, early and late, owed a good deal more to the vast resources of North America—nature's gift, not England's. As for regulations, nobody in the colonies had ever questioned England's right to impose them, and challenging the new round of taxes on the grounds that the colonies were unrepresented in Parliament had no basis whatsoever in tradition. What really annoyed the colonials was the British reason for the tax measures, protection that nobody in America recognized as necessary.

Faulty or not, the argument continued and the opposing positions hardened. The more Parliament insisted on its right to tax, the more the colonials asked themselves what benefits they got from being politically dependent. Their progress in a century and a half on this rich continent gave them confidence and the pride of achievement. The English people, with their own national pride, were too far away to appreciate that progress—in self-sufficiency,

in the trades, in technology, in culture—and it was natural for them to suppose that the colonies still needed their help and guidance. The colonial attitude struck them as the worst kind of ingratitude, and it must have shocked them to read Thomas Paine's masterpiece of propaganda, *Common Sense.* For the colonials, in contrast, this essay merely confirmed what most of them had come to accept. "I challenge the warmest advocate of conciliation," Paine wrote, "to show a single advantage that this continent can reap by being connected with Great Britain."

Paine, the former English corset-maker whom Franklin had encouraged to migrate, had been in America less than two years when he wrote *Common Sense* and had spent most of that time in Philadelphia. He could have had little idea of the vast reaches of the colonial area—two hundred thousand square miles, four times the size of England—or the variety of its regions or of its wealth of resources. A propagandist longer in the land, and well traveled, might have argued, no less tellingly, that this was nature's gift, not England's, and that it rightfully belonged to the people who lived there and had made it prosperous by exploiting its riches. Great powers with overseas possessions never reason that way or even listen to such reasoning; and unless they are very wise and very careful, sooner or later they adopt rash rules that result, as Franklin wrote in one of his political satires, in reducing a great empire to a small one.

The colonial prosperity that the British government sought to tap by taxation came from a combination of natural resources, rich beyond the imagination of most Europeans, and the applied technology of a population determined to get ahead. Just who were they, those people of the Revolutionary generation, the first to think of themselves as Americans?

2

"What Is
the American, This
New Man?"

Collect 2.5 million human beings from three continents, with many different languages and religions and a wide range of developed skills. Color a fifth of them black and a smaller number red. Divide the rest, the 2 million whites, into freemen and bonded servants. Scatter all thinly over two hundred thousand square miles, but not at random; arrange for concentrations by national background and religious conviction. Create thirteen political jurisdictions, each separately administered by agents of a government three thousand miles away, and devise mutual suspicions and hatreds to keep relations between them cool. Make it easy for a few to gain wealth and power, give them political dominance and encourage the disenfranchised majority to struggle bitterly for a voice in decision-making. Pit city against countryside, and older sections against new. The result will be the antithesis of a viable society for which anything like nationhood might seem the remotest of possibilities.

Nobody put the case so bluntly, but thoughtful men everywhere, aware of the diversity and the antagonisms, must have questioned whether the colonies could set their differences aside and carry on, in a joint effort, what had begun at Lexington and Concord. Was the manifest resentment at British measures strong enough? It was one thing to replace acquiescent colonialism with a sense, novel and exciting, of being American, but whether the ferment of nationalism had been working long enough and whether it would extend to overt action was a grave question. The one hope, not at all a certainty, was that men of rebellious spirit in the other colonies would rally to the support of Massachusetts and be willing to pledge their lives, their fortunes and their sacred honor—as Americans—in a common cause.

One man who sought words for the new awareness of being American was a transplanted Frenchman, Michel Guillaume Jean de Crèvecœur, who wrote a series of idyllic essays that he collected in 1782 as *Letters from an American Farmer*. The most famous passage begins with a question, "What then is the American, this new man?" Crèvecœur's answer is the original exposition of the Melting Pot theory: "An American is an European, or the descendant of an European, hence that strange mixture of blood, which you will find in no other country." Intermarriage of people from various national stocks, he thought, had already produced a "promiscuous breed," and he concluded that in the new country, America, "all nations are melted into a new race of men."

What he was really describing was less a new race than a composite of European nationalities, through white intermarriage. This was predictable enough; but for the most part geographic remoteness and difficulty of travel limited opportunities for meeting potential mates with different backgrounds; regional prejudice and mutual antagonism further deterred such unions. Barriers were not too hard to surmount in cities, but the cities were few in number, and none of them large. Religion was everywhere a consideration; it was a rare wedding that made one flesh of an Anglican and a Moravian, a Quaker and a Catholic, a Huguenot and a Jew. Class lines, though far less rigid than in England, also counted; Cinderella had slight chance to meet Prince Charming, and the Horatio Alger hero, yet to be invented, seldom wooed and won the great merchant's daughter.

Interracial marriage and couplings outside of marriage, which Crèvecœur ignored, were much more effective than white unions in creating a new race of men. Crèvecœur, as a slave owner, shared the view of many white colonials that Negroes (and Indians) were not Americans and omitted them from consideration. Indeed, the term *American* was generally limited to individuals of European descent.

Where They Lived

Crèvecœur was more widely traveled than most of the Revolutionary generation, but his observations were limited to a very small part of the colonial area. Nobody else then living, however, could have grasped the full significance of colonial variety; it would have taken years, by the available means of travel, to visit every distinctive section in all the colonies. An armchair traveler, with a substantial library of books and periodicals, can form a better picture than anyone could in 1776.

No national count was taken before 1790, but beginning in 1770 several colonies made body counts, more or less reliable, which, with other evidence like tax lists, provide something better than round-number estimates.

Population by Colony

Colony	Population	Year	Source
Connecticut	297,920	1775	Census
Delaware	37,219	1774–84	Census and tax lists
Georgia	33,054	1775	Governor's estimate and head grants
Maine (a province of Mass.)	47,767	1776	Census
Maryland	254,633	1782	Census
Massachusetts	290,950	1776	Census
New Hampshire	80,950	1775	Census
New Jersey	122,003	1772	Census
New York (including Vermont)	193,167	1775	Census (of 1771 and 1786)
North Carolina	246,580	1770	Tax lists
Pennsylvania	270,518	1779–82	Tax lists
Rhode Island	58,228	1774	Census
South Carolina	169,987	1775	Governor's estimate
Virginia	504,264	1782–85	Census and tax lists

Population maps, with a dot for every fifty or hundred people, show both densities and distribution. Massachusetts, Rhode Island and Connecticut were pretty well filled at the time of the Revolution, with a surprisingly uniform distribution: Only four counties in New England, two each in Massachusetts and Rhode Island, had more than a hundred people to the square mile. Where the dots are closest, indicating greatest density, they become solid black areas—in and near Boston and smaller concentrations at Providence, Newport, New Haven and Hartford and the Piscataqua region, Portsmouth and southernmost Maine from Kittery to Berwick. Nantucket and Cape Cod were also quite well stocked with people.

Most of Maine, New Hampshire and Vermont was still wilderness. So was New York except for concentrations of people on lower Manhattan Island and at Albany, with a scattering on Long Island, up the Hudson and for a short distance along the Mohawk. Most of New Jersey's people lived, as they still do, in a band from Manhattan to Philadelphia; and most Pennsylvanians lived in the southeastern section, between the Delaware and the Susquehanna. Maryland, Delaware and Virginia had the most evenly distributed population of all the colonies, chiefly because cities were so scarce. The Virginia pattern of uniformity carried into northern North Carolina but quickly gave way to sparsity that continued into South Carolina except at Charleston. Georgia's few people lived beside the Savannah River and a short distance southward along the coast. In all the colonies the population dots thin gradually away from the longest-settled areas until their outer line marks the frontier.

Where They Came From

In 1775, as in any other year before the Revolution,

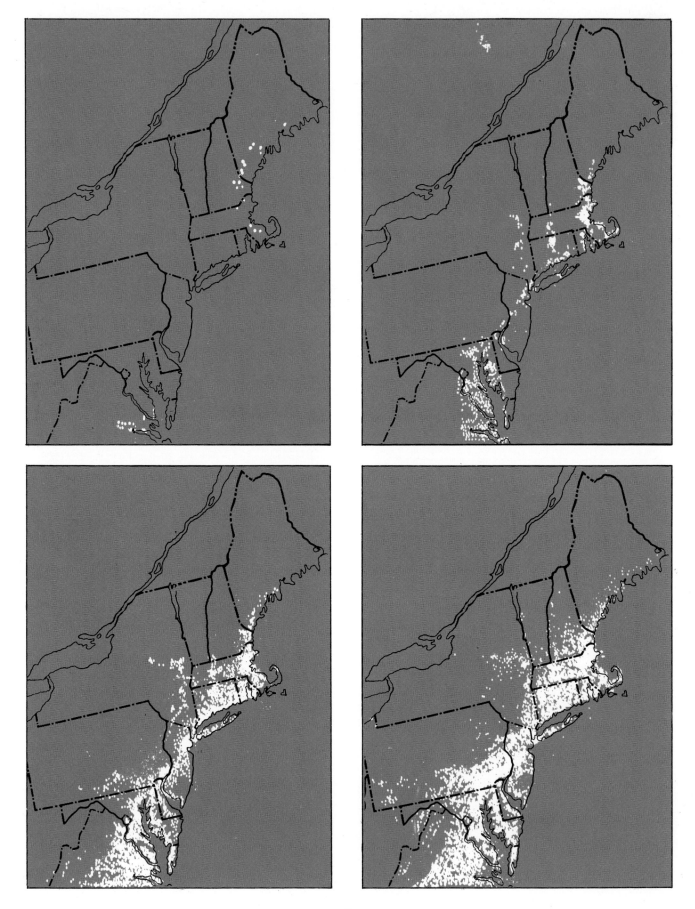

the majority of Americans, perhaps as many as two-thirds, were either immigrants themselves or the children of immigrants. The birthrate was very high, but immigration was continuous, peaking and falling, never stopping. Although exact figures are not available, the population increase estimated at a million, or 80 percent, between 1750 and 1765 suggests that immigration was the factor most responsible for the increase.

Colonials of English descent, once the overwhelming majority, gradually declined in percentage as other countries furnished increasing numbers; by 1775, Anglo-Americans were still the majority but were down to about 60 percent and would have been fewer without a spurt of new arrivals from England in the first years of that decade. The oldest families, dating from the first half of the seventeenth century, had of course multiplied in five or six generations; but if they had forgotten their immigrant heritage or lost track of it, most of the colonials were too new in the land to be unaware of their origins.

The mixing that Crèvecœur spoke about and the mobility that quickened it had, by 1775, barely begun to break up the homogeneity of the different regions. Anglo-Americans were in every colony, but not the same Anglo-Americans; Congregationalists, the heirs of Puritanism, were concentrated in New England, Quakers in Pennsylvania, Catholics in Maryland, Anglicans in Virginia, and their dislike of each other proved to be a handicap for both the conduct of the war and the subsequent creation of a federal union. Immigrants from other nations, with their own religions and particular skills and interests, also tended to flock together. It takes time to scatter elements.

Most of the Dutch in America were in New York and nearby New Jersey, where they could indulge their old love for colorful tiles, handsome painted furniture and fine ironwork. Convivial, materialistic and notably commercial, they had little in common with their serious New England neighbors. A visitor to Manhattan might have found it hard to believe that the Dutch, by 1775, were only 3 percent of the colonial total. The forty years of Dutch control, before the English took over in 1664, had been long enough to plant Dutch culture firmly and to spot the map with Dutch place names —Harlem, the Bowery, Corlear's Hook in Manhattan and outlying New Dorp, Staten Island, the Bronx, Brooklyn, Yonkers and Hackensack, among many more. Families of Dutch origin important in 1775 included the Van Courtlandts and the Rensselaers, the Beekmans and the Schuylers, the Stuyvesants and the Philipses.

The Dutch 3 percent in the Revolutionary population was 3 percent more than could be assigned the Swedes and Finns, who had once had a colony of their own, New Sweden on the lower Delaware (then known as the "South River" as opposed to the Hudson, or "North River"). After the colony was overwhelmed in 1655 by a Dutch force from New Amsterdam, its members were scattered and absorbed into the general white population. Old Swedes Church in Wilmington is one of the very few reminders of their early presence.

The French showed some of the same mixing tendency, but there were more of them, with 2.3 percent of the population in 1775. They crossed the ocean at different times and for different reasons. Some, including Crèvecœur, were members of the French army in America who decided to stay, and others were adventurers seeking fresh opportunity in various colonies. The two largest French migrations resulted from persecution. The Calvinist Protestants, known as Huguenots, fled from France when, in 1685, the government revoked the Edict of Nantes that had given them freedom of worship for very nearly a century. They chose various places to settle but had concentrations in the Carolinas, Pennsylvania and New York, where they founded New Rochelle in 1698. The second mass arrival was in 1755, not from France but from Nova Scotia, where the British broke up the French settlement in Acadia and deliberately scattered its people throughout the thirteen colonies. French extraction is evident in such names as Dana and De Lancey, Du Pont and Delano, Lamar and Laurens, Ravenel and Revere—all prominent in the Revolutionary period.

The Swiss had no special colony to be attracted to, and even though six hundred of them arrived as a group in 1732, they were quickly dispersed, like the French and like the Swedes and Finns after their colony was lost to them. Sober and industrious, the Swiss brought with them well-developed skills—as carpenters, goldsmiths, tool-makers, weavers—that made them particularly welcome.

One very small group, the fewer than three

thousand Jews by the time of the Revolution, was never absorbed, preserving identity and culture even though its members came from no single European country and were so scattered throughout the colonies that only five cities had enough of them—ten men—to organize a synagogue: New York, Newport, Charleston, Savannah and Philadelphia. Most were Sephardic, forced by the Inquisition to leave Spain in 1492 and living elsewhere in Europe until they migrated; almost none were Ashkenazic, from

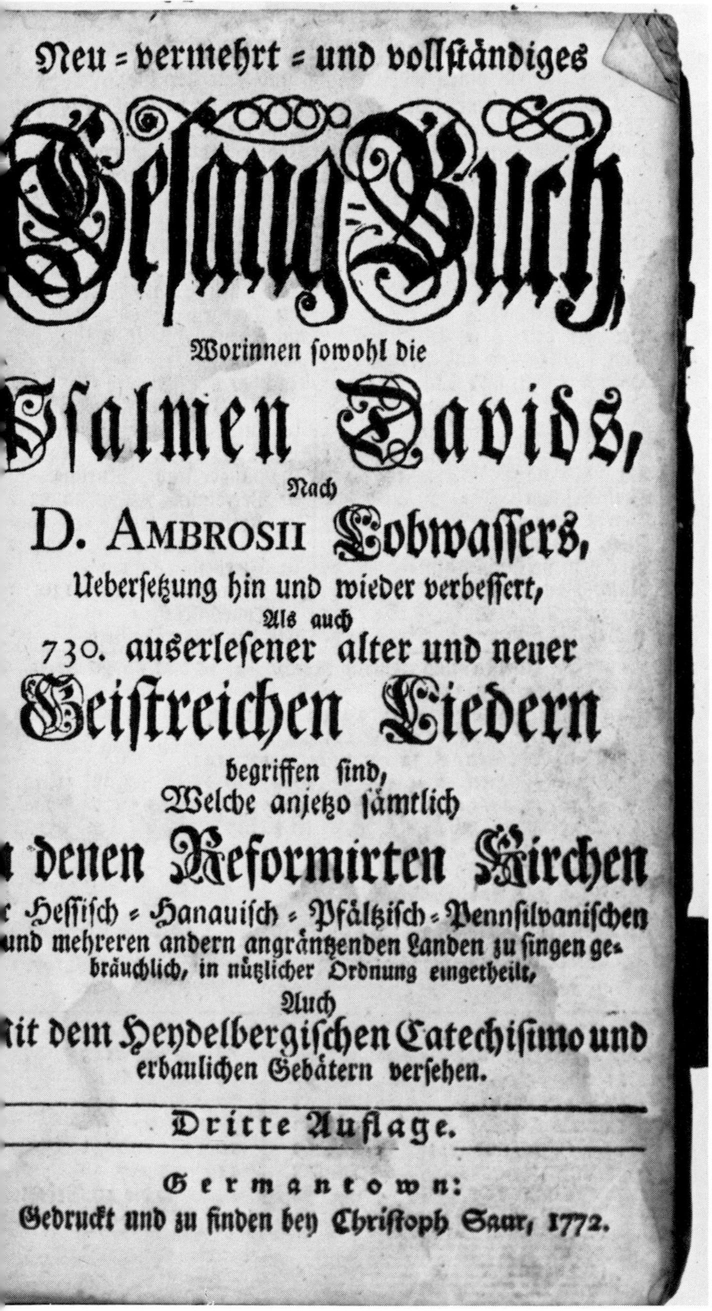

Neu = vermehrt = und vollständiges
Gesang Buch
Worinnen sowohl die
Psalmen Davids,
Nach
D. Ambrosii Lobwassers,
Uebersetzung hin und wieder verbessert,
Als auch
730. auserlesener alter und neuer
Geistreichen Liedern
begriffen sind,
Welche anjetzo sämtlich
denen Reformirten Kirchen
Hessisch = Hanauisch = Pfältzisch = Pennsilvanischen
und mehreren andern angräntzenden Landen zu singen ge-
bräuchlich, in nützlicher Ordnung eingetheilt,
Auch
it dem Heydelbergischen Catechismo und
erbaulichen Gebätern versehen.
Dritte Auflage.
Germantown:
Gedruckt und zu finden bey Christoph Saur, 1772.

Book of Psalms printed in Germantown, Pennsylvania, in 1772, an example of the flourishing German language printing in the colonial period.

Germany or eastern Europe. Not being Christian, they could not take the standard oath, but in some colonies they were permitted to omit the phrase "on the true faith of a Christian" and thus become citizens. They still could not hold office or testify at trials in any colony except Rhode Island, but such handicaps were minor; in their quiet way, as urban businessmen, they made steady progress. Peter Kalm, the Swedish scientist from Åbo Akademi (in what is now Finland), was astonished by their freedom to engage in business and grow wealthy—as they did; in proportion to their numbers they had the highest per capita valuation by the 1770s. Aaron Lopez, a migrant from Portugal in 1754, quickly amassed a fortune as a merchant; his wife's father, Jacob Rivera, made whaling a major industry by introducing the use of spermaceti. James Lucena pioneered the making of fine castile soap. These three all lived in Newport, where the sixty-odd Jewish families, largest such community in the colonies, worshipped in the handsome synagogue their prosperity had built in 1763.

Scots, who could compete successfully with Jews or anyone else in business enterprises, were much more numerous. They arrived in four large waves, the last in 1771–73; the eighteenth-century total, from the Scottish Highlands and Lowlands and from Northern Ireland, was approximately a quarter of a million. Overwhelmingly Presbyterian, they formed the chief opposition to the various English groups—Quaker, Anglican, Puritan—that had dominated colonial politics from the beginning and that resisted any challenge to their continued dominance. The Scots, the second-largest element in the white population with about 10 percent, were too openly shrewd and competitive as businessmen to enjoy the widespread admiration earned by the polite, soft-spoken Jews. With the numerous Scots who became teachers, it was just the opposite; they were admired for their ability to cram information between the ears of their pupils.

South Irish, 3.7 percent of the population in 1775, suffered with other Catholics a degree of prejudice that held them down everywhere. One irony of colonial history is that Maryland, though founded as a Catholic haven under Catholic proprietors, the Calvert family, underwent a long struggle, with religious toleration in and out of favor after Protestants became the numerical majority. Even

with the seesaw, however, Maryland attracted most of the South Irish, although no colony was without a few of them.

The most distinctive regional concentration was of a hundred thousand Germans in Pennsylvania, a third of that colony's population and popularly known as the Pennsylvania Dutch. The oldest settlement was at Germantown, founded in 1683 by a congregation of Mennonites. Others followed, with the migration peaking after 1710: Dunkards and Moravians, Amish and Schwenkfelders, all of them devoted to their particular church doctrines, to their cultural traditions and to their native dialectical German. Whether they would join an open rebellion against the British was yet to be known when the fighting began.

Even more Germans settled in South Carolina, in and near Orangeburg and Charleston, and they could be found elsewhere, with the fewest in New England. Their total, about three hundred sixty-five thousand by 1775, or 8.6 percent of the colonial population, made them the third-largest white group in the colonies.

These, then, were the principal identifiable white groups in the budding "nation of nations," some mixing readily with each other, as Crèvecœur reported, others holding apart as long and as well as they could, the Germans most successfully. But not even the Germans were immune from certain changes that were creating not a new race, but an entity new in the world—the American. More immigrants, from parts of the world not yet represented in 1776, would continue the evolution, but it was already well started when independence was declared. As Thomas Paine observed in *Common Sense,* "Europe and not England is the parent country of America."

It was a good point, even though he ignored Africa.

Top: English tiles with designs by John Sadler from the John Phillips house in Boston. *Middle:* Bed corner of a miller's log house in Delaware, ca. 1740. *Bottom:* A Baptist "immersion" baptismal ceremony in the Schuylkill River near Philadelphia, 1770. *Opposite:* Dutch Delft tiles around a fireplace in New York, with yoke-back chair, tricorn hat and tripod hearth kettle.

Americans by Force

If we divide all migrants to the thirteen colonies into two classes, the free agents and those in bondage, the majority would be in the latter. Transported convicts, exiled political or military prisoners, penniless families willing to repay rapacious ship captains by six-year indenture, children kidnapped off the streets of Europe and slaves from Africa—these comprised a vast army of unfortunates. All except the African slaves could see far off, for their children if not for themselves, the faint hope of becoming, like the lucky ones, free agents, independent colonists.

Blacks in the colonies were a good fifth of the population in 1775. A few were free, by the generosity of white masters (usually by manumission in their wills), by being successful runaways or by completing their terms of indenture—for not all Africans arrived as slaves. One reason for their large number was the tradition, still flourishing today, of counting as black all individuals with a black parent, grandparent or great-grandparent. The peculiar institution of human enslavement was, in retrospect, peculiar indeed. Slaves commonly had a degree of freedom on Sundays for working in their own gardens or for any kind of innocent merriment they wanted, dancing, love-making and singing—but not spirituals, for very few slaves had professed the Christian faith by the time of the Revolution. On no day of the week, however, did the law extend to them such rights as traveling, owning a gun, bringing suit against a white or even marrying.

White colonials by and large approved of the strict controls, to prevent insurrections. They knew little or nothing about the origin of the slaves or about the process of making them slaves in the first place. But the slaves remembered. No one who had

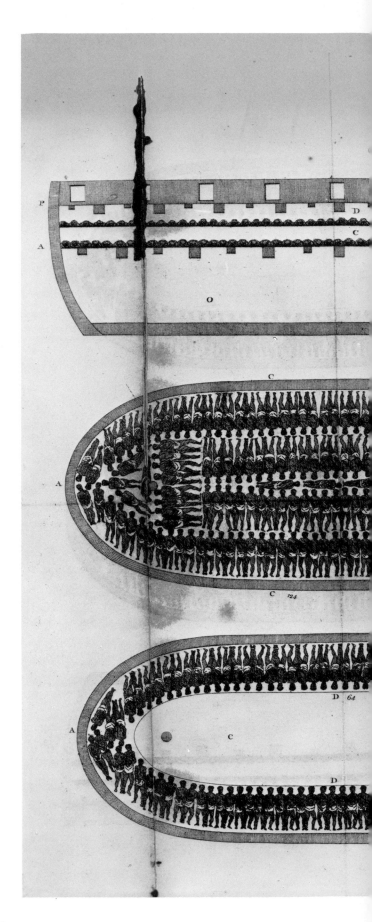

"Packed into the holds of vessels like so many sardines"—diagrams showing
the efficient placement of a slave cargo on the crossing from Africa.

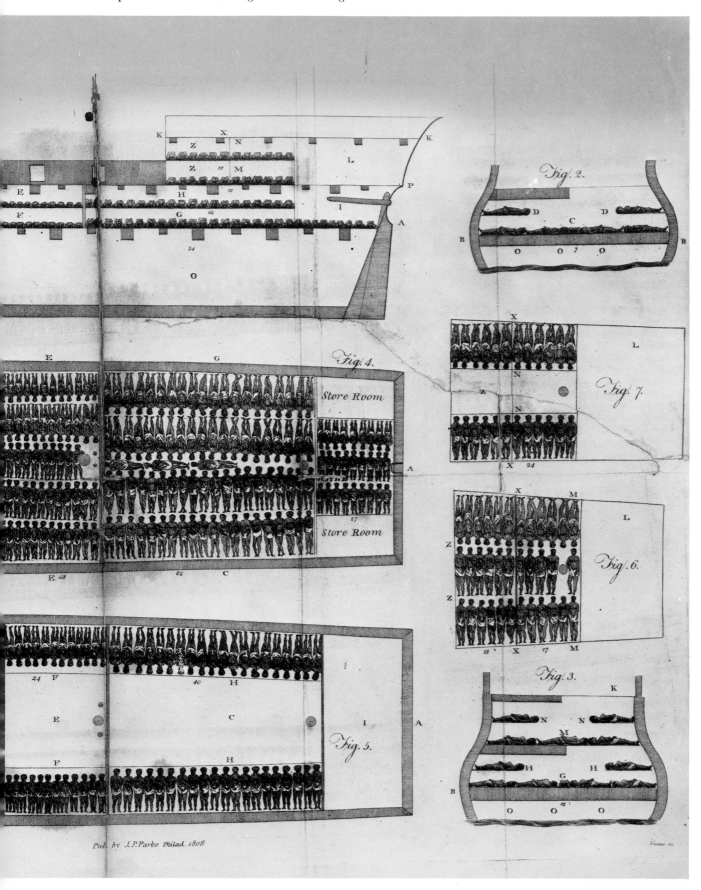

survived such indignities could possibly forget the sequence: kidnapped by slave hunters, wrenched from family and familiar tradition, mixed with other Africans of alien tongues, shipped down one river or another to the coast or force-marched overland in slave coffles, packed into foul-aired slave "castles," like Elmina Castle in what is now Ghana, ruthlessly dehumanized, inspected like cattle to discover defects, branded on the breast with red-hot irons, packed into the holds of vessels like so many sardines and sold off the ship on arrival in America, naked as they had been since their capture. The luckiest were the nubile girls who bought with their bodies a degree of privilege—and began the racial mixing that Crèvecœur ignored. But all shared the tragedy and a bitter hatred of whites.

In the colonies, blacks were handicapped in specific ways. One was having no written language;

no black African did as early as 1775. Even in speech they were disadvantaged; the Bantu, for example, had 182 different languages, a distinct barrier to communication or to possible union against a common enemy. Most of them had no option but to learn the European language spoken on the plantation, just enough of it to understand what their overseers ordered them to do. Nor could they join their former compatriots in particular regions as migrants from Europe could and often did, for deliberate mixing was another means of minimizing the chances of revolt.

British contempt for the colonials was commonly the result of ignorance, but regarding slavery it was soundly based. Thomas Day, author of the famous book for boys *History of Sandford and Merton,* remarked in 1776: "If there be an object truly ridiculous in nature, it is an American patriot sign-

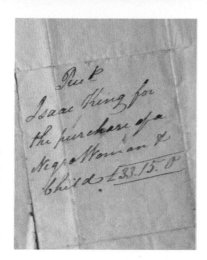

ing resolutions of independence with the one hand, and with the other brandishing a whip over his affrighted slaves." For all that defenders of slavery have written, treatment of slaves was generally harsh. Legal penalties for white offenders were commonly doubled for slaves, and for serious crimes slaves were punished without trial.

The callousness of whites toward slaves was general in the Revolutionary period. Philip Fithian, a Princeton graduate who tutored for a year on a Virginia plantation, was shocked by the severe punishments given to slaves by order of his employer, "King" Carter, otherwise the kindliest of men. At quite a different level, a newspaper item in 1774, from Fithian's native New Jersey, reveals the same callousness by its juxtaposition of commodities offered for sale:

Ship Timber

About 170 trees, knees and other crooked pieces, of different sizes and lengths, properly marked, and cut by the direction of a person acquainted with ship-building. The timber is cut in the rough, and lies ready for hauling, within less than half a mile of the river Delaware, from whence it may be rafted with ease. Any person inclining to purchase the whole together, as it lies on the spot, may have it on very reasonable terms, by applying to Mr. Coxe, at Trenton, and may view the timber at his Bellmont Farm, lying about 12 miles above Trenton Ferry, and opposite to Mr. John Beaumont's, in Bucks county, where his tenant, George Ekenswallow will attend to show the timber upon being applied to.

He has also a young healthy negroe girl, to dispose of, about 16 or 17 years of age, has had the small pox, and capable of much drudgery service in town or country. Enquire as above or of the Printers.

A far more common newspaper notice reported a runaway slave, gave a detailed description for

Huntington, September 20th, 1767.

RUN away from Joseph Lewis of Huntingdon, in Suffolk County, 1 Negro Man, named Daniel, about 21 Years of Age; and 1 Negro Boy, named Ben about 13 Years old:—Daniel, had on when he went away a light brown coat, brown jacket, leather breeches and check linen shirt; wears his hat with a peak cock, and white button; is about 5 feet 7 or 8 inches high, a very likely strait limb'd fellow; the boy had on when he went off, a light blue camblet coat, check shirt and tow trowsers, is remarkable for having one fore eye, and lost one joint of one of his little fingers: Whoever takes up and secures both, or either of said negroes, so that their master may have them again, or notice given to Thomas Tucker in New-York, shall be reasonably rewarded, and all charges paid. JOSEPH LEWIS. 90 93

easy recognition and promised a reward. Reading such notices leaves the strong impression that slaves of mixed ancestry ran away most often. If they were quadroons or octaroons—a quarter black or an eighth—their chances of passing as whites and thereby gaining freedom increased. How many runaways did change their status nobody knows, but since they would never want to admit the fact, a certain fraction of the "whites" in the Revolutionary generation must have had some African blood.

By the time of the Revolution, there were not just three or four possible racial combinations but almost too many to count. "What then is the American, this new man?" Crèvecœur didn't realize what a dangerous question he was asking.

Pureblood Indians, and mixtures recognized as Indians, were few in number within the colonial area and lived wretchedly. At best they were semi-civilized, keeping themselves alive by doing odd jobs. Some sold brooms and baskets they had made; others were adept at reseating chairs. The women were better workers than the men, working in taverns, dipping candles in the winter and helping rural housewives with the unpleasant spring job of making soap. The men did not make good slaves, as a rule, or even satisfactory employees; one disconcerting habit was their wandering off in the summer and returning when the temperature dropped in the fall. Their general behavior was that of "walkabouts," as tramps were then called, but it seems inescapable that their way of life was largely forced upon them by white prejudice. The Moravian practice of baptizing Indians was an anomaly; most whites would have considered it a waste of time.

Americans in Bondage

If slavery means bondage to a master, or involuntary servitude, without any of the personal liberties enjoyed by the master and other free agents in the society, more whites than blacks were slaves when the Revolution began.

New England, inhospitable to all newcomers, had relatively few people in bondage, black or white, but in the other sections they constituted more than half the work force. The blacks could hardly be called immigrants; a better term might be merchandise. It was a large and profitable business, buying the merchandise from coastal African traders and selling it to Americans who needed labor, and many New England fortunes were made in the process. But trade in whites was also profitable, although the profits were declining by 1775 after regulatory laws had been passed. Not until after 1800 did blacks overtake whites, numerically, as the primary source of involuntary servitude.

Redemptioners were whites who left Europe without a contract specifying the number of years they would be required to serve in return for the cost of their passage. William Eddis, surveyor of customs at Annapolis, called them "free-willers," and in a letter he wrote in 1770, he expressed the opinion that their lot was "more to be lamented than that of the convict and the indented servant." Upon arrival at an American port, they could not leave the ship until they were redeemed, by friends or relatives if they were lucky; all that was needed was cash enough to pay what the captain asked. Most redemptioners were not so fortunate; they had to redeem themselves by agreeing to a term of servitude to whoever would pay the captain. The few with skills in demand could drive a reasonable bargain, but the majority, many of whom knew no English, were at a great disadvantage.

People leaving England without money to pay for passage were required by law to have a written contract, which is what indenture really meant. But

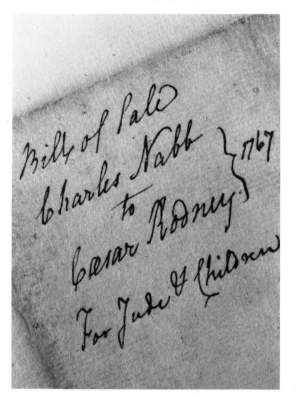

British officials did not always observe the law; the *Emigration Records* in the Public Record Office listed as redemptioners ninety-nine emigrants during the week of June 12–19, 1775, with the notation: "These people, on their arrival at Maryland, are to be disposed of for a Number of Years, provided they are not found capable to pay the Captn for their passage as P Agreement."

Redemptioners who entered indenture upon arrival, as most of them were forced to do, were henceforth no different from indentured servants with prior contracts. Ship captains made a good profit from both. The actual cost per individual of the transportation seldom exceeded ten pounds, but the minimum price the future master had to pay was fifteen, which meant a 50 percent profit to the captain. The average dockside price in Maryland was twenty pounds, but in Virginia, where bidding was most competitive, buyers sometimes paid forty or fifty. Even that was a bargain, for the buyer got several years of service with no expenses except for housing, clothing and food. John Harrower, who shipped as a redemptioner, was lucky; the captain was friendly, and the man who bought his service proved very generous, giving him pocket money for visits to town and making Christmas merry for him with a present of sugar and two bottles of the very best rum.

While still on shipboard awaiting a bidder, Harrower had observed other kinds of American behavior. When one indentured servant went ashore, got drunk and abused the ship's officers when he returned, he was horsewhipped, put in irons, thumbscrewed for an hour and gagged for a day. About a week later two "soul-drivers" came aboard; these were men who bought all or part of a cargo "and then they drive them through the Country like a parcell of Sheep until they can sell them to advantage." It was all quite legal: Inden-

tured servants, like slaves, were property. During the war, owners of servants who enlisted in the Continental army were given "appropriate compensation" for the loss of their services. Other patriots were paid for army use of their oxen.

Most terms of indenture were far from ideal—so very far that white runaways were as often reported in the newspapers as runaway slaves.

Four Dollars Reward.
Philadelphia, August 5, 1775
Ran away on Thursday evening, the 3rd inst. from the subscriber, a Dutch servant girl named Maria Catherine Mamro, eighteen years of age. . . . She goes by the name of Caty, and supposed to be gone with one Conrad Konigsfold to Mr. Wistar's glass-house in the Jerseys. Whoever secures said servant so that her master may have her again shall be entitled to the above Reward.
Richard Footman

Most notices showed greater urgency, and more detail, like this one from the preceding year:

33

Run away, last night, from the subscribers, in Lower Penn's Neck, Salem county, West New-Jersey, the following servants, viz. William Ingle, an English lad, about 18 or 19 years of age, about 5 feet 5 or 6 inches high, a thick well set fellow, fair complexion, smooth faced, straight black hair; has been in the country four years; had on a redish brown coat, that has been turned, with mohair buttons on the wrong side, new striped blue and white homespun jacket, without sleeves, one homespun linen shirt, one old tow ditto, new tow and linen trowsers, shoes and stockings, a good felt hat. Richard Brown, about 18 years of age, country-born, five feet 4 or 5 inches high, a slim spare lad, dark brown hair, a down look, and something near sighted: had on, and took with him, a brown half-worn outside jacket, one pale blue coatee, striped home made trowsers, one fine shirt, one homespun ditto, shoes and stockings, and an old beaver hat. Whoever takes up said servants, and secures them in any gaol on the continent, so as their masters may have them again, shall have four pounds reward, or forty shillings for either and reasonable charges, if brought home, paid by Andrew Sinnickson, junior, and Ezra Firth.

N.B. It is probable they may sell or change some of their clothes. All masters of vessels, and others, are forbid to harbour or carry them off.   *June 14, 1774*

Two other newspaper notices, also from New Jersey, are typical of many to be found in the "For Sale" column:

To be Sold,

About five years time of an indented servant girl, born in Jersey, about 14 years old; honest, good tempered, fond of children, and handy at most kind of work about a house. Enquire of the Printer.

A Dutch girl, that has 5 years and a half to serve, together with a male child, two months old, that will be bound till 30 years of age, are to be sold by Arney Lippincut of Springfield, in Burlington county. The price will be twelve pounds.

Girls ran away less often than men, especially skilled men who could readily find work in distant communities. Those that avoided recapture joined the growing force of free labor; it was a form of quick upward mobility.

White servants could be advertised for sale or as runaways just as slaves could, but they did have a few advantages over the blacks: They were not usually branded, they seldom worked as field hands, their children did not ordinarily inherit their status and they could look forward to eventual freedom. But even the most generous contracts were for several years, four at the minimum, of total subjection to a master without any of the privileges common to free agents, such as the right to vote, to run for office, to move about freely or to acquire property. This last point is a reminder of an important secondary advantage to the master. Several of the colonies offered land grants, usually fifty acres, for importing immigrants. South Carolina was particularly openhanded, giving a headright of 150 acres to every migrating freeman, another 150 for every able manservant he brought and 100 for each womanservant and each male under sixteen. The intent of the grants was to increase the population, not to encourage purchase of immigrants after they arrived, but the provision did both. White bondsmen were usually promised land grants when their indenture expired, along with an agreed-upon sum of money, tools, clothing and food, which they often had difficulty collecting. The years of bondage so reduced hope and ambition, however, that not many accepted the land. By one estimate, only one former bondsman in ten settled on the land; a second took up trade, while the other eight died in service, returned to Europe or became the first "poor whites"—shiftless, ruined, without ambition. The women did better than the men, for they could marry established citizens.

These whites in bondage were a varied lot. Many were convicts who had been condemned to death for any of some 169 crimes as Sir William Blackstone reported in his famous *Commentaries on the Laws of England* (1765–69). Offered a choice between hanging and lifetime bondage in the colonies, most convicts chose the latter—30,000 of them in the eighteenth century, by one estimate, with most going to Maryland and Virginia. Their transportation, by contract with the government, continued until the outbreak of war in 1775 and made fortunes for the contractors. Laws passed by some of the colonies to end the practice were voided by the British government, and petitions to the Crown and Parliament were ignored.

In addition to felons convicted of capital crimes, there were assorted rogues and rascals, whores, cheats and vagabonds, whose loss, at a time of widespread poverty and mounting crime in England, few Englishmen regretted. Nor were English tears shed for children kidnapped off the streets or for unattached women (in constant demand as colonial wives) or for entire families tricked into indenture or for such public enemies as political and military prisoners, like the Highland Scots who

had joined Bonnie Prince Charlie in the abortive uprising of 1745. The British government did little to suppress the vicious forms of coercion, for the net result relieved the land of its surplus population, which cost more to keep alive than it contributed to the economy.

Not all candidates for white bondage were English. Scottish farmers racked by high rents, Irishmen perpetually hungry and Germans in hopeless poverty saw indenture as a lesser evil. Illiterates and people who knew no English were often victimized, signing papers they could not read and without recourse to government agencies at home or immigrant aid bureaus where they landed.

The indenture system was the chief source of labor in the Revolutionary period; free men in general preferred it to slavery out of fear that blacks might one day outnumber whites if more slaves than white servants were imported. Both were preferable, in the thinking of men needing

labor, to free workmen, who had to be paid. Free labor was gaining slowly, however, because free men generally do better work than men in servitude and because members of self-sufficient rural families increasingly adopted trades in their eagerness to share in the rising prosperity.

"Doers, Planners, Achievers"

With so very many individuals in bondage, the free agents comprised only about half the Revolutionary generation. Being free, they could take part in the resistance to British pressure as black slaves and most whites in bondage could not; and if the Revolution was complete before 1775, it was in the minds not of all the people but almost exclusively of the freemen, who alone could speak and act for themselves, without restraint from masters.

There were limitations, however; the status of freemen did not carry with it automatically the

right to share in political action. Every colony limited the right to vote or hold office to freemen with property; paupers and debtors were excluded, along with women, but so were men unable, by their youth, their lack of skill or their improvidence, to acquire the minimum of valuation set by each colony. Within the class of free agents, as a result, there were two subclasses: men with property enough to enjoy political freedom and men without enough property. Paralleling the rebellion against the British government was an internal contest between the disenfranchised, who wanted a voice in local government, and the politically privileged, who saw the enlargement of the electorate as a threat to their dominance. The most familiar such conflict was in Virginia, where the House of Burgesses was a virtual private club of aristocrats resisting every demand for more representation by the growing majority of small farmers in western areas. Conditions were actually much worse in South Carolina, where the great planters and Charleston merchants ignored both the backcountry and the city itself, even though most of them lived there.

Virtually everything of importance was in the hands of free agents; the hands of slaves and bondsmen were effectually tied. Wherever we turn our focus of attention, to art or religion, to village life or urban business, to travel or housing or domestic felicity, it is the free agents we chiefly observe. They were the doers, the planners, the achievers. People in bondage did the menial work—for the free agents. Whether we speak of rural self-sufficiency or culture or the professions, they counted most; for amounting to something is what freedom really means. Not for some years would America be described as "the land of the free and the home of the brave."

3
The
American
Life – Cradle
to Grave

Left: Closet with a window, blue-and-white Delft flower pot on the sill. Diamond panes were yielding to rectangular ones in double-hung windows by 1770.
Right: Child's cradle of the period—part of the "borning-room" furniture. *Opposite:* Bedroom in a South Carolina home of some wealth, as attested to by the handsome carved furniture and the elaborate sleeping gown on the chair.

unfinished second floor), where the closest thing to privacy was a sheet or blanket suspended from a rafter. In cold weather, when the prize location was beside the chimney, quilts and puffs and blankets were heaped on the beds in profusion. Mattresses, thick enough to even out the spaces between the rope cording that preceded metal springs, were of cornhusks; on top, if the sleeper was lucky, was a mattress stuffed with feathers—the famous featherbed. If his luck was fantastic, a second featherbed served as a cover. For extra warmth several children slept together; the coldest bed was one without a companion. Sheets, if used at all, were of linen. All the bedclothes, of course, had to be woven, kept in repair, and replaced when worn out, by the women in the household; the men's share in this business was making the wooden bedsteads and reroping them when they began to sag from long use. All the material, even the rope, could be produced at home; the only store-bought items were needles for quilting and for sewing the hand-woven ticking together to make mattress covers.

Larger and more elaborate houses might have additional finished bedrooms, downstairs or upstairs or both. The usual pattern of two dormitories, the parents' crowded bedroom downstairs and the unheated attic, was intimate and public but convenient, especially when a sleeper woke in the night and had to use a chamber pot. Toilet training was largely a matter of teaching children to find that object in the dark, for it was a long way to the privy, outdoors or in some corner of the woodshed or barn.

Manuals for raising children were numerous, but most of them were long on moral advice and short on practical suggestions. An exception was John Locke's *Some Thoughts Concerning Education,* first issued in 1693. Locke recommended brown bread and cheese for breakfast and supper and also water-gruel, milk porridge and flummery—soft bland food such as custard or blancmange. Drinks he limited to milk and small-beer, which was ordinary beer diluted with water. Apples were good for children, he thought, but not peaches, plums, melons or grapes. Beds should be hard, with quilts but never feathers.

Most children, however, were seated at the family table once they were weaned, which was often after the second birthday, and ate what the adults ate—the hearty fare of farm tradition that survived both migration to cities and acquisition of wealth. Meat twice a day, vegetables in profusion, fresh from the garden, brought up from storage bins in the cellar or in the city bought daily at the public market, all sorts of fruit and berries and always pastry in abundance—homemade bread and pies and puddings. The colonial diet was varied and rich and kept the digestive tract busy. As for drink, children and adults alike shunned water, which was feared as diluting physical vigor, and washed down their food with apple cider or beer, or tea—until the British slapped a tax on it. Milk was all right for babies, or for calves, but not for children with chores to handle. A little more milk might have reduced the dental woes that few colonials escaped.

The work ethic was instilled early; as soon as a boy or girl could do any work at all, specific household chores were assigned. The principle was not the only reason, however; maintaining a large household without laborsaving gadgets was roughly equivalent to operating a man-of-war. Where there were slaves or indentured servants, children were spared the incessant toil and had time for play; but play as such got little encouragement, especially in New England. Childhood everywhere was viewed as a prelude to adulthood, and if girls had dolls or played hopscotch while their brothers played marbles for keeps, both were dressed like miniature adults, drilled in adult behavior and judged by adult standards. In sober fact, childhood was brief; boys joined the working force at fourteen and at sixteen assumed their militia obligation, and most girls were married by seventeen or eighteen.

Left: Kitchen in a masonry house, Chester County, Pennsylvania. A large crane supports trammel and pothooks in the fireplace, which has a massive beam over the hearth. Exposed ceiling beams, pewter and earthenware eating utensils and the children's table off to one side are all typical of the times. *Above:* Needlework wall pocket. This one holds *Poor Will's Almanack* for the year 1740.

Colonial Schooling

There were radical ideas in the late colonial period, like inoculation for smallpox, the superiority of natural rights to the divine right of kings and the even more startling suggestion that all men, simply by being born, are equal. But nobody in 1775 had gone so far in radicalism as to propose that all children should be provided with, and required to accept, schooling to a fixed age at public expense. For some children, in some of the colonies, schooling was available or even compulsory, but the majority of youngsters grew up without ever seeing the inside of a schoolroom. The best education, in the sense of preparation for contemporary needs, was not in schools at all but in the shops of tradesmen.

By 1671, Massachusetts, New Hampshire and Connecticut had compulsory education laws; but these did not mean compulsory school attendance, for families had three options: instructing their children at home, sending them to a private or public school or putting them out as apprentices. Enforcement of the education law relaxed with time, however, and by the Revolution numerous Massachusetts towns had abandoned their public schools without being penalized. What remained, in much of rural New England, was home instruction, which the authorities never closely supervised, or apprenticeship, which was increasingly valued as the trades expanded and flourished. The apprentice laws called for some formal instruction—in simple arithmetic, reading and writing—at the master's expense, although towns usually paid part of the cost.

The well-to-do, in any age or country, can always manage to educate their children in the ways they wish, even if it means sending them abroad. Boston's private schools were good enough to attract pupils from outlying colonies, especially Barbados. One such visiting pupil, twelve-year-old Anna

Green Winslow, kept a sprightly diary that she sent, in batches, to her parents in Nova Scotia. She attended not one school but three: Mrs. Whitwell's for standard subjects, a sewing school and a dancing school; and in her spare time she found plenty to do to keep busy. In 1772, she was reading an abridged version of *Joseph Andrews,* in "nice Guilt and flowers covers," and on the evening of March 6, with her work all done, she wrote with satisfaction, "I think this day's work may be called a piece meal for in the first place I sew'd on the bosom of unkle's shirt, mended two pairs of gloves, mended for the wash two handkerchiefs, (one cambric) sewed on half a border of lawn apron of aunts, read part of the XXIst Chapter of Exodus, & a story in the Mother's gift." The weather had been wretched that

Kitchen in Williamsburg shows plastered fireplace, cooking utensils, basket for fruit and vegetables.

day, and she hadn't gone to school, for attendance was optional. Her spelling was better than the average of the period. Good penmanship was considered essential, but nobody worried much about how words were spelled, and teachers were often judged primarily by their competence in teaching handsome penmanship.

In the Middle Colonies, education was most fully developed in Pennsylvania, but it was curiously fragmented. The academy proposed by Franklin was supposed to be nonsectarian, but when it opened in 1751 three-quarters of its board of trustees were Anglican, and as a result the Quakers held aloof. It was two schools in one—the Latin School and the English School. The first of these, like the Boston Latin School and most of its younger rivals

Oil portrait of William Beekman of New York, a "good boy at his books," by John Durand. As most children were at the time, he is dressed like an adult.

in New England, prepared students for college; and since all colleges in the eighteenth century stressed the classics, the private schools had to also if college was the goal. The English School was a reflection of the dominant regional attitude; colleges and classics were not set on a pedestal above trades and practical subjects in Pennsylvania. Of some hundred private schools in and near Philadelphia in 1775, the majority stressed instruction in surveying, navigation, accounting and business arithmetic—tools for the practical man of affairs. The best private school in all Pennsylvania was kept by Andrew Porter, a mathematics school enrolling more than a hundred boys.

Like Boston, Philadelphia was well supplied with competent teachers and could attract the best from the older colleges and from abroad. Public schools, though less respected, and a solid program in apprenticeship gave the city a well-rounded educational system; even girls were provided for, though they were more likely to study French and dancing than navigation and accounting. Quakers, Moravians and Swedes, if not Anglicans, saw virtue in educating women; but all groups, in all the colonies, were much more concerned with education for boys.

The German settlements west of Philadelphia developed their own schools without direction or help from the colonial government. The variety of schools matched the variety of sects; some viewed education for girls with horror, others shunned worldly subjects, but in general the schools were as good as any in other rural sections. The Schwenkfelders, a very small community easily overlooked, had perhaps the most democratic school system of the period. It was wholly secular, open to all children, free to children of indigent parents and centrally administered, thus resembling public schools of later times.

"Good Boys at Their Books"

Schools varied greatly in 1775. It would astonish nobody to learn that facilities were primitive, but the specifics of primitivism may produce a jolt or two. Heavy pencils were just then coming on the market, made of pulverized graphite mixed with clay, but the common writing implement was the quill pen, which a schoolmaster with any experience could quickly cut from a goose quill with his penknife. The best ink was imported from Europe; it came in powdered form and had to be dissolved in vinegar. Soot, which cost nothing, was often substituted for the imported powder, but more rural families made ink by boiling down swamp-maple bark and adding copperas, an inexpensive ferrous sulphate, to make it darker. Pupils carried their ink to and from school, in inkhorns that were like powder horns but smaller or in small leather bottles. There were no blackboards or chalk, and individual slates were a luxury. Except in the best private schools, the available paper was rough and dark—and costly; to save expense some children ciphered or practiced writing on birch bark. The paper, unruled, came in foolscap size; doubled over twice, one sheet made four leaves, or eight pages. Slipped into each other, given a cover of brown wrapping paper and sewed together at the spine, they made a booklet that could be kept for later review or reference. The preliminaries to learning, it is obvious, took time and patience. One technique the pupil had to acquire was lining the paper with an individually owned lead plummet tied to a ruler.

Schools were not built for comfort. The first seats were planks set on legs, but by the 1770s, most were benches with backs, both flat. If there was any heat, it was from a large fireplace; the potbellied stove associated with "the little red schoolhouse" was still unknown. There were no maps; none were

Inside a colonial classroom. Textbooks were bound in leather for durability. Goose-quill pen and ink pot were universal, but the slate was a rarity. The globe was virtually the only visual aid to learning.

needed because geography was not at that time in the curriculum.

The textbooks, handed down from one pupil generation to the next, suggest the subject matter. The most durable was the *New England Primer,* first published before 1690 and reissued, with slight changes, many times in the next two centuries. It introduced the alphabet with a "syllabarium," a series of syllables somewhat more difficult than the ABC hornbooks that beginners used. Another major section of the *Primer* was the "Shorter Catechism," 107 religious questions and answers. From 1737 on, the *Primer* carried the familiar children's prayer (by an unknown author):

> *Now I lay me down to sleep,*
> *I pray the Lord my soul to keep,*
> *If I should die before I wake,*
> *I pray the Lord my soul to take.*

An even more lugubrious poem, on the same page, must have reminded many pupils of dead brothers and sisters in that time of high infant mortality:

> *I in the burying place may see*
> *Graves shorter there than I;*
> *From Death's arrest no age is free,*
> *Young children too may die.*
> *My God, may such an awful sight,*
> *Awakening be to me!*
> *Oh! that by early grace I might*
> *For Death prepared be.*

What was most conspicuous in the *Primer* was moral didacticism. The very first entry, even before the alphabet, promised the student a reward for classroom diligence:

Above: Jane Beekman (later Mrs. Stephen Van Cortlandt), painted by John Durand. *Opposite top:* Poor Richard's sayings were never illustrated in Franklin's almanacs. They were still very popular in the eighteenth century and were then set down on a single sheet and given the title *Bowles Moral Pictures or, Poor Richard Illustrated.* *Opposite bottom:* Double page from 1767 edition of the colonial schoolbook, the *New England Primer.*

T		Young *Timothy* Learnt Sin to fly.

Young *Timothy*
Learnt Sin to fly.

Vashti for Pride,
Was set aside.

Whales in the Sea,
GOD's Voice obey.

Xerxes did die,
And so must I.

While Youth do cheer
Death may be near.

Zaccheus he
Did climb the Tree,
Our Lord to see.

T
U
W
X
Y
Z

WHO was the first Man?   *Adam.*
     Who was the first Woman?   *Eve.*
Who was the first Murderer?   *Cain.*
Who was the first Martyr?   *Abel.*
Who was the first tra flated?   *Enoch.*
Who was the oldest Man?   *Methuselah.*
Who built the Ark?   *Noah.*
Who was the patientest Man?   *Job.*
Who was the meekest Man?   *Moses.*
Who led *Israel* into *Canaan*?   *Joshua.*
Who was the strongest Man?   *Samson.*
Who kill'd *Goliah*?   *David.*
Who was the wisest Man?   *Solomon.*
Who was in the Whale's Belly?   *Jonah.*
Who saves lost Men?   *Jesus Christ.*
Who is *Jesus Christ*?   *The Son of God.*
Who was the Mother of Christ?   *Mary.*
Who betray'd his Master?   *Judas.*
Who deny'd his Master?   *Peter.*
Who was the first Christian Martyr?   *Stephen.*
Who was chief Apostle of the Gentiles?   *Paul.*

The Infant's Grace before and after Meat.

BLess me, O Lord, and let my Food strengthen me to serve thee, for Jesus Christ's sake. *Amen.*

I Desire to thank God who gives me Food to eat every Day of my Life. *Amen.*

Good Boys at their Books.
He who ne'er learns his A, B, C,
Forever will a Blockhead be;
But he who to his Book's inclin'd,
Will soon a Golden Treasure find.

Diligence alone was not enough, however; vice had to be actively shunned in the unceasing drive toward virtue:

> *Wo to the Wicked, it shall be ill with him, for*
> *the Reward of his hands shall be given him.*

Another "lesson" is clear enough, in justifying the use of corporal punishment in virtually every school in the colonies:

> *Foolishness is bound up in the Heart of a Child,*
> *but the Rod of Correction shall drive it*
> *from him.*

The most explicit section of the entire *Primer* reminded its young readers that

Good Children must
Fear God all day,
Parents obey,
No false thing say,
By no sin stray,
Love Christ alway,
In secret pray,
Mind little play,
Make no delay
In doing Good.

Children were taught and expected to obey their parents without question. The father held supreme authority; a mother's best means of quelling revolt and restoring good order was to threaten to report the misconduct to father.

Other textbooks widely used in the 1770s approached the *Primer* in longevity. Thomas Dilworth's *A New Guide to the English Tongue* was first issued in 1740, and J. Hodder's *Arithmetic: or, that Necessary Art Made Most Easy* in 1739. American schoolbooks were printed on poor paper, and the illustrations were crude, yet they were usually

Assorted colonial classroom equipment: a set of paints, which had to be dissolved in water, two pens and a stick with string, which was used for lining paper.

bound in full leather and obviously intended for long use.

Good teachers were scarce. Some of the best were clergymen with college degrees who eked out their clerical stipends by conducting schools. Even more in demand were transplanted Scots. The poorest teachers were uneducated men unable or unwilling to hold other jobs, giving substance to the old gibe:

Those who can, do;
Those who can't, teach.

To inspire the respect their credentials seldom justified, many schoolmasters adopted a kind of uniform: three-cornered hat, long dark coat with square skirts reaching to the calves, white silk stockings, paste knee and shoe buckles, gray wig down to the shoulders and a gold-headed cane. They permitted no nonsense and were skilled in the use of ferule, rattan, cowhide or even cat-o'-nine-tails and in devising more imaginative punishments. Seatmates addicted to private conversation were sometimes yoked together and their mouths gagged by "whispering sticks"—strips of wood tied by strings around the neck. Sitting on a unipod, a stool with one leg, or standing on a dunce stool or being forced to wear a dunce cap were reserved for backward pupils. Other lads spent periods of time labeled with placards—Idle Boy, Tell-Tale, Lying Ananias—or holding heavy wooden blocks by a ring in the center for several minutes.

Girls were seldom punished, perhaps because they realized it was a concession to hold school for them at all and behaved with decorum. In some of the Dame schools, on the kindergarten level, they were mixed with boys, as was usual also under family tutors; but the general school practice was to instruct them when the boys were not in attendance —early morning or late afternoon or in the summer when their brothers were working. There was plenty of time, for the school year was short, a few months only. Nathan Hale held summer school for girls, in the morning from five o'clock until seven; since the parents paid him twenty shillings for the session, his class of twenty yielded twenty pounds, considerably above the average, though not, perhaps, for Yale graduates who turned to teaching.

Schooling in the South

Travelers venturing into the Southern colonies were invariably struck by the regional peculiarities and their effect on education. The almost total reliance on agriculture, the widely scattered homesteads, the large size of parishes—averaging more than five hundred square miles and seldom with a central village—the paucity of towns and cities, the political control by large plantation owners who fancied themselves an aristocracy and defended the neo-feudal social structure, the sheer numbers of black slaves and indentured whites, the relative lack of education among the first settlers and, by extension, the continuing indifference to an educated public—all these conspired to limit education severely in the plantation colonies. Instead of laws requiring political units to create and maintain public schools, Virginia legislated education for certain disadvantaged children. Seventeen laws affected orphans; New England needed no such laws and had none. The seventeenth of these laws, passed in 1748 and embracing all the others, required all orphans without means to be indentured. Another set of laws, passed from 1646 to 1769, ordered parish vestrymen to give religious instruction to poor children and to see that they learned trades. Such children increased rapidly in number because so many parents, uneducated themselves and not prosperous, were shiftless, ignorant and given to deserting their children. The county court was required to bind out to tradesmen all children who were permitted by their parents to become vagrants. The courts had even more power over illegitimate children, numerous because of the laws forbidding the marriage of servants. No legal provision was made for the education of mulattoes and other racial mixtures, any more than for the slaves themselves.

What these laws add up to is education in the trades, as apprentices or bondsmen, for children who otherwise might become antisocial or wards of the colony. A few private schools existed, established by philanthropy, among others the Syms-Eaton School in Virginia and the Bethesda Orphan Home in Georgia. Apart from a grammar school at William and Mary College, Virginia had no publicly supported schools. English schools advertised in Virginia, but families that could afford them were increasingly reluctant before the Revolution to send their darlings to a country of such reputed corruption and dissipation, bad manners and worse morals. Private schools in the Northern colonies were preferable. One final possibility was to enroll children under the tutor hired by a wealthy neighbor, *if* the tutor and the neighbor consented and if the great neighbor lived near enough.

Charleston was the one Southern city well stocked with schools. One was called "The Free School," founded under the Free School Act of 1712, but with only twelve pupils paid for out of public funds, twenty more supported by donors and others admitted for four pounds a year, it wasn't really free. The others were all private, including one for girls opened in 1770 by Mrs. Elizabeth Duneau, "a gentlewoman lately from England." Its curriculum was trivial. Most of the schools, for boys only, offered substantial practical instruction. This urban pattern developed because the South Carolina

aristocracy spent much of the year in Charleston instead of on their plantations, located as most of them were in humid and unhealthful lowlands.

The older aristocracy in Virginia seldom visited cities and relied on tutors instead. The plantation tutor, indeed, has a place in our mythology almost equal to that of the one-room rural school in the North. The myth includes the assertion, which seems improbable, that most of the tutors were transported felons or redemptioners. Yet of two plantation tutors whose journals have been published, one was a bondsman, John Harrower; his master, Col. William Dangerfield, owner of a large plantation near Petersburg, needed a tutor at once and found Harrower acceptable because he was a Scot. The other was Philip Fithian, who served as tutor for one year, 1773–74, for the Robert Carter family at Nomini Hall and then returned to New Jersey to marry and enter the ministry.

Both men ate with the master and mistress, were assigned slaves to tend their quarters and accompanied the household to church and on visits to neighboring plantations. Harrower's schoolhouse, a neat structure twenty by twelve feet at the end of one of the avenues leading from the mansion, doubled as his private quarters; early every morning a "bonny blackbairn" came to clean up and make the bed. No blackbairn, however, was among the pupils, but the colonel's carpenter, Thomas Brooks, attended the lessons in writing and arithmetic. For brief periods there were also children from the neighborhood, rounded up by the colonel as a means of helping the tutor; the going tuition fee for such outsiders was five shillings a quarter. At term's end, collecting the money proved very difficult, if possible at all.

Harrower's one misadventure related to corporal punishment. Like every teacher in the land he could whip an insolent pupil, but the mistress of the plantation became very angry when he whipped one of her sons, and she hinted at dismissal. A few days later her husband chided Harrower for *not* whipping another son who he believed deserved it.

The Carter plantation was on a much grander scale, with about five hundred slaves, assorted stewards, clerks, craftsmen and artisans. Carter himself was a parish vestryman and church warden, a onetime member of the governor's council and a militia colonel. His seven children, two boys and five girls, and a resident nephew made up Philip Fithian's school, which occupied one of several outbuildings collectively known as "offices." The two sons lived in one of these buildings and enjoyed a degree of freedom not in the experience of most boys. The girls gave Fithian only occasional trouble, but he was hard pushed to keep the boys in line. In reporting one of their heated arguments, he quoted the older boy as taunting the younger for taking a slave girl to bed with him, and it was not denied; but by that time Fithian was so used to their devilment that he recorded no particular shock.

Whatever education took place that year was more important for the tutor than for his pupils. He talked often with amiable Mrs. Carter; they agreed that if all the slaves were sold and the proceeds put at interest, the family income would be greater. Fithian's private opinion, no doubt reflecting his Northern background, was that the poor slaves should have remained in Africa, their places taken by industrious white tenants.

College—for the Few

Scots and Princetonians were favored as tutors by plantation owners who hoped their sons would qualify for Oxford or Cambridge. In the Northern colonies, boys heading for college studied under local clergymen or attended one of the few preparatory schools. Of these, the Boston Latin School and the Dummer Academy in Byfield, Massachusetts, were considered the best in New England, furnishing about half the Harvard freshman class year after year. A smaller academy in Lebanon, Connecticut, was a close rival; according to local tradition Yale waived the entrance examinations for its graduates.

Jonathan Trumbull, Connecticut's wartime governor, had helped found the Lebanon school, but as a Harvard alumnus he wasn't chagrined when his sons chose Harvard over Yale. One son, John, decided not to go on to college at all because his chief interests, modern languages and painting, were not yet in the curriculum. But at sixteen he changed his mind, enrolling at Harvard as a junior —a practice fairly common in those days and the only way to escape the hazing of freshman year. Course work proved so easy that he arranged with a family of relocated Acadians to teach him French. The most significant event of his Harvard experience was his meeting, sometime in 1772, with John Singleton Copley, who revived his ambition to become an artist—as he subsequently did, with conspicuous success.

Graduates of Harvard and the eight other colleges founded before the Revolution commonly became men of distinction but not because college prepared them for particular occupations. The social value of college in those days came less from the curriculum, which had almost no relation to current realities, than from the unique opportunity for boys from different regions and classes to mingle on an equal footing and exchange ideas. Thomas Jefferson, at William and Mary in the early 1760s, was confirmed in his democratic views by acquaintance with sons of backcountry farmers, and Philip Fithian, a decade later at Princeton, reported that

"I have the Opportunity of acquainting myself with Mankind by observing the Conduct and Temper of the Students in this Seminary."

At Harvard, the members of each class were ranked until 1773 in a strict order of seniority, based not on the modern "accumulated grade-point average" but rather on status in colonial society. Students recited, marched in processions and were seated at meals in this order; it even determined their placement in the catalog of graduates. Sons of governors (John Trumbull among them) came first, then sons of lieutenant governors, members of legislatures (in the chronological order of their election), justices of the peace and lesser officials, then the sons of college graduates in the order of *their* graduation and finally the sons of nobody in particular, with charity students at the tail end. Until agitation for greater democracy, as part of the revolutionary fervor, whittled away at such ranking, the Harvard system merely reflected accepted practice in colonial society.

There weren't many choices in the 1770s for boys who wanted a college education: Harvard and Yale in New England and two others less than ten years old, The College of Rhode Island (now Brown) and Dartmouth; Kings in New York, which waited until 1784 to change its name to Columbia; two in New Jersey, Queen's at New Brunswick, which became Rutgers in 1825, and the College of New Jersey at Princeton, better known as Nassau Hall; the College of Philadelphia, soon to be renamed the University of Pennsylvania; and, alone in the entire South, William and Mary at Williamsburg, Virginia. None existed, except on paper, in Delaware, North or South Carolina or Georgia. But the fact that nine were in operation was one more evidence that the colonies were not the raw wilderness of British imagination.

Love and Marriage

Early marriage was encouraged. Deferral, in the

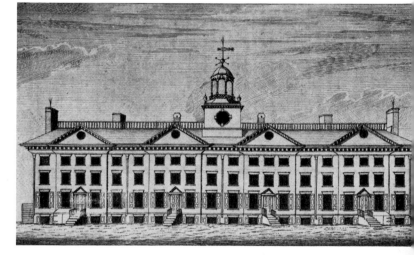

logic of practicality, was like failure to open good land to husbandry, with a resulting loss of harvests. The crop most in demand was children. The fact had a bearing on social customs and on attitudes, including the scorn heaped on bachelors and spinsters and the tolerance of premarital intimacy.

Whether the Dutch or the English invented bundling nobody seems quite certain, but by the late eighteenth century, it was an accepted part of courtship in New England and the Middle Colonies. Jonathan Edwards had firmly opposed it, but most clergymen, if pushed for an opinion, endorsed it for engaged couples. In warm months, lovers could walk off into the woods or meet in the barn or the springhouse, but on cold or stormy nights they could be together only indoors—and it was pretty crowded around the fireplace. Simple hospitality and a genuine wish to hasten the courtship prompted an invitation to stay and share the girl's bed; it was usually the only place where the boy could have slept, and the center board kept for such occasions theoretically discouraged close intimacy.

One obvious advantage was that the parents knew where the girl was and who was with her, whether or not the centerboard stayed in place. If she was pregnant at her wedding, the ceremony more or less sanctified it; and besides, bearing children was a woman's duty. The arrangement greatly reduced the incidence of illegitimacy. But even when the couple couldn't marry—if, for example, the boy was killed in an accident—an unmarried mother brought no great shame to the family, no lasting stigma, whatever *The Scarlet Letter* said about the matter in a later (Victorian) generation.

In colonies where bundling was not a practice, "natural children" were quite numerous. One set of laws in the Southern colonies severely limited the freedom of indentured servants to marry; as an inevitable result, other laws had to be passed to prevent their offspring from becoming public charges. A passage in Harrower's journal no doubt reflects, in its matter-of-fact wording, the casual attitude of most colonials in the Revolutionary era:

Yesterday came Mary Fitzgyls to spin flax. She is an Irish girl and has now been Nine years in Virginia. She is still unmarried but has a child to one Dolton a Taylor in Fredericksburg. The boy is with her and is now two years old.

In certain New England churches, approval of a marriage was contingent on full confession of sins by the prospective bride and groom. In the hierarchy of sins, lying was apparently worse than unsanctified sex, for the records of one church, over a period of years, show that almost half the couples admitted carnal knowledge of each other. Once that technicality was out of the way, the wedding date could be set. The reading of banns on successive Sundays had been generally abandoned by 1760,

but the Stamp Act revived it: Oral announcement of intention to marry cost nothing, but a published statement, according to the act, carried a tax. Church disapproval was reserved for what were called "disorderly marriages," meaning any not sanctioned by the church or by civil authorities. One old reprobate defied public opinion, insisting on keeping a girl as his wife with no ceremony whatsoever; but as Alice Morse Earle relates the story, a magistrate outfoxed him. Meeting the two on the street, he spoke sharply:

"John Rogers, do you persist in calling this woman, a servant, so much younger than yourself, your wife?"

"Yes, I do."

"And do you, Mary, wish such an old man to be your husband?"

"Indeed I do."

"Then, by the laws of God and this commonwealth, I as a magistrate pronounce you man and wife."

Rogers, thus wedded despite himself, could only answer, "Thee's a cunning fellow." His bride was hardly alone in having a much older husband; a girl given the chance of becoming the second (or third) wife of a clergyman or a prominent merchant was encouraged by her parents to accept, as a quick step upward on society's ladder. Young men sometimes took aged wives. On May 15, 1775, the *Virginia Gazette* reported that "Yesterday was married, in Henrico, Mr. William Carter, third son of John Carter, to Mrs. Sarah Ellyson . . . aged eighty five, a sprightly old Tit, with three Thousand Pounds Fortune."

If money was young Carter's motive, financial considerations were also basic to what were called "smock marriages." An old English tradition held that a husband did not have to assume any debts the bride might have accumulated if she wore only a smock at the wedding. Some brides, to make doubly sure, dispensed with the smock and stood naked in a closet or behind a screen, with only a hand extended to receive the ring. It also helped, some believed, to hold the ceremony on a public road; in 1774, several marriages were performed on the main highway in York, in coastal Maine. At one of them, in February, the minister took pity on the shivering bride, clad only in her chemise, and threw his coat over her shoulders. Smock marriages were also reported in Vermont, Rhode Island, Pennsylvania and New York.

Newlyweds, whatever their social status or the form of their wedding, began housekeeping at once; a honeymoon trip was extremely rare. Where there was money enough, the couple moved into a house built or bought for them; more commonly, they shared the home of one set of parents until they accumulated cash enough for a house of their own. At a midway economic stage, the double house was quite common: parents on one side, son and family on the other. No arrangement, however, could guarantee perfect harmony; especially with marriage at so early an age, incompatibility could develop, and often did. One oddity of the times was that estrangement was announced in public, in the form of notices like this:

West New-Jersey, July 27, 1774
Whereas Honnor, my wife, hath for some time past behaved in an unbecoming manner, hath carried away some of my wearing apparel, and eloped from my bed; these are therefore to forewarn all persons not to trust her any thing or lend her on my account, for I will not pay any debts or answer any contracts of hers after the date hereof.

Abraham Whitworth

More astonishing, in a period when a wife was expected to be obedient and subordinate to her husband, were the numerous notices published by aggrieved wives. One submitted by a New Jersey schoolmistress in 1775 is unusual for lapsing into rhyme:

Salem County, December 18, 1775
I, Sarah Smith, School-mistress, the wife of William Smith, take this method to inform the public not to trust or credit the said Smith on my account, for I shall never pay any of his contractions; my living shall go no more after that rate as it did last March. . . . I will not trust it to that false man. I nine years have been his wife, tho' he for a widower doth pass, when he meets a suitable lass; for his wicked doings I never more can him abide, nor he never more shall lie by my side.

Sarah Smith.

If a prize had been offered for the frankest, most detailed statement of wifely grievance, one printed in 1774 would have won it hands down:

Whereas John Ludeman, of Newark, my supposed husband, has advertised and exposed me in the public news-papers, accusing me with leaving his bed, whereunto I declare the same to be a wilful lie, because I never was bedded by him, it is true I parted from him for the following reasons:

I. He is a liar and a drunkard, and keeping company with those, who, with their flattery to gratify their vicious and drunken appetites, have instilled the spirit of jealousy into his breast, and by reason of his inability to perform the duties of a husband to a wife in the marriage bed, confirmed the same jealousy to be true, and therefore I was ill-treated by him.

II. The unnatural and beastly usage wherewith I was used from the time we were married till now, I thought it proper and lawful for me to part, to avoid future miseries, and the scandal which threatened me. I

Tapestry depicting a New England wedding in 1765. The bride and groom appear ready to leave in the waiting coach, while one late-arriving lady rides up sidesaddle.

therefore disclaim all right and title to him as a husband, and likewise free him from all obligations to me as a wife. I shall not trouble his credit, because no body will trust him without an order from Mr. Ogden, I shall only content myself with getting rid of so vile, base, treacherous, unnatural, beastly and drunken fool.

Marriage two centuries ago was obviously not the same as marriage today. Most wives accepted their status of subordination to their husbands and with it the almost-continuous pregnancies that aged them rapidly. Some had to contend with brutality and other mistreatment, and of these a few were quite prepared to report it, however shameful the details, in the newspapers. Others, able to endure abuse no longer, ran away; but it is only fair to add that some eloped in bigamous unions. Divorce was possible in some of the colonies, but difficult; only the most flagrant behavior was accepted as grounds. For roughly half the population, to round out this summary, marriage itself was not possible; slave unions had no legal standing, and many whites in bondage were barred from marrying.

Food in Abundance

The new bride, assuming her responsibilities of managing a household immediately after the wedding, simply maintained the pattern her social status had prepared her for. If there was wealth, she was the manager, with slaves or servants to do most of the work, and she would have on her table the best cuts of meat, the choice fruits and vegetables, the greatest delicacies, local or imported, that money could buy, along with the finest wines from Spain or Madeira. Without such wealth, the bride could apply her long apprenticeship to her mother, as cook and general manager, with the hope of gaining a reputation as a "frugal housewife."

Further down the social ladder, field hands owned by tight-fisted planters got weekly doles, seldom generous. But as a rule they had plots assigned to them, where they could raise food of their own, and they could cook their own meals, in whatever way they wished, in the quarter. Indentured servants were variously treated, some living like the slaves, others taking their meals in the mansion kitchens, a few eating with the family. But all Americans fared well—better, certainly, than people of their equivalent status in Europe—for here was a land of plenty and of general prosperity.

Eating habits were basically European, with American modifications and regional variations. Meat or seafood or poultry was served twice a day in most regions. Many families kept "dung-hill fowl," unfenced hens that fended for themselves. The old tried-and-true barter system helped; neighbors slaughtered by turn, exchanging with each other and keeping tallies of who owed what to whom. It reduced the number of animals any one man had to maintain. Where winters were cold enough, choice pieces could be frozen and packed with snow; and preserving by salting was increasingly helpful, now that salt was more plentiful and reasonable in price than earlier.

Sugar, however, was still a luxury; even molasses was expensive for the ordinary family. In the sections where "sugar maple" trees grew, the families with large pans in which to boil down the sap could make their own maple syrup or maple sugar, but such pans were scarce. Sugaring-off parties were a thing of the future. Even honey was not available to many people. But nobody grumbled; for the simple fact is that Americans in that period weren't the sweet tooths most of us are today. Baked beans, for example, were prepared without the molasses now considered essential in the home of the bean and the cod. In lieu of standard sweeteners, housewives added to cake batter (which was about the same as rich bread dough) chopped-up apples, currants, dried blueberries or the sections of squash and pumpkin nearest the seeds. Rose water sometimes was added. The effect of all these was flavor as well as sweetening.

Yeast was the only leavening; soda and baking powder entered the kitchen only later, well after 1800. Ginger, of various kinds, and West Indian nutmeg and allspice were familiar to most housewives, who also knew the flavoring virtues of common herbs, wild or domesticated. Some needed pulverizing with a mortar and pestle, as the Indians had done.

Cookbooks were scarce before the Revolution; some published in London had a few American recipes. Helpful hints might be included, such as what to do with tainted venison: "Bury it in the ground in a clean cloth a whole night, and it will take away the corruption, savour, or stink." Women exchanged and carefully kept recipes of their own written out on paper. Isolation accounted for regional specialties, not yet victimized by commercialized cookery; a New Englander traveling down through the colonies could be confident of a culinary surprise at each city en route—sausage and scrapple in Pennsylvania, terrapin and beaten biscuits in Maryland, ham in Virginia like no other he had ever tasted and in Charleston that queen of desserts, the syllabub made of cream, Rhenish wine, strong dry sack from the Canary Islands, lemon juice and sugar. If his visit was extended, however, he would come to miss the New England lobster stew, with its liberal chunks cut from cold-water lobsters that ran, in those days, to twenty pounds or more, or the Yankee oyster pie. After the oysters were parboiled and seasoned, "the pye being made, put a few currans in the bottom, and lay on the oysters, with some slic't dates in halves,

some large mace, slic't lemon, barberries, and butter, close it up and bake it, then liquor it with white wine, sugar, and butter."

If our traveler went from Philadelphia westward to the German region, he would have even greater culinary surprises: the "wurst" family of meats, for example—knackwurst, bratwurst, blutwurst and liverwurst—fine-cut sauerkraut and creamed potato salad. One compiler of Pennsylvania Dutch customs listed 264 traditional recipes, more than half of them for meat, vegetables and cereals. Others were for noodles and pickles, pretzels and zweiback, scrapple, cheeses and a wide variety of pastries—fastnachts (raised crullers), dumplings, shoofly pie (molasses crumb cake), rye bread, pumpernickel, anise-flavored cookies. The real Dutch, in and near New York, had fewer distinctive foods: smearcase (cottage cheese), olykoeks (doughnuts), Dutch apple cake, waffles and caudle. This last was made chiefly for sizable occasions, such as weddings; one recipe read as follows:

> 3 gallons of water
> 7 pounds of sugar
> oatmeal by the pound
> spice, raisins, and lemons by the quart
> 2 gallons of the very best Madeira wine

If that did not produce sociability, nothing could.

Travelers were sometimes overwhelmed, as John Adams was when Justice Chew invited him to Cliveden, his county seat near Germantown:

About four o'clock we were called to dinner. Turtle and every other thing, flummery, jellies, sweetmeats of twenty sorts, trifles, whipped syllabubs, floating islands, fools, etc., with a dessert of fruits, raisins, almonds, pears, peaches. A most sinful feast again! everything which could delight the eye or allure the taste. . . . Parmesan cheese, punch, wine, porter, beer.

Not many Americans dined that well in the Revolutionary period; but succulent dishes were familiar in all the colonies, in a variety that no one country in Europe could have provided. Not all these, unfortunately, have survived. The sora rail, "rather bigger than a lark," as one British visitor reported in 1775, is one of many delicacies no longer on menus, and few of us know the taste of rabbit stewed until tender with mace, a little flour, a quarter of a pound of butter and half a pint of port wine. Roast quail has survived; the recipe from the eighteenth century is simple:

Pluck and draw the Birds, rub a little
Butter over them, tie a strip of Bacon
over the Breasts, set them in the oven for
twenty or twenty-five minutes.

Anything not consumed while hot might appear next morning at breakfast. In Virginia our 1775 British traveler was astonished to find the breakfast table loaded with various "roasted fowls, ham, venison, game, and other dainties. Even at Williamsburg," he continued, "it is the custom to have a plate of cold ham on the table; and there is scarcely a Virginia lady who breakfasts without it." Philip Fithian reported the same custom of meat for breakfast at the Carter plantation, but he also spoke of fish on Wednesdays and Saturdays all summer long. For the evening meal, the Carters served only coffee with bread and butter.

Among Virginia Anglicans, Sunday was marked by a brief, formal church service followed by a great feast and then hearty exercise to work it off or a long nap to sleep it off. In extreme contrast, loyal New England churchgoers breakfasted on baked beans, kept warm overnight in the brick oven, and in cold weather carried to the unheated meetinghouse foot stoves or heated stones that warded off the chill during the three-hour morning service. For the noon meal they walked to a tavern, if one was near by, or crowded into a "nooning house" next to the church, where they could warm up a lunch brought from home in preparation for the afternoon service, also three hours long.

Lyman Beecher, father of Harriet, Henry Ward and the rest of that famous tribe, remembered the meals of his boyhood in North Guilford, Connecticut. Breakfast was a gourmand's delight of rye bread with fresh butter, buckwheat cakes and pie; and both dinner and supper meant salt pork or corned beef, vegetables and pie or pudding. On Sunday there was always a boiled Indian pudding. Beecher's mother made up a large stock of pies at Thanksgiving and froze them for winter use; they lasted until March. Life for the boy was strenuous, as he helped his father with the endless chores, but the heavy food supplied more than enough energy, and he often had heartburn after eating pie. Whether he drank milk with his meals he neglected to mention, but there was always plenty of cider; for a day of sheepshearing he and his father took a gallon of cider along and a little water. But when his Uncle Lot invited seven or eight neighbors to help with the haying, the gallon jug held not cider but rum, for there was a superstition, widely shared, that rum was essential when men were working together out of doors.

In many parts of the country the noon meal began with pudding followed by meat and vegetables. The pudding, however, was not like a modern dessert, for it was commonly unsweetened: hasty pudding (cornmeal mush) or a steamed dumpling-like concoction. Pies, in contrast, were often served for breakfast. As in so much else in the Revolutionary period, foods and meal patterns varied greatly, region by region, class by class. Most people ate at home; dining out was rare, something less to

The colonials ate well. All these are native American foods—nuts, cider, Indian corn, squash and pumpkin.

enjoy than to put up with when away from home. Taverns had their solid place in late colonial life, but less for the food they served than to slake what seems to have been a most amazing national thirst.

"To Ward Off Chills and Malarial Fevers"

Like their British models, colonial taverns were easy to find in any city: Hanging conspicuously above or beside the door was a sign with a picture representing the name—Blue Anchor, Three Cranes, Dragon, Beehive, Eagle, among many others. Waterfront taverns, to attract sailors, had such names as Dolphin, The Jolly Sailor, The Wounded Tar. Some names were corruptions: Bag o' Nails from Bacchanalians, Cat and Wheel from St. Catherine's Wheel, Goat and Compasses from God Encompasseth Us. Keeping them freshly painted put money in the pockets of young artists. During the early 1770s, names related to British royalty were dropped and less obnoxious ones substituted. King's Arms, The George and others that had formerly been common became Pig and Whistle or Indian Queen or anything else the owners could think of. A few, to save money, kept the royal portrait but assigned it a new name. Where Loyalists were locally strong, such a change would have meant loss of patronage. The Golden Bowl at Weston, some fifteen miles west of Boston, was a noted Tory house; and Tory spies could be safe at any of several taverns owned by men named Jones —an oddity that defies explanation. Once the shooting began, however, ardent patriots gave the Tory owners the choice of changing offensive signs or going out of business, which explains in part the sudden popularity of taverns named after rebel generals, Washington in particular.

Not all taverns served meals, but all sold liquor. The taproom was always the largest room in the place and the most crowded, night after night. The bar, as the center of interest, was usually protected by a contraption resembling a portcullis that could be lowered at closing time. Over the bar there was often a rhymed reminder that drinks were not sold on credit:

> *I've trusted many, to my sorrow.*
> *Pay today. I'll trust tomorrow.*
>
> *My liquor's good, my measure just;*
> *But, honest Sirs, I will not trust.*

Among the few things free in most taverns was the pipe tongs on peg beside the great fireplace; the user could pick up a live coal with it and light his pipe from the coal, tamping the lighted tobacco down with the other end. Some taverns also provided a small metal brazier called a "comfortier"; it held several live coals and could be passed around a table from one pipe smoker to the next, saving trips to the fireplace.

Drinks were served in containers of many shapes and sizes. The flip glass without handles might hold as much as a quart, but most mugs and tumblers were smaller. The common American version of flip, mixed in a large earthen pitcher, was two-thirds strong beer sweetened with sugar, molasses or dried pumpkin fortified with a gill of rum and given its special quality by the immersion of a red-hot poker called a "loggerhead." Cider was sometimes used instead of beer. Toddy, sling and grog, all with a rum base, had numerous variations, the result of the great increase of intercolonial travel, and the barkeep had to keep his wits about him. If the buyer insisted on a lump of sugar, he got it readily enough but had to crush it himself, using the toddy stick, six or eight inches long, that hung on a wall beside the fire tongs and the comfortier.

Punches were popular, made of rum, sugar and "sourings," the word for lemon, orange or lime juice or pineapple juice imported from the West Indies or Portugal in demijohns. Anyone willing to pay the difference could have brandy instead of rum, but a few recipes required both and also Madeira wine. One elegant punch called for sugar, hot water, lemon juice and peel, spice, brandy, porter and Jamaica rum. The spice most in demand was nutmeg, and yet another tool for tavern patrons was the nutmeg holder, shaped to hold one nutmeg and with a grater on one surface. Only the hardiest tipplers tried certain far-out concoctions, like "whistle-belly-vengeance," made by simmering sour beer in a kettle, adding molasses for a sweetener and filling the kettle with bread crumbs, or the ominous-sounding "stone-wall," half rum and half hard cider.

At the Wolfe Tavern in Newburyport, on the main road from Boston to Portsmouth, a number of local men gathered on September 26, 1765, to discuss the Stamp Act. How many were there we do not know, but they ran up a fifty-nine pound bill by downing thirty-three double and three "thribble" bowls of punch, an unspecified number of egg toddies, along with supper and breakfast the next morning. Stamp Acts, of course, aren't everyday events. But good rebels needed no special occasion to assemble, as more than three hundred did on August 14, 1769, at Robinson's Tavern in Dorchester, where they feasted on barbecued pig and drank no fewer than forty-five toasts. The forty-fifth and last was a scorcher: "Strong halters, firm blocks, and sharp axes to all such as deserve them."

Moderate drinkers could order what was called "small drink"—beer or wine or mead made from fermented honey or, in Virginia, from the long beans of the locust tree. From surviving tavern records, however, it would seem that moderate drinkers and teetotalers stayed at home or visited taverns only for special occasions like weddings, funerals, lottery drawings, church raisings or ordinations of clergymen. One ordination at Beverly, northeast of Boston, must have made the tavern owner happy, for his account in pounds, shillings and pence was as follows:

	£	s.	d.
30 Bowles of Punch before the People went to meeting	3		
10 bottles of wine before they went to meeting	1	10	
44 bowles of punch while at dinner	4	8	
8 bowles of brandy	1	2	
Cherry Rum	1	10	
6 people drank tea		6	

When some ministers were ordained, an "ordination beer" was brewed, from a forgotten recipe but presumably less heady than contemporary punches. But ordination parties for which tavern records survive stuck to standard drinks—toddy, punch, flip and wine. The records, incidentally, concern New England clergymen; in the Southern colonies, where taverns were scarce, comparable ceremonies for Anglican priests went unrecorded.

Strong drink, quite obviously, was an integral part of being alive. Not all colonial Americans drank, but a good many of them habitually took a morning dram before breakfast, to ward off chills and malarial fevers. Prohibition sentiment barely existed; one tract published in 1774, by the "Quaker Saint" Anthony Benezet, bore the impressive title *The Mighty Destroyer Displayed, in Some Account of the Dreadful Havock made by the mistaken Use as well as Abuse of Distilled Spiritous Liquors.* But most clergymen viewed alcohol as a "creature of God," not to be despised. As for the moderates, Ben Franklin provided a theme song in one of his rare

attempts at verse; entitled "A Drinking Song," it
includes these stanzas:

'Twas honest old Noah first planted the Vine,
And mended his Morals by drinking its Wine;
And justly the drinking of water decry'd,
For he knew that all Mankind, by drinking it dy'd.

From this Piece of History plainly we find
That Water's good neither for Body nor Mind;
That Virtue & Safety in Wine-bibbing's found
While all that drink Water deserve to be drown'd.

Diversions and Entertainments

A book for sale in the Revolutionary period, *The
Pretty Little Pocket Book,* told young readers all
they needed to know about play and games and
must have been a welcome relief from the moral
austerity of the *New England Primer,* which
equated play with idleness and sin. Hopscotch,
marbles, kite flying, jacks, cat's cradle, jumping
rope, dolls, sledding, blindman's buff and five kinds
of tag, one of them played in the snow—the book
had enough in it to keep life from ever becoming
dull, indoors or out, summer or winter, for any boy
or girl. Imaginative children could always invent
other games; Anna Green Winslow in her 1771
diary tells of a party she gave for eight girls and of
settling down, after minuets and other dances, to
pawns, hunt the whistle, thread the needle and woo
the widow.

Dolls were in short supply. A boy good at whit-
tling, as most boys were, could have cut from soft
pine a better doll than shops ever offered for sale;
most were wooden in appearance as well as in
material. The best dolls were not for sale but were
imported by dressmakers and milliners as fashion
models, in the absence of books and magazines with
fashion plates. Sent out to one prospective customer
after another, these dolls gradually lost their value
for business and eventually found permanent homes
with loving foster mothers.

The Pretty Little Pocket Book had no counter-
part describing adult play. The work week in the
Revolutionary period was so long, and most of the
work so hard, that it's a wonder men and women had
any time or desire for active diversions. Except for
dancing, people preferred to be spectators, as at
hangings and horse races, or to engage in sedentary
activities like card games, or to match skills that required no rapid movement, such as at quoits and
turkey shoots.

Dancing, the one great exception, was almost a
mania in the colonies. In any community large
enough to support a dancing teacher, the art was
taught to youngsters with the full encouragement,
if not the prodding, of parents; for skill on the
dance floor, like the fine penmanship prized more
highly than correct spelling, was a hallmark of
social superiority, and upward mobility was a general ambition. Some public schools and more private schools made dancing a regular part of the
curriculum. But when the Dummer Academy introduced dancing and hired a Frenchman as instruc-
tor, it produced a great uproar; one critic even
composed a poem on the subject:

Ye sons of Byfield now draw near,
Leave worship for the dance,
Nor farther walk in wisdom's ways,
But in the ways of France.

The old religious hostility to dance had largely
relaxed by 1770; most clergymen now approved and
even recommended dancing as a proper and healthy
exercise, although they drew the line against "pro-
fane and promiscuous dancing." The fox trot and

the bunny hug would no doubt have been banned but not jitterbugging, for the basic contredance pattern of two lines facing each other and performing in unison was interrupted now and then as individual pairs broke loose in solo gyrations but not in close embrace. Balls began at six o'clock, whether in Boston or Charleston, giving plenty of time before nine or ten to run through all the favorite dances. Their names, unfortunately, give no clues to their specific natures—Orange Tree, High Betty Martin, Miss Foster's Delight, Old Father George. All were probably American versions of traditional English dances. Other traditions survived in various regions—German forms in Pennsylvania, for example, and among the slaves who could relax only on Sunday, the Calinda and similar riotous dances imported chiefly from the West Indies.

Aristocratic Virginians, self-conscious heirs of Cavalier tradition, took pride in their dancing. Philip Fithian, at a ball given by Colonel Carter at Nomini Hall, reported every detail with enthusiasm —the alternate rounds of minuets and country dances; the game called "Button" that yielded pawns to be redeemed and the several kisses he got with his pawns; the excitement as Col. Philip Lee arrived from Williamsburg in his "traveling chariot"; and the supper at candle-lit tables—"a gay, sociable Assembly, & four well instructed waiters!" But Nicholas Cresswell, with his English standards, found nothing to praise at a similar ball in Alexandria. The ladies were overdressed and vain, he thought; and though they loved to dance, they did so without elegance. Jigs danced by one couple after another seemed endless; but what offended him more was the mixture of old women, young wives with children on their laps, widows and unmarried girls. Cresswell recorded that he "went home about two o'clock," after the cold supper, "but part of the company stayed, got drunk

Left: Open cupboard displaying wares used by an average family, including plate scoops (declining in use), earthenware (quite popular) and pewter (in increasing use). Mortar and pestle were essential to food preparation.
Above: Display rack in an affluent household, showing tablespoons with feather edge and porringer—both made by Joseph Richardson of Philadelphia—plates probably of Dutch Delft and opaque air-twist wineglass.

and had a fight." This was seven weeks after the British rout at Concord and Lexington, a fact that may have affected Cresswell's attitude.

Dancing appealed equally to both sexes. Few women, however, shared with men the passion for gambling that travelers noted throughout the colonies. Men would bet on anything—dice, card games, cockfights, horse races, target contests, election returns, the weather—and lotteries. These were widely used to raise money for reputable causes, not only by churches and colleges but by towns and colonies —to pay off public debts, perhaps, or to build bridges. When Faneuil Hall was rebuilt several years after it was gutted by fire in 1761, a lottery yielded much of the needed money, even though 90 percent of the proceeds went for prizes. Harvard College was somewhat less generous, keeping an eighth of what its own lotteries brought in.

Deceptive practices in private lotteries, which offered books, furniture, jewelry or real estate instead of cash prizes, undermined and eventually destroyed public confidence in all lotteries. By 1774, it was necessary for reputable institutions to explain in print precisely how their lotteries would operate. Thus, when the Dutch Reformed Congregation of Millstone, New Jersey, wanted money for a parsonage, it promised a total of 2,002 prizes, ranging in value from $2,000 down to $4 and totaling $12,-000, the very amount the 6,000 two-dollar tickets would yield; the church's share was a 15 percent deduction on every prize, or $1,800. Fair enough. In March of the same year the College of New Jersey and two nearby Presbyterian churches announced a joint lottery, with 20,000 five-dollar tickets, prizes equaling the proceeds of $100,000 and 15 percent deducted for "expenses." Buyers had to get their tickets by May 1, the notice continued, for on that date a New Jersey law against lotteries was to take effect.

October 1.

TO BE SOLD,

Or rented for a Term of Years,

A Commodious Brew-house, Malt-House and Dwelling-House contiguous, situated at the upper end of Water-street, between Race and Vine-streets, bounded on the river, and by two wide alleys, one being a public alley: The buildings & implements are all in good order, & every article wanted for carrying on the business, may be landed at the wharf, without the heavy charge of carting. The works are so calculated that they may be managed with as much ease, & as little expence, as any brewery in the city. Any person inclining to purchase, or rent the said premises, may inquire for further particulars of JOHN JONES.

N: B: The business is carried on as usual; where may be had different kinds of BEER, at the customary prices.

September 10.

TO BE SOLD,

Top: Advertisement offering a Philadelphia brewhouse for sale. *Bottom:* Utensils used in a tavern—bottle, tankard, porringer, spoon, Delft posset pot. Posset was a drink made of hot milk, sweetened and spiced, then curdled with wine. Sometimes it was thickened with bread crumbs or with eggs. *Opposite:* Tavern sign.

J. ALDERMAN

Tavern sign for The Duke of Cumberland, owned by John and Sarah Robbins of Rocky Hill, Connecticut. Musket balls, believed to have been fired by the rebels in opposition to British royalty, remain embedded in the walls of the building, which is still standing. *Opposite:* Engraved decanter and wineglass on a piecrust table.

formal, rising out of a congenital male impulse to organize, and were devoted to conviviality, keeping the taverns crowded if they had no quarters of their own. Some clubs grew around special interests—exclusive racing and hunting clubs in the plantation colonies, workingmen's clubs in Northern cities and patriotic groups such as the Sons of Liberty.

Wives got their sociability as they could, at quilting bees or informal neighborhood gatherings. A few women, at the upper economic levels, had time for the card games then in fashion, four-handed quadrille and the older ombre, with three players and forty-card decks; but women showed less interest in formalizing their activities by organizing. Men didn't rely wholly on clubs, however; they could assemble spontaneously enough for local horse races or even travel some distance to watch and bet on major contests like the pacing races at Little Neck Beach near Narragansett or the open races staged by the Race Club and the Jockey Club at Charleston or the innumerable weekly race meets in Virginia and at local fairs held in many places throughout the colonies.

Any "shoot" or "baiting" always drew a crowd of males. In a modern turkey shoot, a live turkey is awarded to the winning marksman; in Revolutionary times the turkey itself was the target. The range differed with the firearms used—110 yards for a musket, 165 yards for a rifle. Bears were other popular marks, as a notice in the *Boston Evening Post* for January 11, 1773, indicates: "This is to give Notice That there will be a Bear and a Number of Turkeys set up as a Mark next Thursday Beforenoon at the Punch Bowl Tavern in Brookline." Baiting was no less popular but somewhat more savage. Wolves, the most hated and destructive of all natural enemies, were hunted down in a "wolf rout" or caught in pits or traps, but instead of being killed outright, they were tortured for the

Lotteries could come or go, however, with no appreciable effect on the rich subculture of male amusements. Clubs of all sorts flourished. Freemasons were the only fraternal order with formal organization; the proliferation of secret societies began after 1800. Franklin belonged to the first Masonic lodge in America, founded in Philadelphia in 1730. Washington joined a lodge in Virginia in 1752. St. Andrew's Lodge in Boston, with Paul Revere, John Hancock and other rebel leaders on its rolls, was a virtual cell of patriotic activism. The Masonic order as a whole leaned toward the rebel side, and links between lodges all up and down the coast helped unify the anti-British movement. When the war began, American Masons cut loose from the older lodges in Great Britain.

Irish in the colonies formed a number of independent societies, such as the Sons of St. Patrick who entertained Josiah Quincy on his Charleston visit. Most clubs, however, were both local and in-entertainment it provided. The most common form of this baiting was to tie the wolf to a stake and let dogs attack it on every side. Bears, never as numerous as wolves, were also baited, and on rare occasions a bull or a horse. By the time of the Revolution, baiting was on the decline, not because men were growing soft but rather because the larger carnivores were approaching extinction in older settled areas.

The blood lust, or whatever it was that made baiting popular with colonial men, had another outlet in the public execution of criminals; but women and children were also attracted. One of the most memorable was the hanging of Levi Ames on October 21, 1773, at the age of twenty-one. His conviction on a burglary charge won him considerable popular sympathy because his partners in the crime were never caught. On successive Sundays for two months he was carried through the streets of Boston, handcuffed and with his ankles chained, to be exhibited at one church or another, according to long-standing practice, while the minister preached on the wages of sin; and a large crowd of men, women and children always walked beside his cart. Several broadsides were printed and quickly sold. "The Dying Groans of Levi Ames," twelve quatrains of remorse and admonition, possibly of the hero's own composition, ended with the hope of salvation that he actually entertained:

> *Farewell to Earth, farewell to Sin,*
> *One pang will set me free;*
> *Support me, O! thou Rock divine,*
> *And snatch my Soul to Thee.*

Another broadside poem, in four-beat couplets, was "The Speech of Death to Levi Ames"; Death indicts the youth for idleness, drunkenness, foul language and evil company and closes by observing:

Above: Plates from an instruction book on dancing.
Opposite: Drawing by Dr. Alexander Hamilton illustrating his minutes for the Ancient and Honourable Tuesday Club, a social group organized by a number of prominent Annapolis, Maryland, gentlemen in 1745.

Grand Rehearsal of the Anniversary Ode.

Ruin advances by Degrees:
The youth with lesser Crimes begins,
And then proceeds to grosser Sins,
From Step to Step he travels on
And sees himself at once undone:
Surpriz'd! unthought on! finds his Fate,
His Ruin final, and compleat.

Holidays and Festivals

Slaves worked six days a week and had Sunday free; so did indentured whites and so did free agents with steady employment—it was one of the few things all workers had in common. The free agents could also relax on holidays and certain festive days:Whether the others could depended on the nature of the celebration and the relative generosity of their owners. Such days differed from colony to colony; some were limited to particular communities, and only a very few were recognized by all the population on the same date each year.

Christmas was one of these; it had been celebrated on December 25 since the fourth century. But Puritans disapproved of what one of them called "wanton Bacchanallian Christmases," and only in one Anglican stronghold in Rhode Island was the day a holiday anywhere in New England. Families could observe it privately, but people with jobs had to work. In other sections, especially those dominated by Anglicans, the traditional English Christmas held firm. Thanksgiving, in contrast, was not a general holiday; and even in New England, where it originated, it was a "moveable feast" with a vengeance, observed in different months—January, perhaps, or October or December—until President Washington, in 1789, proclaimed it a national holiday to be observed the last Thursday in November. The one constant through all its history, the serving of turkey as the main course, took

Opposite: Colonial dolls, crude of manufacture but doubtless loved none the less. *Above left:* A handsome wooden rocking horse, brought from England and used by the family of Lieutenant–Governor Samuel Phipps of Boston. *Top right:* A peg game called "merek," similar to tick-tack-toe. *Bottom:* Iron puzzle made by a blacksmith.

79

on a special significance in the Revolutionary period as a repudiation of Britain's traditional beef.

Religious festivals varied, from colony to colony, in the ways they were observed. Where the Anglican church was established, not only Christmas but Epiphany, Lent and Easter followed the practice in England. The same calendar dates were observed among the Pennsylvania Dutch but with the traditional German stress on food: *Fastnachtskuechlen* on Shrove Tuesday, *lebkuchen* "by the crockful" at Christmas. In adopting Thanksgiving, these sturdy people assigned it a particular kind of food, *Schwenkfelder* bread. They also saved the ashes from the fireplace on Good Friday for special farm purposes, to keep their livestock well and to keep lice from the fruit trees.

One annual holiday, notable for its fireworks, was the King's Birthday, celebrated everywhere until it came to an abrupt end with independence. Its logical replacement, the Fourth of July, was not established at once but was in growing favor before the war ended. Another relic of British tradition, Guy Fawkes Day (November 5), survived the break with England, largely because it had come to be known as Pope's Day and served to reaffirm Protestant feelings. During the day, boys in fantastic costumes formed parades, and after dark straw figures representing the pope and the devil were burned in bonfires; when Benedict Arnold was exposed as a traitor in 1780, he was burned in effigy beside them. Pope's Day, it hardly needs to be said, was not observed in Catholic areas.

What had once been called Training Day, when militia companies assembled to demonstrate their continued battle readiness, was better known as Muster Day in the years before the Revolution, but it had degenerated into an occasion for rough humor and hard drinking. The Stamp Act abruptly restored its seriousness. Election Day, however, the noisiest and least dignified of all holidays, retained its social character. In Framingham, Massachusetts, on March 5, 1770, the freeholders who could vote were busy electing selectmen, a town clerk, constables and collectors, wardens, overseers of the workhouse and of the poor, surveyors of highways, tithingmen, fence viewers, sealers of leather, hogreeves, deerreeves, plus committees to procure a grammar-school master, a writing master and school dames. Other committees were chosen to take care of the schoolhouses and to devise a new seating plan for the meetinghouse, which had to be done "without degrading any man." This meant that they had to consider specifically what estate each man had paid taxes on in the years 1768 and 1769 and assess on that basis, "allowing four pence per year for age after forty years old." They then adopted a budget of £209—£30 for support of grammar and writing schools, £20 for repair of schoolhouses, £20 for support of the poor, £25 for repairs of highways, £114 to pay the town's creditors. This done they could join their wives and all the others who had no civic duties for a holiday celebration. There may have been an Election Day sermon; in any case, Martha Brown, whose husband had been elected one of the six hogreeves, had baked her election cake for the special dinner.

Grandmother Brown's Election Cake
A piece of butter, twice its weight of sugar, twice their weight of flour, eggs, spice of cinnamon and nutmeg. Raisins. Malt yeast. Set to rise in warm place. Bake in thin loaves and glaze when hot with molasses.

A major occasion in college towns was commencement, which opened the academic year. Headmaster Moody of the Dummer Academy loved to attend the ceremony at Harvard, where he basked in the attention of his former students and was an

An Exhortation to young and old to be cautious of small Crimes, left they become habitual, and lead them before they are aware into those of the most heinous Nature. Occasioned by the unhappy Case of *Levi Ames*, Executed on *Boston*-Neck, *October* 21st, 1773, for the Crime of Burglary.

I.

BEWARE young People, look at me,
   Before it be too late,
And see Sin's End is Misery:
   Oh! shun poor *Ames*'s Fate.

II.

I warn you all (beware betimes)
   With my now dying Breath,
To shun Theft, Burglaries, heinous Crimes;
   They bring untimely Death.

III.

Shun vain and idle Company;
   They'll lead you soon astray;
From ill-fam'd Houses ever flee,
   And keep yourselves away.

IV.

With honest Labor earn your Bread,
   While in your youthful Prime;
Nor come you near the Harlot's Bed,
   Nor idly waste your Time.

V.

Nor meddle with another's Wealth,
   In a defrauding Way:
A Curse is with what's got by stealth,
   Which makes your Life a Prey.

VI.

Shun Things that seem but little Sins,
   For they lead on to great;
From Sporting many Times begins
   Ill Blood, and poisonous Hate.

VII.

The Sabbath-Day do not prophane,
   By wickedness and Plays;
By needless Walking Streets or Lanes
   Upon such Holy days.

VIII.

To you that have the care of Youth,
   Parents and Masters too,
Teach them betimes to know the Truth,
   And Righteousness to do.

IX.

The dreadful Deed for which I die,
   Arose from small Beginning;
My Idleness brought poverty,
   And so I took to Stealing.

X.

Thus I went on in sinning fast,
   And tho' I'm young 'tis true,
I'm old in Sin, but catcht at last,
   And here receive my due.

XI.

Alas for my unhappy Fall,
   The Rigs that I have run!
Justice aloud for vengeance calls,
   Hang him for what he's done.

XII.

O may it have some good Effect,
   And warn each wicked one,
That they God's righteous Laws respect,
   And Sinful Courses Shun.

Broadside printed and sold at the
time of the execution of Levi Ames,
condemned to death for burglary.

Above: Imported Chinese porcelain teapot, cup, spoon tray and tea caddy; silver teaspoons made in Philadelphia; pierced creamware plate from England. *Opposite top:* A woman's sidesaddle, used in Pennsylvania; stirrup has footrest and toe cover. *Opposite bottom:* Pipe stand with clay pipes and Delft tobacco jar; "Varinas" was a Venezuelan tobacco.

honored guest at the annual dinner. He wrote:

A Public Commencement I conceive by far the most glorious Show in America, and when the Exhibitions are fine and well-conducted, reflect the greatest Lustre on the Officers of the College, raise to the highest pitch the Ambition and Efforts of the Youth, carry the Applause of a large Assembly of brilliant, learned and respectable Spectators, spread the Fame of the University far and wide, and make large Accessions to the Numbers.

Anniversaries of the appointment of distinguished clergymen were seldom holidays but attracted crowds of the faithful. More outward enthusiasm, however, was evident in rural festivals of many sorts, some planned, others spontaneous, but all keyed to the sequence of the seasons: haying and berrying parties in the summer, apple-picking and cornhusking contests in the fall, sliding or skating parties in the winter and the gatherings of the annual run of shad and salmon in the spring. These were not holidays, in the strict sense, but any day when people deserted their work became a holiday in fact if not by tradition or employer consent. A generation that worked as these Americans did deserved all the holidays they could get.

"An Acquisitive Age"

Gold sovereigns, silver. crowns and shillings and copper pennies were scarce in the colonies, drained off year after year by England's profit-minded merchants. But coins of other nations, especially Spain and the Netherlands, circulated freely. Spanish-milled dollars, the famous "pieces of eight," came close to being the standard for colonial exchange. But when a country is prospering, it manages to devise new forms of money. Several colonies issued paper currency; it had a bad habit of depreciating

in value, but the Pennsylvania issues held firm. People also used letters of credit, individual drafts, promissory notes and bills of exchange, some of them representing so many pounds of tobacco or beaver pelts. The most visible proof that shortage of specie, though a nuisance, was no serious handicap was the way people adorned their bodies. Even the old Quaker stress on simplicity yielded to the current richness of fashion.

The great merchants and landlords could live as extravagantly as they liked, with extensive wardrobes and fancy chariots, trips abroad and weeks at exclusive spas, without denting their vast fortunes; but in the 1770s more and more tradesmen, shopkeepers and professional men broke out of the subsistence bind and had money to accumulate for future use, money to invest in land or other speculative property, money to spend freely on diversions and commodities they didn't really need. Skilled labor made the greatest gains in the Revolutionary era and contributed the most to the increasing flow of money and to the expanding total wealth.

On Sundays and holidays, and for special events on week nights, tradesmen laid their leather aprons aside and showed that they knew how to dress in the accepted social mode. The ultimate goal, which few commoners could really hope to reach, was the elegance of the aristocrats—enormous cocked hat, cloak or cape of scarlet broadcloth lined with silk and faced with velvet, embroidered vests with deep pockets, shirts ruffled in front and at the wrists, silk knee breeches and stockings, polished shoes with square silver buckles, gloves of doeskin or beaver and a glossy black cane, six feet long with a carved ivory head. The fact that fashions were set in England did not trouble the patriots; ability to acquire such an outfit was more important, as a proof of success. One by-product of the impulse toward finery was a marked increase

in ready-made clothing. An enterprising Boston tailor, Jolley Allen, advertised in 1768 a stock of "Coats, Silk Jackets, Shapes and Cloth ditto; Stocking Breeches of all sizes & most colours. Velvet Cotton Thickest Durory [corduroy] Everlasting & Plush Breeches." Newspaper editors, moreover, stimulated interest by describing individual garb; here's a report from 1782:

He wore a red velvet cap within which was one of fine linen, the last turned up two or three inches over the lower edge of the velvet. He also wore a blue damask gown lined with velvet, a white stock, a white satin embroidered waistcoat, black satin small-clothes, white silk stockings and red morocco slippers.

The man thus dressed was John Hancock. With his wealth he could have had an entire wardrobe of striking garb; but the details above suggest a shift from English influence to French, a fine gesture to a wartime ally that he could well afford.

No ready-made clothing, not even underclothing, was yet available for women; instead of trying on one dress after another in sedate shops or jostling each other in bargain basements, they made their own clothes or called in dressmakers. Skill in sewing was taught to every girl as part of her education, but professional help was needed for an outfit that would attract the gaze of girl-watchers and rouse the envy of rivals. Fabrics from many countries—silks, satins, laces, velvets, brocades—found eager buyers in colonial cities, where wages were considerably higher than for the same work in Europe. Wives of prospering tradesmen did not balk at the standard five-shilling fee to examine the newest "babies," as the fashion dolls were called; and in working out details with the seamstress (or mantua-maker, or itinerant tailoress), the prime thought was getting the most suitable ensemble; cost was secondary.

It was an acquisitive age; it was also a time when people kept inventories of their possessions—clothing, furniture, art objects and whatever else they spent their money on. The inventories that survive, however, never list any bathing facilities. Standards change; one general practice at the time of the Revolution was to wash underclothes once a month and to rely heavily on perfume. The best perfumes were imported; their unavailability during the war forced colonials to fall back on homemade products. Technological progress was not so advanced that people had forgotten special qualities of herbs and roots and blossoms; bunches of "simples" hanging from attic rafters could contribute as much to cosmetic as to medicinal needs. Pea-sized pellets made of fragrant gums and oils were burned to freshen the air in rooms. Rose petals had at least two uses: Set in holders on the mantel or in sconces, they gave off a pleasing aroma; ground up and formed into little cakes, they helped to overcome mustiness in storage chests.

The British blockade also reduced the supply of good soap. The soft lye soap made, with much grumbling, by rural housewives was unfit for marketing, while the fine castile produced in Rhode Island could not begin to meet the demand. But "gentlemen's Fine Washballs," "Scented Marble Washballs" and similar substitutes for soap were on sale as early as 1771, and old recipes were trotted out for experimentation. One of these called for forty pounds of powdered rice, twenty-eight pounds each of fine flour and starch powder, twelve pounds of white lead and four pounds of orris root, all thoroughly mixed and sifted, formed into balls of desired size and colored by Dutch pink or brown damask powder. So much white lead must have hurt complexions more than the other ingredients helped.

Some aids to personal hygiene had to be

bought: nail clippers (called "knippers"), silk or worsted powder puffs, toothpick cases, curling irons and pinching tongs, flesh brushes, ivory back scratchers and razors—for men shaved (and insisted to their wives that it was a daily agony as great as childbirth). These utensils were all widely advertised in the newspapers, along with the face patches fashionable after 1760, ointments to eliminate freckles and hair rollers weighing from eight to fourteen ounces. One Salem barbershop employing twelve barbers advertised in 1773: "Ladies shall be attended to in the polite constructions of rolls such as may tend to raise their heads to any pitch they desire." Anna Green Winslow complained that the heavy rolls made her head "ach and itch like anything"; but if fashion was a tyrant, any girl or woman aspiring to be a lady had to submit.

As with flamboyant clothing, the old opposition to elaborate hair styles gave way totally in the eighteenth century. By the time of the Revolution, the fantastic wigs worn by men in the earlier 1700s had shrunk to a small tight-fitting wig and then to powdered natural hair, shoulder-length and with a queue down the back. But wigs for women grew in popularity. As a rule, the wig was only part of the tower, as the elaborate hairdo came to be known; the hairdresser worked wig and natural hair together, as high as possible. The report of a street accident in 1771 reveals the absurdity of the fashion: When a young woman was knocked to the ground by a runaway horse, her tower disintegrated, scattering bits of cotton, wool and tow stuffing, strands of false hair and loops of gauze and ribbon—to the vast delight of young street arabs.

Extravagance in dress was found in every colony, though mostly in the cities. In Charleston, as Josiah Quincy noticed, men at formal affairs wore swords to show their military rank. Most fashionable women wore stays—whalebone covered with stiff buckram and known as "ironclads." In Philadelphia even the Quakers submitted to fashion; and certain ladies in that city, when Franklin was abroad, received gifts from him that he knew they would like—silk, plumes, satin, shoe buckles. George Washington, wherever he set up headquarters during the war, maintained the social amenities and showed in his own attire that Virginia gentlemen knew how to dress. At home, however, where aristocrats were above the need for rivalry, he followed the regional custom of wearing casual attire among friends. The pinnacle of flamboyant costume, as all travelers agreed, was not in plantation Virginia but in New York.

Rural families got the word and followed it to the limit of their resources; the "best clothes" laid away for wear on important occasions, like weddings and funerals, were of the same cut and pattern as in the cities, differing only in their lower cost and lesser elegance. Even slaves had "Sunday clothes" of the basic fashion. The only people who dressed in a completely different way were the Mennonites and other small religious sects that required simple clothing, and the more numerous frontiersmen, who wore on all occasions the same very practical clothing: broad-sleeved hunting shirts, capes fringed in various colors, deerskin moccasins; breeches hanging, like trousers today, to the ankles and the all-important belt, buckled behind the body, which supported the breeches, held tomahawk, knife and strips of tow to clean the rifle barrel and enclosed a looped end of the shirt to form an ample pocket. The sensation made by frontier militia companies marching east in 1775 to join the Continental army resulted not only from their incredible skill with rifles but also from their dress, so unfamiliar to other colonials.

Fashionable display and regional variations were forgotten when colonials retired for the night.

If the meager evidence can be relied on, every man, woman and child donned a long, loose garment, usually made of linen, known by one name or another: rail (or rayle), night-rail, bed-coat or bed-gown (but not nightgown, which then meant what we now call an evening gown). Most were plain; the only decorative touches were occasional embroidery and lace edging, but in the dark, who cared? Thus clad, they closed the windows tightly (for night air was thought to be unhealthful), blew out the candles and drifted off to the kind of sleep they deserved.

"Living—and Staying Alive"

Not every American on the eve of the war could enjoy in full measure the varied pleasures of living. Children died at an alarming rate, and the mature were never quite without anxiety. Keeping in good health wasn't easy.

Whatever rights a woman had were surrendered when she married. Her basic duty, as spelled out in the marriage ceremony and as approved by society, was to honor and obey; and her husband's "conjugal rights" outweighed any thoughts she may have had of increasing the intervals between pregnancies. Increasing the population was no longer as crucial as it had been in the early years of settlement, but society still applauded prolific production. Nobody, apparently, saw anything immoral in a first wife's dying after bearing a dozen children in as many years and being promptly replaced by a young second wife until she too died of exhaustion and yielded to a third. Contraceptive devices were openly sold in London in the Revolutionary period and were probably available, though not advertised, in the colonies. Few wives, however, would have been able to insist on their use if their husbands were opposed. Since another phenomenon of the period was a sudden upsurge of population, it

Top: Watch box, probably from New Hampshire. Watches were rare and were carefully treated. *Bottom:* Same watch box with the front removed. *Opposite:* Coat hanging on a door with H-L hinges and raised panels.

would seem that few husbands were interested in limiting family size. So strong was the approval given to parenthood, indeed, that bachelors and spinsters were objects of scorn.

As a natural result of the prevailing attitudes, the proud father of a large brood was often a patriarch by the time his last child was born; but he was also likely to be a man with sad memories of frequent deaths, for children so close in age tended to lack the robustness helpful in resisting childhood diseases. It was not uncommon for only two or three out of twenty children in a family to reach maturity.

When we look at the facts about health and medical care in the colonies, we may wonder how as many children grew up as did and why there was a population explosion just before the Revolution. At any given moment, the majority of Americans must have been feeling well and functioning normally; if they hadn't been, they could hardly have continued to prosper and progress, let alone mount a successful war for independence. But illness was a constant threat, cures were uncertain and the current crop of medical practitioners inspired very little confidence. When someone fell ill, the family's first resort was likely to be prayer—and given the wretched medical attention in most areas, this may have been as reasonable a course as any.

The annual death rate in the 1770s was about 35 per 1,000 for whites and twice that number for blacks. (The comparable figures today are roughly 10 and 12.) What may strike home more forcefully is life expectancy at birth; in 1775, it was thirty-four years for males and thirty-six for females—about the same as in today's underdeveloped nations. This doesn't mean, of course, that on the eve of independence most Americans died in their thirties; that would have been sad enough, but the even sadder fact, starkly familiar to most American fami-

lies then, was that most deaths occurred before the age of ten. For those who survived to their twentieth birthday, the prospect was a good deal brighter: At that age men could expect to reach fifty-four and women fifty-six. Some people did far better, living to a ripe old age as at any time in human history. But nobody worried about geriatric problems: The paramount question for colonial families was how to keep the children alive until they were ten. Childhood had always been known as a hazardous period, and more youngsters had always died than lived; these were accepted facts of life. It was prudent, men must have believed, to have large families in order to avoid dying without leaving heirs.

There were medical practitioners enough but few with any training or competence. Only the sons of well-to-do families could go abroad for the only good training available, and once they were back home, with a respectable diploma to hang on the office wall, they were so few in number that they could care for only a fraction of the population. Of some thirty-five hundred established practitioners in the colonies when the Revolution began, only about four hundred had been exposed to medical education of any sort, and of these fewer than half held medical degrees. Well-trained Europeans saw little advantage in migrating to the colonies, where the ancient guild distinctions went unrecognized: A surgeon or apothecary this side of the Atlantic enjoyed all the rights and privileges that in England were reserved for the elitist physician, who usually had a university degree, was called "Doctor" and never worked with his hands like the lowly "surgeon," who was called "Mister" to his face and "bonesetter" behind his back. All too many colonials didn't even recognize this distinction.

The numerous practitioners who migrated in the late eighteenth century were commonly surgeon-apothecaries, men with limited skill who recognized a good thing when they saw it—a demand for sure-cure medication and a public resistance to all efforts to license practitioners, as smacking of monopoly and limiting individual freedom. The public attitude was so permissive that anybody at all, native or newcomer, could set himself up in practice; it was an easier way to make a living than most kinds of work in the 1770s. Most of the incompetents would have been disbarred by even the most elementary examination for a license. Many of them practiced only part-time, to eke out an income from some more legitimate work like currying horses or making soap.

Medicine was far from scientific; even the most reputable physicians in 1775, trained in Leyden or Edinburgh, were hardly reliable. They prescribed a few drugs in great quantities—ipecac, calomel, mercury, opium and quinine (then known as "Jesuit's bark") not only for symptoms they specifically alleviated but for others as well. Diagnosis was inexact, and when it was in error, which was often, the medicine prescribed might aggravate the illness —or kill the patient. Overdosage was also commonplace, sometimes the result of vague directions like "enough to lie on a penknife's point" or "the bigth of a walnut." Little was known, moreover, of the side effects of particular drugs; mercury could arrest syphilis, but it could also leave mercury poisoning in the body. Venereal disease never reached epidemic proportions before the Revolution, but during the war its incidence rose sharply; it is usually associated with outsiders, and not all contacts with European soldiers were on the battlefield.

Quacks, with only the haziest knowledge of standard drugs, were more inclined to rely on old folk remedies or to concoct their own nostrums. But physicians at all levels of competence practiced "strenuous medicine"—bleeding their patients, dipping them in cold water, sweating and blistering them and evacuating their digestive tracts with strong purgatives. Bleeding was a relic of the Middle Ages, when everybody was positive that health depended on a proper balance of the four body fluids. The method that was still widely used reflected failure to accept Harvey's discovery in 1616 that blood circulated: Blood was drawn simultaneously from opposite sides of the body so that neither side would be depleted. In sickness as in health, it was an heroic age.

One fairly common childhood disease was rickets, caused by lack of vitamin D and too little exposure to sunshine and marked by fevers and defective bone development. Since nobody knew about vitamins, physicians tried anything they could think of, including one complicated procedure recommended in 1769:

In ye Rickets the best Corrective I have ever found is a Syrup made of Black Cherrys. Thus. Take of Cherrys (dry'd ones are as good as any) & put them into a vessel with water. Set ye vessel near ye fire and let ye water be Scalding hot. Then take ye Cherrys into a thin Cloth and squeeze them into ye Vessell, & sweeten ye Liquor with Melosses. Give 2 Spoonfuls of this 2 or 3 times in a day. If you Dip your Child, Do it in this manner: viz; naked, in ye morning, head foremost in Cold Water, don't dress it Immediately, but let it be made warm in ye Cradle & sweat at least half an Hour moderately. Do this 3 mornings going & if one or both feet are Cold while other Parts sweat (which is sometimes ye Case) Let a little blood be taken out of ye feet ye 2nd Morning and yt will cause them to sweat afterwards. Before ye dips of ye Child give it some Snakeroot and Saffern Steep'd in Rum & Water, give this Immediately before Diping and after you have dipt ye Child 3 Mornings Give it several times a Day ye following Syrup made of Comfry, Hartshorn, Red Roses, Hog-brake roots, knot-grass, pettymoral roots,

sweeten ye Syrup with Melosses. Physicians are generally fearful about diping when ye Fever is hard, but oftentimes all attemps to lower it without diping are vain. Experience has taught me that these fears are groundless, yt many have about diping in Rickety Fevers; I have found in a multitude of Instances of diping is most effectual means to break a Rickety Fever. These Directions are agreable to what I have practiced for many years.

Other panaceas, for various illnesses, have the ring of medieval sorcery, anachronistic in the Age of Enlightenment. Pulverized grasshoppers, the scrapings of human skulls, the viscera of poisonous snakes and the ground-up remains of toads boiled the night of the full moon in August were a few of the weird ingredients used by ignorant practitioners and consumed by their credulous clients. The fouler the taste, for such people, the greater the confidence in the treatment. If the patient recovered, medicine and practitioner got the credit; if he died, it was God's will.

Some of the wordiest newspaper advertisements of the period were inserted by "doctors," usually with testimonials from satisfied patients, as in this example from 1775:

Doctor Yeldall,

Has for Sale, at his Medicinal Ware-House, three doors from the Bank-Meeting-House in Front-street, most kinds of medicines, both chemical and galenical. Likewise most patent medicines now in use, which may be depended on to be genuine; together with the Doctor's Family Medicines, which are well known in most parts of the continent, and where any person in the country may, by sending an account of their disorder, either in writing or otherwise, have advice and medicines as the nature of their complaint may require. Those that live in the city may be waited on at their houses, and due attendance given through the cure of their disorder, on the most moderate terms. Advice is given gratis to all who chuse to apply; and none will be under taken but where there is a probability of success. . . .

For the benefit of others, be it made public, that I, Alexander Martin, of King's-woods county, New Jersey, was afflicted with a comsumptive disorder for upwards of three years. I applied to every man of skill that I

Opposite: A physician's portable medicine chest. *Left:* Physician taking the pulse of a woman modestly hidden. *Below:* Assorted apothecary tools.

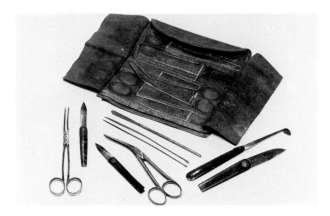

Surgical instruments in leather case,
used during revolutionary
war by Dr. Eliphalet Downer.

*could, but to no purpose; and when my money and
strength were gone, they desired I might go to the hospital at Philadelphia, where I continued upwards of three
months, went through a course of mercury, and tried
many other things in vain, and at length was discharged.
I then applied to Doctor Yeldall, who, in a short time,
recovered me to my perfect health.*

Alexander Martin

In two respects the colonial population was
lucky: Leprosy and bubonic plague, the worst diseases in Europe, did not accompany the migrants
crossing the Atlantic, and diseases indigenous to
America, for which the newcomers could have no
inherited immunity, were so mild as to be virtually
nonexistent. But several diseases were imported
from Africa with the slaves—hookworm and dengue,
confined to the South, and yellow fever, which
spread throughout the colonies. The favored people
also brought with them such scourges as typhoid and
dysentary, and worst of all, "chills and fever," as
malaria was called.

Food, clothing and shelter have their bearing
on health and illnesses. The urban poor, least able
to maintain a varied diet, especially in cold
weather, were easy victims of scurvy and other diseases of malnutrition. More properous city people,
and farm and village families generally, could enjoy
a reasonably good diet year round. Clothing was
warm enough, made chiefly of wool, leather and
linen; but hygienic washable materials such as mus-
lins and cottons weren't available for underclothing
or for hot weather until after 1800. Washing the
entire body was something almost nobody did, particularly in winter. The resulting body odors,
stronger by the week, could be politely ignored,
as unavoidable, but no living person could ignore
"the itch"—scabies—that accumulating dirt all but
guaranteed. Some radicals advocated public baths

like those in European cities; but the people who
could have profited most were strongly opposed because they were positive that such baths spread
venereal disease.

Another widespread notion, hardly less du-
bious, was that the longer and harder one worked,
the less likely he was to be sick. The converse, that
hard labor drains energy and lowers resistance to
disease, would not have been popular at a time of
such headlong economic growth and fierce competition; work, not cleanliness, was next to Godliness.
Nobody seemed to suspect any connection between
all that work and the common cold, which was very
common indeed, or the ailments of the intestinal
and respiratory tracts that rivaled malaria for dead-
liness or the epidemics feared even more or the
heart and vascular conditions that went by such
whimsical names as fits, dropsy and decay. Play,
though it carried Poor Richard's endorsement, had
a poor reputation; organized sports went begging.
Who needed more exercise than work provided?

Environment was important, too. Philadelphia
began to clean its streets, as a public service, in
1762, but in New York and other cities the residents
were expected to sweep the trash into piles, in
front of their property, and to pay a cartman to
haul it away. Still, no method, public or private,
could remove all the horse dung or urine or all the
dried sputum from the streets and roads. Water
came from wells, mostly private, but some of them
were public in the more settled urban districts
and often perilously close to privies and open
drains; water closets and buried sewers did not
yet exist in British America. Efforts in a few communities to safeguard public health ran afoul of the
strong tradition of individual freedom; the only
measure not opposed was quarantine during epidemics. Inoculation was voluntary; fear of smallpox
and fear of inoculation were roughly in balance,

and men soliciting business for their inoculating parlors had to word their advertisements carefully. Here's how one man, who made no claim at all to being a physician, attracted clients:

Inoculation.

The subscriber begs leave to inform the public that he continues with his usual success to inoculate for the small pox in the most approved method, at the pleasantly situated house, near the City of New-Brunswick, as formerly advertised in this paper. The strictest attention is given, and every thing necessary provided, at a moderate and easy rate, by the public's most obedient, humble servant,

John Cochran

New Brunswick, May 27, 1775

The theory of inoculation was that the very mild case it produced was preferable to contracting a serious, perhaps fatal, case in the future.

As for dentistry, an occasional surgeon-dentist from England visited the colonies for short periods, but colonial dentists were nonexistent; there were not even ignorant quacks pretending to a knowledge of the subject. This was particularly deplorable because Americans in general had very poor teeth, as Peter Kalm reported in 1748: "Girls not above twenty years old frequently had lost half their teeth, without hopes of getting new ones." Most of the suggested reasons made no sense. Some colonials thought tooth decay was due to the air or to the rapid changes in weather; but the native Indians had excellent teeth. Others put the blame on drinking tea and eating fruit; but young people who drank no tea and ate little fruit lost their teeth at the same alarming rate. Another suggested cause was the sheer amount of hot food that most Americans consumed, far more than Europeans were used to. Nobody then knew about calcium deficiency; milk was not a popular beverage, and women actively producing children accepted as inevitable the saying, "A tooth for every child."

One man advertised "the Famous Anodyne Necklace," priced at twenty shillings, which he insisted would

open and ease the foregums of teething children and bring their teeth safely out. Children on the very brink of the grave and thought past recovery with their teeth, fits, fevers, and convulsions, hooping and other violent coughs, gripes, looseness, and all proceeding from their teeth who cannot tell what they suffer nor make known their pains any other way [than] by crying and moans, have miraculously recovered after having worn the famous Anodyne Necklace but one night's time.

Out of folklore came other sage advice: carrying the tooth of a dead man to stop a toothache; rinsing the mouth with lemon juice and rubbing the teeth with a sage leaf to prevent decay; chewing mastic until it was soft enough to press into a cavity. Extraction was a last resort, one that was feared and deferred because the clumsy "tooth wrenches" the barber-surgeons used often broke not only the offending tooth but sometimes the jaw.

It was possible, by the late 1760s, to fill the embarrassing gaps with false teeth. A London surgeon-dentist, John Baker, during a year he spent in Boston taught the technique to Paul Revere. It called for the kind of skill that Revere had developed as a goldsmith: precise shaping of the new tooth, preferably cut from hippopotamus ivory, which kept its color, and attaching it to adjacent teeth with gold or silver wire or silk thread. A customer with less money to spend could settle for the tooth of some animal; it was better than nothing. Revere's advertisement in the *Boston Gazette* (September 19, 1768) gives some idea of how satisfactory these false teeth were:

WHEREAS many Persons are so unfortunate as to lose their Fore-Teeth by Accident, and otherways, to their great Detriment, not only in Looks, but speaking both in Public and Private:—This is to inform all such, that they may have them replaced with artificial ones, that looks as well as Natural, & answeres the End of Speaking to all Intents, by PAUL REVERE Goldsmith, near the Head of Dr Clark's wharf, Boston.

All persons who have had false teeth fixt by Mr John Baker, Surgeon-Dentist, and they have got loose (as they will in Time) may have them fastened by the above, who learned the method of fixing them from Mr Baker.

After the war, an expert ivory-turner and instrument-maker named Isaac Greenwood took over Revere's dental business and so improved the technique that he earned the title of our first native-born dentist. It was high time.

"Watering Places"

In 1775, the Virginia burgesses passed an act to create a spa, on land donated by Lord Fairfax, on the model of Bath in England. They tried to name it Bath, but its former name, Warm Springs, persisted. During the Revolution it served as a detention center for captured British soldiers, who joined the aristocratic summer clientele in all the diversions the well-to-do considered essential to the restoration of health: billiards, gambling, theatricals and music, horseback riding, formal teas and, when the spirit moved, bathing in the warm water for its alleged therapeutic value.

Ordinary people, much earlier, had gone on holiday to springs in all parts of the colonial area; springs numbered in the thousands, but only a few hundred were big enough to accommodate bathers, and fewer yet had unusual mineral content. Some were warm, which made them popular in colder sections; others were cold and crystal clear, encouraging entrepreneurs to bottle the water and sell it in cities where the local drinking water was of poor quality. Most were in attractive natural settings. Sooner or later it was inevitable that some of them would become resorts, and this happened in the Revolutionary period.

Above: Aquatint of the hotel and other buildings at the mineral springs in Stafford, Connecticut, the earliest popular spa. *Opposite:* Engine Company No. 4 was so proud of its new engine that it had its portrait painted.

The first to gain this happy status was Stafford Springs in northern Connecticut. (The plural was almost always preferred, perhaps out of fear that nobody would travel to a mere "spring.") What gave Stafford its priority, and a reputation that drew patrons from as far away as the West Indies, was an interesting combination of promoters providing special coach excursions from Boston and physicians settling on the grounds, opening clinics, promising cures for any ailment and inserting testimonial advertising in the newspapers. By 1770, Stafford was *the* spa to visit in New England. John Adams, suffering from overwork and depression, went there on horseback, spurning the coach, and profited from the visit; the trip itself, to any spa, was beneficial, whether or not the water actually helped, as was claimed, to cure gout or phthisis or vapors or any of the numerous other afflictions then popular.

The quest for health was one obvious reason for the success of the spas; but if one contemporary cynic called Stafford Springs a "mecca of hypochondriacs," he might have added the adjective "rich," for as any spa became popular, attracting more people than it could accommodate, the cost began to rise until only the wealthy could go there. The majority of lesser affluence continued to enjoy the undeveloped springs, as they did particularly in the Philadelphia area; the gap between these and the fashionable spas widened steadily. In the process, ironically, the original reasons for the spas, the restoration of health, receded in importance for their patrons.

No other diversion available in the Revolutionary period, unless it was crossing the Atlantic for the Grand Tour of the Continent, so firmly accented the difference between rich and poor in America.

"The Universal Gamble"

The place, the City of New York; the date, September 21, 1776:

This Morning about 1 o'Clock, we were alarmed with the Appearance of a Fire in the Town; and presently after it burst out, at several Places, into a most tremendous Blaze. The Wind was rather strong, which increased the Rapidity of the Flames; & these extended in a Line for almost the Length of a mile, consuming onward from the East River, for several Hours together, to the North River up to St Paul's Church, which wonderfully escaped, while Trinity Church (called the Old English Church, being the oldest Fabric upon the Establishment in the Town) which was less, was utterly destroyed. Many Houses were consumed in and about Whitehall

Top: Leather fire bucket, used by the Library Company of Philadelphia. *Bottom:* Detail from a notice of meeting of the Hand-in-Hand Fire Company of New York about 1750, showing a fire company in action. The bucket brigade passes water from the well pump at the left to the engine, where a fireman directs the hand-pumped water toward the flames. The hook-and-ladder men are in the foreground. The fire chief, to the right of the engine, calls directions while neighborly citizens retrieve belongings from the burning building.

near the Fort. Some Rebels, who lurked about the Town, set it on Fire: and some of them were caught with Matches, and Fire-balls about them. One Man, detected in the act, was knocked down by a Grenadier & thrown into the Flames for his Reward: Another, who was found cutting off the Handles of the Water-Buckets to prevent their Use, was first hung up by the Neck till he was dead and afterwards by the Heels upon a Sign-Post by the Sailors. Many others were seized, on account of Combustibles found upon them, and secured; and, but for the officers, most of them would have been killed by the enraged Populace & Soldiery. The New England People are maintained to be at the Bottom of this Plot, which they have long since threatened to put into Execution.

I walked on Shore about Noon, surveyed the Devastation, which has taken in, 'tis supposed, about one fifth Part of the City. . . . The attack upon Powley's Hook was deferred on account of this vast Conflagration, most of our Sailors being engaged in extinguishing the Fire.

This account of New York's worst fire—worst, at least, in proportion to the city's size—is from the journal of Ambrose Serle, the British civilian who served as secretary to Lord Howe. The cause of the holocaust has never been determined, though one hypothesis, that it started in a brothel, has considerable support. If the large royal garrison in the city could not suppress the fire before it destroyed a third of the city, not a fifth as Serle estimated, the skeletal fire department most certainly could not have. Fire was a constant threat everywhere, something to be dreaded by every last colonial in those days of no fire insurance whatsoever.

When a house burned, its owner suffered the loss, whatever it amounted to; and with no banks, his money and valuable papers were likely to be destroyed in the fire. No insurance was available, moreover, for any other catastrophe—death from illness or accident, destruction or theft of property, loss of limbs or eyesight through mishaps at work or what are still called collectively "acts of God"—floods, lightning, falling trees, high winds. No unemployment compensation kept the household going when jobs collapsed. It was an age of rugged individualism, and often it was rugged indeed, beyond normal capacity to accept. Men took their chances whatever their occupation, and if gambling was virtually a national vice, living itself was a gamble. The only solace, if it ever was a solace, came from awareness that the gamble was universal.

People generally, however, enjoyed a fair degree of security. Gangs of ruffians plagued the major cities, but rural America was virtually free of crime; most villages had no law enforcement personnel and needed none. Complaints by citizens to the "courts of first instances," meaning county or district courts, received prompt attention. Sheriffs or other agents of the courts investigated and made arrests as circumstances warranted. At the preliminary hearings and subsequent formal trials, if these became necessary, plaintiff and defendant confronted each other in person, for the relatively few lawyers seldom represented clients in court. Court dockets were not crowded, and speedy verdicts were the rule.

Crime—and Punishment

Whether severe penalties deter miscreants is a perennial question, but it wasn't much discussed in colonial times, although abolition of the death penalty was an occasional college debating topic. The general desire for population increase tempered the impulse to punish; a Massachusetts law actually forbade cruel and unusual punishments. A fine carpenter or brick-maker was more useful alive and free to work than dead or in prison, whatever crime he might have committed. Fewer crimes were punishable by death than in England, but the list became much more extensive after 1800. Levi Ames was hanged for burglary; other men were hanged for such crimes as rape, arson, adultery, kidnapping, inhuman treatment of children resulting in death, sodomy, forgery and counterfeiting. The list varied; Pennsylvania had only two capital offenses, murder and treason.

The accused could ordinarily depend on a fair trial; the judges, appointed by colonial governors, were often more lenient than the enraged populace. Not in the case of Ebenezer Richardson. As a lesser officer in the Boston Custom House, he was already notorious as "the informer" before a random shot from his gun fatally wounded a boy of eleven, early in 1770. He was tried and found guilty of murder. Governor Hutchinson, however, refused to sign the death warrant, on the reasonable grounds that the charge should have been manslaughter, and Richardson was freed after two years in prison. A better example of contemporary justice was the trial of nine British soldiers implicated in the Boston Massacre of 1770; two were found guilty and were discharged from the army, but Captain Preston and six others were acquitted despite strong public demand for punishment. John Adams and Josiah Quincy, by defending the accused, lost no standing among patriots, which in itself speaks very well for the contemporary sense of fairness.

In New Jersey, at least, trials for capital offenses were conducted by the state supreme court, and execution of the sentence was relatively speedy, as this report from 1774 indicates:

New-York, Nov. 24. On Saturday last the 12th instant, the Supreme Court for the province of New-Jersey ended at Burlington, when Peter Galwin (a schoolmaster) was convicted of a rape on an infant under the age of

A few LINES on
Magnus Mode, Richard Hodges & J. Newington Clark.
Who are Sentenc'd to ſtand one Hour in the
Pillory at Charleſtown;

To have one of their EARS cut off, and to be Whipped 20 Stripes at the public Whipping-Poſt, for making and paſſing Counterfeit DOLLARS, &c.

BEHOLD the villains rais'd on high !
(The *Poſt* they've got attracts the eye :)
Both Jews and Gentiles all appear
To ſee them ſtand exalted here ;
Both rich and poor, both young and old,
The dirty ſlut, the common ſcold :
What multitudes do them ſurround,
Many as bad as can be found.
And to encreaſe their ſad diſgrace,
Throw rotten eggs into their face,
And pelt them ſore with dirt and ſtones,
Nay, if they could wou'd break their bones.
Their malice to ſuch height ariſe,
Who knows but they'll put out their eyes :
But pray conſider what you do
While thus expos'd to public view.
Juſtice has often done its part,
And made the guilty rebels ſmart ;
But they went on did ſtill rebel,
And ſeem'd to ſtorm the gates of hell.
To no good counſel would they hear ;
But now each one muſt looſe an EAR,

And they although againſt their will
Are forc'd to chew this bitter pill ;
And this day brings the villains hence
To ſuffer for their late offence ;
They on th' Pillory ſtand in view :
A warning ſirs to me and you !
The drunkards ſong, the harlots ſcorn,
Reproach of ſome as yet unborn.
But now the *Poſt* they're forc'd to hug,
But loath to take that nauſeous drug
Which brings the blood from out their veins,
And marks their back with purple ſtains.
   From their diſgrace, now warning take,
And never do your ruin make
By ſtealing, or unlawful ways ;
(If you would live out all your days)
But keep ſecure from Theft and Pride ;
Strive to have virtue on your ſide.
Deſpiſe the harlot's flattering airs,
And hate her ways, avoid her ſnares ;
Keep clear from Sin of every kind,
And then you'll have true peace of Mind.

ten years, and three other indictments preferred against him, one for the same offence, and two others on infants for an assault, with an intent to ravish; and John Taylor, alias John Philip Snider, was also convicted of that detestable crime bestiality, which the law terms "a crime not to be mentioned among Christians;" he was likewise indicted for murder; both of which criminals received sentence of death, and are to be executed on Monday the 5th of December next.

Public hangings were becoming relatively rare by the Revolutionary period, but other punishments in the open provided popular entertainment. Magnus Mode, Richard Hodges and J. Newington Clark, convicted in 1767 of counterfeiting Spanish milled dollars, escaped hanging; each stood for an hour in the pillory, had one ear cut off, received twenty lashes and spent a year in prison at hard labor, after which the counterfeiters were required to pay all the court costs.

Women were as often punished in public as were men. The ducking stool, reserved chiefly for scolds or gossips, was still in some use as late as 1800, but stocks and the pillory were more common instruments of punishment. In the pillory, the culprit stood with neck and wrists encased in holes; in stocks he or she sat with legs encased. Neither caused severe pain, but both were humiliating, and there was always the chance of being pelted with garbage, to the accompaniment of insults. Whipping was more serious, whatever the implement used; ten or fifty lashes on the bare back caused very painful stripes and welts that never disappeared. Whipping posts were still functioning in major cities until after the Revolution. Branding was also permanent; the intense pain did not last long, but the letter burnt into thumb or cheek or forehead—A for adultery, B for burglary or blasphemy, C for counterfeiting, and so on, could never be concealed.

Slander, name calling and scandalmongering were actionable. Abusive newspaper notices sometimes drew retorts, like this one in the *Pennsylvania Journal* for April 20, 1774:

To the great Boar, at his Sty in Borden-Town, Joseph, Joseph, why hast thou so furiously pricked up *the* bristles *of thy wit?—Although the* maw *of thy understanding is plentiful* gorged, *with the* wash *of slander, yet be it known unto thee, oh* Joseph! *thou wilt not be permitted so to* wallow *in the* mire *of vanity, and* cram *thyself with the* husks *of conceit, as to* squeak out puns *in triumph against the miller of Chesterfield with impunity!* stagger, *therefore, back again into the* pen *of obscurity, lest the* miller, *to prevent thy* rooting up the ground of thy neighbour's reputation, *should cut off the* snout of thy sagacity, *yoke* thee with the collar of infamy, *wring from thee a confession of thy guilt,* steep *thee in the* lye of thy own manufacture, *put thee in such a* pickle *as will make thee* grunt out an acknowledgment *that thou are sufficiently* smoked, *and thoroughly* gammoned, *—then* barrel *thee up, and* brand *thee with the* letters J. B. *to prevent counterfeits.—*

These few hints I hope will cure *thee of the* mange *of witticism, and be a warning to thee not to* crawl out *again from the sphere in which Providence hath wisely appointed thee to move, this being the surest way to* save *thy bacon.*

> *From thy Friend,*
> *Rasher Ham.*

On occasion, however, somebody retracted what he had published, perhaps because his temper had cooled, although fear of arrest and trial may have prompted the admission of error. Here's an example from the *Pennsylvania Gazette,* March 30, 1774:

Whereas I have highly injured Mr. William Lawrence, of Mantua-creek, Gloucester county, by certain de-

Opposite: Broadside commemorating pillory sentence
of three convicted criminals in Charlestown.

99

famatory words by me spoken, to wit, that he was a thief and stole a calf, and at other times that he was a murderer, &c. which words tends to do him the greatest harm, by injuring his character; now in justice to him, I here publicly declare, that the words I spoke are totally false and groundless, that I am sincerely sorry for my imprudence in propagating so bad a report, and that I never will do the same again.

William Tennant

Witnesses present, James Bowman, Richard Johnson

A final example, from the *New York Journal* of December 28, 1775, reflects the heightened tension in the months following the first battles of the war. Tories with wealth and influence enough could oppose the rebels with impunity, at least until independence was declared, but tradesmen apparently could not at

Quibble Town, Middlesex County,
Piscataqua Township, N.Jersey

Thomas Randolph, cooper, who had publickly proved himself an enemy to his country, by reviling and using his utmost endeavours to oppose the proceedings of the Continental and Provincial Conventions and Committees in defence of their rights and liberties; and he being judged a person of not consequence enough for a severer punishment, was ordered to be stripped naked, well coated with tar and feathers and carried in a waggon publickly round the town; which punishment was accordingly inflicted; and as he soon became duly sensible of his offence, for which he earnestly begged pardon, and promised to atone, so far as he was able, by a contrary behaviour for the future, he was released and suffered to return to his house in less than half an hour. The whole was conducted with that regularity and decorum that ought to be observed in all public punishments.

The great majority of free agents never had to worry about punishment of any sort; due process protected those who behaved themselves, and despite Dr. Samuel Johnson's slur that the colonies were peopled chiefly by criminals, most Americans were orderly and law-abiding. But bankruptcy, which has never been willfully sought, could land a man behind bars until he paid off his debts. Paupers, commonly orphans who had never had a chance or oldsters no longer able to support themselves, were put up at auction, usually at a tavern, if relatives could not or would not assume their care. The young were bound out to their purchasers, just like indentured servants arriving from Europe, for a specified period of years; the old and infirm went to the lowest bidders—that is, whoever would accept the smallest amounts for keeping them alive.

A generation that watched hangings with mingled horror and sympathy might be expected to be fascinated by tales of famous criminals. Like eclipses or comets, they were rare; most of the population never saw one, and they seemed immune to social control. Henry Tufts, whose long and varied career in crime was recorded in what was alleged to be his autobiography, published after 1800, was well known to his victims, to his scattered wives and other bedfellows and to law officers in several states; though he was often jailed, and sometimes tried and found guilty, he always managed to escape. He was operating throughout the Revolutionary period, part of the time in the uniform of the Continental army; but most of his crimes were petty, and he was more admired as a rascal than hated or feared as a threat to the peace.

Another scoundrel who lived by his wits and earned considerable fame was Tom Cook. His mischievous behavior in boyhood was obvious proof, for the credulous, of a compact with the devil, who gained his soul in return for snatching him from death in a serious illness. When the devil arrived to claim him, Tom said to him, "Wait till I get my galluses on." The devil agreed, but it was a mistake; for Tom threw the galluses in the fire and hence could never put them on. Thus freed, he set out on a career that earned him the reputation of "the honest thief," though he preferred to be known as "the leveler." Food that he stole from the rich, he gave to the poor. Children liked him; he was quite personable, and, besides, he stole toys to give to them. His income was from annual tolls paid by wealthy farmers as a price for exemption from his raids. He was finally caught, tried and sentenced to death. When the judge completed his verdict, "I sentence you to be hanged by the neck till you are dead, dead, dead," Tom answered cheerfully, "I shall not be there on that day, day, day," and he was not, for he escaped.

How much of the story people really believed matters less than the pleasure they got from hearing it told and retold. Novels, for those who read them, were set in distant countries; Henry Tufts and Tom Cook and other picturesque villains of the time were flesh-and-blood Americans, and their success despite all the odds gave vicarious pleasure to hard-working colonials just as eager to succeed.

Last Rites

On the tenth of May, 1775, a woman on the Dangerfield plantation near Petersburg died of the effects of dropsy. She was not, apparently, related to Colonel Dangerfield, for no member of his family "sat up" with the corpse. That duty fell instead to the overseer, two girls and the indentured tutor, John Harrower. On the twelfth, the body was dressed in a calico gown and white apron, wrapped in a sheet and laid in a walnut coffin lined with "flannen" (flannel) and with pinchback handles. The next day Harrower screwed down the lid, and

the coffin was taken on a chair carriage to the Snow Creek graveyard nearby. There it was lowered into a grave about six feet deep and then partly covered with dirt. On the fourteenth, somebody read the brief service for the dead, and the grave was at last filled in.

Walnut coffin, assignment of the arrangements to a white tutor and lack of emotion at the interment all suggest that the dead woman was not a slave. Such funerals were no doubt common enough for whites at the lower social strata—paupers, indentured servants, members of isolated frontier families hard put to break even. For anyone of consequence, any member of a family with the slightest regard for what was appropriate, such minimal attention would have been unthinkable.

Sitting up with the corpse took the form of a funeral feast, similar to a wake, the night before the service, with the residence overflowing with relatives, friends and neighbors. Since the crowd returned to the house after the interment, the family was often left with a substantial bill for rum and other strong waters, not to mention sugar, spices and lemons. If the departed was a clergyman, the cost of the liquor was assumed by the church or the town; what was more, an experienced committee was on hand to superintend the mixing of the funeral punch and to dispense it. Nobody objected: It was a case of giving honor to whom honor was due.

The procession from house to church, and later from church to graveyard, was usually on foot behind the coffin. The man of greatest eminence among the mourners walked beside the widow (or widower or parents), and behind them the others walked in the accepted order of social ranking. Two sets of bearers were the rule: the underbearers, young men who actually carried the coffin on a bier, and the older pallbearers, who held in place the pall (alternately known as the bier cloth or mort cloth)

Three New England gravestones. *Opposite:* Rutland, Vermont. *Top:* Windsor, Vermont. Location of the third gravestone is unknown.

that covered not only the coffin but the heads and shoulders of the underbearers. This cloth of heavy black velvet or broadcloth was church or town property, as was the bier, a frame or stand of durable construction. If the distance was great, a second set of underbearers alternated with the first. Burial under the church floor, or in the yard of the church, of course reduced their labor. For the funeral of an important person, the "quality" rode in carriages; for the 1778 funeral of the Rev. Andrew Eliot, the Boston divine who preached the execution sermon for Levi Ames in 1773, four hundred couples walked behind thirty-two carriages, from his home to Corpse Hill, as Copps Hill was called.

Details varied. Above-ground interment in tombs or family vaults, preferred by Southern families, especially where the burying grounds were low and subject to flooding, was not unknown in New England. It posed one problem: When a tomb was opened for its newest occupant, the stench from the lack of ventilation could be sickening. Not much better were the vaults under major city churches; a burial under Trinity Church in Boston stamped on one eight-year-old mourner an unforgettable memory of dim light and chilly dampness. Rural families

had the best idea: burial in a private plot, somewhere on the farm, strengthening the link between the land and its owners and providing a sense of family continuity.

Burials might differ, but one expense of most funerals was the distribution of gloves. Not to give them to the officiating minister and other local worthies was to risk the loss of social standing. They served often as a kind of invitation to the funeral; but they were also used as rewards for services—expensive gloves to the pallbearers, cheaper quality to the underbearers. Some were white, others black or purple. Most were imported until the Stamp Act prompted nonimportation resolutions like one that James Otis introduced at Faneuil Hall on October 28, 1767: "And we further agree strictly to adhere to the late regulations respecting funerals, and will not use any gloves but what are manufactured here, nor procure any new garments upon such occasions, but what shall be absolutely necessary."

Clergymen were also given gloves at weddings and christenings, and during extended careers they accumulated great numbers of pairs. The aforementioned Reverend Eliot, who was the pastor at Boston's new North Church for over thirty years, kept an "almanac" in which, among other things, he recorded every pair of gloves he received. The total for thirty-two years came to 2,940 pairs; during this time he sold most of them to shopkeepers and netted £1,441 18s. 1d. even though some remained unsold.

He also sold off his collection of "burying rings." These were far less numerous than gloves, being given only by wealthy families. Made usually of gold with black (or black and white) enameling, they displayed such suitable figures as a winged skull, a death's head, a serpent or a coffin with a skeleton, together with a motto: Prepare for Death, Death Parts United Hearts or Death Conquers All. Goldsmiths stocked them and, for a sale, engraved the name or initials and the date of death; sometimes a minute lock of the dead person's hair was added. The recipient of a ring was likely to say in conversation or note in his journal, "Made a ring at the funeral." One will dated in 1775 included a bequest to a grandson, "a ring I made at his father's death."

A common adjunct of a funeral was the elegy written by a friend or relative. Since deaths, like births and weddings, went unnoticed by newspapers unless the deceased or his family was quite prominent, these mournful verses seldom appeared in print; those that did only prove that genuine poets were rare. Here's an obituary for the daughter of a "gentleman" (as the courtesy title of "Esq." indicates), which may be read as typical of the period:

On the 11th inst. died at Hopewell, aged 20 years, Miss Sally Temple, daughter of Benjamin Temple, Esq., of Hunterdon county, New-Jersey, and on the 13th her remains were interred in the old Presbyterian burying-ground, near Trenton, attended by a number of her intimate acquaintance. The suddenness of her death, the nature of her disorder, her blooming age as well as pe-

culiar excellencies, made it the occasion of general sympathy. To the thoughtless and dissipated let this be a solemn lesson of instruction, that life is fleeting as the passing cloud, but death and retribution as certain as the returning morn; nor can any virtue, any accomplishment, procrastinate the destined and fatal hour, or this beloved object might have yet continued to gladden the heart of her dejected parent:

> *The conflict's o'er, the lovely Sarah's dead,*
> *In that soft sigh th'immortal spirit fled,*
> *No more, alas! the pleasing power we find*
> *Of those bright eyes that spoke th'embellished mind.*
> *From her pale lips we now no more shall hear*
> *Those flows of wit that charm'd the listening ear.*
> *When'er she spoke attention catch'd the sound,*
> *And spread the smile of approbation round.*
> *Her voice was sweetness, and her judgment strong,*
> *And soft persuasion dwelt upon her tongue.*

Funerals could be dirt cheap for a pauper with no family intent on keeping up appearances or very costly for a man of distinction. Economy entered the picture with the erection of a gravestone, usually after some time had passed and initial grief had subsided. Unmarked fieldstone was less and less used, being limited to lowly slave field hands, children born dead or dying very young and people in isolated areas where there were no means of cutting stone. In the 1770s, the typical gravestone was slate, with a smooth surface easily engraved. The best was imported from North Wales; it arrived already decorated with cherubs, death's heads, hourglasses and other funereal motifs. A few of the very wealthy ordered marble stones from England. Most colonial families, however, used native stone, either because of the high price and heavy duty on the marble imports or out of patriotic sentiment. There was quite a variety to choose from: fieldstone, local slate, quartzite, green or mica schist, limestone and sandstone, which disintegrated rapidly. Very little marble was used until the last years of the century. Adding the inscription to an imported stone gave work to a stonecutter; giving him a stone fresh from stream bed or quarry made a sculptor of him. American sculpture may not have begun with the carving of gravestones, as has been suggested, but it certainly dominated that art until after the Revolution. Most of it simply imitated foreign models, but with freedom to improvise, some men developed genuine talent, as in low-relief portraits, and were proud enough of their work to sign it.

Inscriptions varied greatly. One in Concord from 1773 recited, in twenty pompous lines, the virtues of a slave, John Jack, freed shortly before

DEATH, THE GRAND TYRANT,
GAVE HIM HIS FINAL EMANCIPATION
AND PUT HIM ON A FOOTING WITH KINGS.

Most slaves went to eternity beneath unmarked fieldstones or wooden markers bearing only their names and dates, partly because very few of them were christianized before the close of the Revolution, but also because nobody wanted to pay for anything better.

Most epitaphs, understandably, were deadly serious, reciting virtues that were sometimes exaggerated and reminding survivors that their own lives were limited. Some have for latter-day pilgrims a humor that was never intended, while a few reflect a grim defiance of respectable tradition:

IN MEMORY OF
ABRAHAM RICE

WHO DEPARTED THIS LIFE IN A SUDDEN
& AWFUL MANNER & WE TRUST ENTERD
A BETTER JUNE YE 3 ANNO D. 1777
YE 81ST YEAR OF HIS AGE.
MY TREMBLING HEART WITH GRIEF
O'ERFLOWS
WHILE I RECORD THE LIFE OF THOSE
WHO DIED BY THUNDER SENT FROM HEAVEN
IN SEVENTEEN HUNDRED & SEVENTY SEVEN.
LET ALL PREPARE FOR JUDGEMENT DAY
AS WE MAY BE CALLED OUT OF TIME
AND IN A SUDDEN AND AWFUL WAY
WHILE IN OUR YOUTH AND IN OUR PRIME.

A man of eighty-one is hardly in his youth or prime, but put it to poetic license. Quite different was the story suggested by twin stones side by side in Little Compton, Rhode Island:

IN MEMORY OF
ELIZABETH WHO
SHOULD HAVE BEEN THE
WIFE OF MR.
SIMEON PALMER
WHO DIED AUG. 14TH
1776 IN THE 64TH YEAR
OF HER AGE.

IN MEMORY OF
LYDIA YE WIFE OF
MR. SIMEON PALMER
WHO DIED DECEM
YE 26 1754 IN YE 35TH
YEAR OF HER AGE.

To all that Revolutionary generation, whatever their epitaphs, "Rest in well-earned peace!"

In his famous "Concord Hymn," Ralph Waldo Emerson saluted the "embattled farmers" who opened the war for independence. Stirring words but misleading, for many of the men in that engagement were no more farmers than Emerson himself was, sixty years later. Like him, they lived in the self-sufficient rural tradition, but also like him they made their livings in occupations other than farming. A nation of farmers could not have gained the high level of prosperity and technology that gave the war a chance of succeeding.

Emerson was neither the first nor the last to speak of the rebels as farmers. Sometime in the 1780s, Benjamin Franklin remarked that farming was "the great business of the country," and historians down to the present have kept the notion alive. In fact, by 1775, the skilled trades were overtaking agriculture as the economic base of colonial life in all sections except the plantation South, and technology was already well advanced and gaining steadily. It was the seed time not only of the Republic but also of industrial America as we know it.

Farming, to break even, to keep alive, was one thing; we call it subsistence farming, and we haven't much use for it today. Neither did our forebears in the 1770s. Like us, they dreamed of getting ahead, of rising on the economic ladder, of having money to spend. Standing still was not enough. So they turned, more of them each year, to the skilled trades, which promised income and financial security, and to business. The dream came true, for those who had the choice; when the war for independence began, free Americans, on the average, were the world's most prosperous people. Farm self-sufficiency could never have produced such wealth.

A Self-Sufficient People

There is really no mystery, not even a paradox, in

4

Rural Americans

Below: Masonry headquarters of Washington and Lafayette at Chadd's Ford, Pennsylvania—lower left is beehive oven. *Opposite:* Portion of first-floor master bedroom, with miniature chair, Delft ware.

calling Americans farmers and, almost in the same breath, reporting their conversion to the trades and to business. Nine-tenths of all colonials lived on farms or in small villages in the Revolutionary years, and whatever else they did, they *were* tillers of the soil, some of the time at least. The diversion of interest and energy to other work made poor farmers of many of them, but this hardly mattered; the rural pattern was a way of life they would have abandoned only with great reluctance. Throughout the colonies, except in the cities and where large plantations dominated, most free-agent families clung to homestead self-sufficiency by preference or because they saw no advantage in other modes of living. Some families, in undeveloped regions, had no choice. The pattern was most successful in rural New England and least successful in the backcountry South.

Self-sufficiency, which can still prompt nostalgia when cities and routine jobs grow irksome, is familiar in general outline; but the specifics may need reviewing.

For the prospective colonial homeowner in a developing community, the help of neighbors was essential. The framed house, all but universal in rural America, simply could not be "raised" by one man working alone. He might dig the cellar hole himself, fell the oak trees, haul the logs behind his own oxen to the site, rough hew them to approximate squareness, shape their ends for mortise-and-tenon connection and complete each side, flat on the ground. But raising each side to an upright position and joining the four sides when they were raised called for many hands, which were needed also to set in place the various heavy timbers—sills, joists, beams, rafters, braces. The occasion was usually a social one, with a great deal of rum flowing freely and lasting friendships being formed. Neighbors also lent their oxen to drag the huge granite foundation stones,

which had to be set in place. There was a great deal to be done before the raising could begin.

Once the walls were raised and the house framed, the owner could do all the rest by himself if he had average capacity with tools. A man who was all thumbs was likely to end up with a clumsy house, hard to heat, drafty, with uneven floors, smoky chimney, ill-fitting windows, a roof that leaked in heavy rains; but until the culture was converted to specialization, most men *could* do most of the kinds of work involved in home construction. The one essential skill few men would have had was in working iron; the first tradesman in a village was therefore likely to be a blacksmith, for without a swinging crane and other fireplace iron, cookery would have been primitive and severely limited.

Winter was a time for repairing tools, replacing shingles on the roof and stopping leaks and replenishing the wood supply for the fireplace, from the homestead woodlot or the town forest owned in common. Large trees were best cut down with a two-man saw, but an axe, with its edge newly sharpened on a grindstone turned by foot, was enough for most trees. Once felled, the tree was sawed into cord lengths, four feet, which most fireplaces could easily accommodate. But green wood doesn't burn; it had to be stocked and seasoned for a number of months or a year. Some lengths up to a foot in diameter were reserved as backlogs, which, placed against the back of the fireplace, lasted a week or more. Another four-foot length, no more than half as thick, was placed in front, as a forestick; between the two, on the hearth or on andirons, was the fire. Most wood for the fire was in shorter lengths, which were split for easy burning. Early and late in this process there was considerable hauling, by wagon if the ground was bare, by sledge if snow was deep enough.

Overnight, in those days, the fire was banked with ashes; come morning these were carefully raked away and kindling was laid on the pink coals to revive the fire, with the help of a bellows. The ashes, when cool, were taken down cellar and stored until the annual soap-making. If for any reason the banked coals did not last through the night, somebody was sent with a fire pan to the nearest neighbor for a few live coals; the alternative, producing fire with a tinderbox, was more difficult. There was a knack to it that many people never acquired. It was not hard to make a spark by striking the flint and the piece of iron together, but aiming the spark at the bits of thin dry cloth, getting the cloth to smolder and bringing the smolder to a flame called for skill and great patience.

The big central chimney, usually of brick by the eighteenth century, created a draft that gave all the ventilation anyone could have asked for. Too much of it, often, for comfort. The hotter the fire, the cooler the parts of the kitchen farthest from the hearth, from cold air drawn by the draft through uninsulated walls. This effect could be somewhat offset by a settle, which was three things in one: a long chest, for storage; a bench, using the cover of the chest; and, most important, a solid back the width of the chest and extending from the floor

almost to the ceiling. The settle not only deflected the cold air currents but caught the heat from the fire and, as a consequence, was a favorite place to sit on cold winter evenings.

Heat was only one function of the fire; cooking was the other, and it was not seasonal. The various operations combined in a modern stove were separate in colonial homes. Boiling and stewing required pots or kettles, of different sizes, suspended from a swinging crane by a simple pot hook or a trammel with its several notches. For mere simmering or brewing tea, the pot was put on the hearth or perhaps on a trivet near the coals. Meats were grilled directly over the fire, in a rack with a long handle, or boiled in a suspended pot or roasted either on a spit or within a curved reflector at hearth level. Eggs, corn and potatoes were wrapped in wet leaves and covered with coals to roast. A heavy skillet resting on the coals was fine for frying and, when covered, for pot-roasting. An odd-looking utensil called a Dutch oven, with a long handle, long legs and a depressed cover for holding hot coals, was efficient for baking, whether set atop the coals or suspended from a pot hook.

All these terms had regional variants, and an

easy way to start an argument was to insist that a skillet was more properly a spider or a spider a frying pan or a Dutch oven a domed brick vault built into the chimney wall. Whatever the terms, the function was what mattered. The brick oven, long familiar in Europe, excelled any cast-iron implement for baking. Preheated by a fire of well-seasoned twigs, it was considered warm enough when the carbon deposit on the upper bricks was burned off. Then the burned twigs were removed and the interior swept clean, shaped bread dough was placed on the floor and the hinged iron door was closed except for a tiny crack to permit a draft. When the loaves were well baked, they were removed with a long-handled flat spade called a peel. This was traditionally a job for Saturday; the oven was also used for baking meat, pies and beans.

One great advantage of country living was the wide variety of available food. City people might be better acquainted with exotic imports, but there wasn't much chance on city streets to shoot a deer or a game bird or to gather wild fruits and berries. More city people then than now had small gardens and orchards, but farm families had much more land to cultivate or to use as pasture.

All the European foods were available, brought along, in the form of seeds or cuttings, poultry and domestic animals and honeybees, by the early migrants. There was little thought, at the outset, of living off the land, and some of the unfamiliar indigenous foods took time to be appreciated. Among the distinctive natural foods the Indians liked were strawberries, plums, persimmons, grapes, groundnuts, wampee or tuckahoe (a root of the arum family growing in Virginia and farther south), Indian rice and cane. From the Indians the settlers had learned the culture and use of the unfamiliar vegetables, especially maize (or Indian corn), which had been improved by plant breeding and cultivation

through the years. The Indians had also improved the varieties of peas and beans, squash, pumpkin and other plants they domesticated. One species popular in the 1770s was the Jerusalem artichoke, which was neither an artichoke nor from Jerusalem but the bulbous root of the common eastern sunflower. Another, still prized as a rural spring delicacy, was the fiddlehead fern, a substitute for asparagus. Cornmeal became for the colonists the basis of many kinds of bread with such regional names as corn cake, johnnycake, hoecake, corn pone and simply corn bread. Cornmeal was also made into hasty pudding (cornmeal mush) and Indian pudding—cornmeal, molasses and milk well spiced and baked very slowly.

At some point in the remote past, the males in a family were called the spear side and the females the distaff side. The first term dropped out with the spear, but the latter persisted as long as spinning was a universal function in the household. Any modern woman yearning to regain the self-sufficiency of 1775 must become proficient in many occupations, including the various steps in turning wool, fresh from the sheep, into clothing and blankets. Men did the shearing, but women took over after that. Wool was important in colonial America for two chief reasons: The finished material was stronger, warmer and more durable than any other fabric then available, and any farm could produce sheep.

The most unpleasant part was the first—cleaning the wool by scouring it with lye soap. Sheep are not the cleanest of animals, and a lifetime of gamboling through thickets and rolling luxuriously in mud filled the wool with dirt and pebbles, thorns and twigs, all well matted with suint, a greasy substance formed of dried sweat and peculiar to sheep. No disinfectant sheep-dip was yet on the market to destroy parasites before shearing. Next came card-

ing, which completed what the washing began. The card (or carder) was a wire-toothed brush that had to be vigorously applied to remove stubborn particles and disentangle the wool fibers. The third step, spinning the fibers into thread or yarn, is properly associated with quiet candlelight evenings, a dying fire on the hearth and, of course, the spinning wheel, one of the dominant reminders of colonial life. Like the grindstone used to hone the axe, it was powered by a treadle worked up and down by foot and geared by wooden screws to the wheel, about four feet in diameter, with its flat outer surface two or three inches wide. The washed and carded wool was drawn by hand from the notched distaff at the farther end of the apparatus, worked by dexterous fingers into a continuous strand of consistent thickness and fed to the slowly revolving wheel. When the wheel held all it could take or all that was wanted, the material was taken off, again by hand, and folded into skeins of yarn—loops perhaps a foot long—or, if very fine, rolled onto spools as thread. Slight variations in thickness mattered less than the firm connection of the filaments.

What remained was working the spun wool into material and shaping the material into garments or flat ware, like blankets. Weaving woolen thread was tedious work, gladly hired out to the village weaver, if there was one, who had more efficient looms than most households could boast, or to one of the numerous itinerant weavers. Four or five yards of cloth was a very good day's work, whoever did it. Yarn intended for knitting was colored first, in an earthenware dye pot kept warm in a chimney corner. The dye itself was usually made of indigo dissolved in urine, a mixture that gave no offense until the time came to remove the soaking yarn and wring it out. The resulting stench was dreadful, but our forebears couldn't afford to be overly sensitive about odors. Even so, news that a dyer had opened for business down by the village green must have signaled general rejoicing among the womenfolk.

For men's clothing, woven goods were taken to a clothier, if one was handy, who beat fuller's earth, an absorbent claylike substance, into the cloth to remove the last animal grease and to make it easier to cut and shape into trousers, coats and vests; wool particularly needed this fulling because without it pressing and creasing were next to impossible.

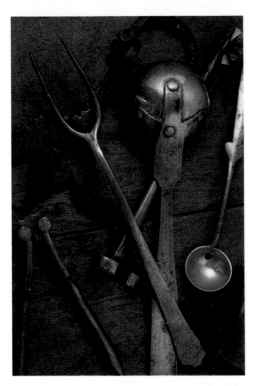

Above: Blacksmith's products—
nutcracker, door knocker, pie
crimper, spoons and fork.
Right: Fireplace with forelog
and backlog, andirons, crane,
trammel, pots. There is a
toaster on the floor between
the andirons. Large kettle was
used for making soap or apple
butter. *Opposite:* An unusual
settle—it opened up into a bed.

Woolen cloth for women's wear was not fulled but simply dyed and pressed (and was thus called "pressed cloth").

The other common material for clothing, until cotton came onto the retail market well after 1775, was linen. Like wool it could be produced on the home farm, although flax had the bad reputation of exhausting the soil. Men did most of the work, pulling the flax in the fall, working it into a plot of loose dirt to let the woody parts rot away, then crushing the fibers on a flax brake, beating them with a wooden paddle called a "swingle knife" and combing out the tow (the short or broken pieces) on a hackle, a wicked-looking implement made of strong metal spikes set close together (and the source of that useful verb *heckle*). The surviving fibers were put on a distaff and spun on a wheel somewhat smaller than was used for wool—only about twenty inches in diameter. The tow separated by the hackle was also spun, making twine that served well for bagging. Linen thread, from the long fibers, was woven into a stiff cloth most useful for sheets, ticking, table linen, handkerchiefs and men's dress shirts. Cloth made of linen and cotton was called "fustian"; the term *homespun* refers to woolen material not fulled or pressed but made into garments for rough wear about the farm. In summer, when homespun became much too warm for comfort, men preferred linen.

A once-a-year task that usually fell to the women, who heartily despised it, was making up the year's supply of soap. On one of the first spring days warm enough to work outdoors and always before the annual spring housecleaning, a washtub big enough to hold sixty or seventy gallons was put together and bound with stout hoops of wood or iron. The bottom was lined with bricks set on edge, which were covered with straw or hemlock branches and then with a porous cloth. The ashes carefully saved and stored all winter, from any wood except pine or beech, were then dumped in, and boiling water was added at intervals and allowed to settle. When the tub could take no more water, the noisome mixture was left alone for one or two hours, undergoing a chemical process known as leaching. A sample was drawn off, and if an egg broken and dropped into it floated, what the tub contained was lye. If the egg sank, more time was allowed. Once ready, the lye was mixed with the winter's accumulation of grease from cooking and boiled down to the gooey consistency of soft soap, not very good but the best that most families could expect.

Milking and churning butter were skills common to both sexes, but the men preferred keeping tools and farm implements in repair and patching the holes in shoes and slaughtering the animals for food and tanning the hides if the village had no tanner. If the town touched on salt water or a good river, the men spent some time fishing; they also ran traplines for furs they could use or sell. Each family worked out its own division of labor, but there was always enough to go around. If in a year's time the great endless circle of domestic economy threw off short tangents of profit from selling a little farm produce, and if this profit exceeded the cash outlay

Below: Flax hackle (or hatchel) with flax beaten to remove the outer layer. Foreground, flax before beating. *Right top:* Loom for weaving yarn. *Right bottom:* Tape loom—a child could operate one—to make such things as shoestrings, decorative tapes and fringes for clothing and bed hangings. *Opposite:* Rear of loom.

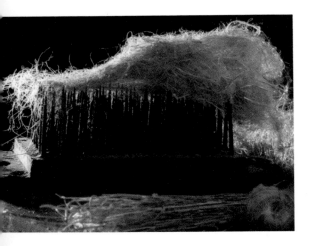

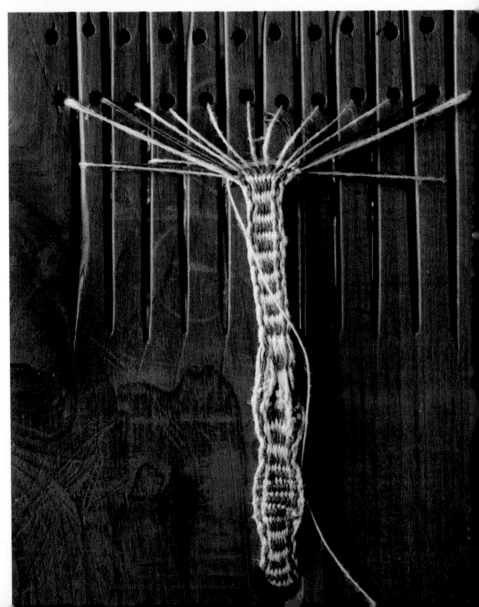

for salt and implements and taxes and tithes to the local church and rum and an occasional luxury, colonial families could not complain; but the steady expansion of work opportunities away from home, in trades that were increasing in variety and demand in the late colonial period, was undermining self-sufficiency as the basic pattern of economic survival. Getting ahead in life meant external income.

Farmers—Competent and Not?

There was good money in truck farming near every city, replenishing day by day the stalls of public markets, and anyone developing a specialty and applying scientific methods could expect a good income—from carefully tended orchards, for example, or from systematic breeding of cattle and horses. Resourceful apple men turned their windfall fruit into the sweet cider that was the common drink with every meal or the hard cider that rivaled rum as the favorite alcoholic drink or the vinegar used to preserve certain foods and to make ink. Industrious cattlemen had no trouble producing better bulls and cows than the underfed average; they not only took good care of their stock but experimented with new English grasses that gradually replaced salt-marsh hay and other nonnutritious natural forage. But the landmark success of colonial agriculture was the breeding of excellent horses.

The most competent farmers in all the colonies, the Germans in Pennsylvania, saw the need for a sturdy workhorse for farm operations and for hauling produce to Philadelphia; oxen might do for plowing but were too slow on the highway. Selective breeding yielded the magnificent Conestoga horse, named for a stream near Lancaster and a rival of the great draft horses of Europe—Shire and Clydesdale and Percheron. The horse, perhaps unfairly, has not shared the fame of the Conestoga wagon, a later product of those energetic people, nor did it gain the international renown of the Narragansett trotter, bred on the great landed estates along the west shore of Narragansett Bay in Rhode Island and sold in large numbers, especially to planters in the West Indies. The fame of these trotters was their undoing, however, for the breeders unwisely sold too many of the mares out of the country and the business slowed to a halt.

The Germans in the population were mostly from the Rhine Valley and other parts of Germany noted for progressive farming; in America they were continuing a great tradition. Anglo-Americans, in contrast, had a strong urban heritage and looked on farming as a temporary expedient until the skilled trades had time to expand. This is an oversimplification of the facts, for many Germans were excellent craftsmen and some Americans of English descent were good farmers. Regional attitudes differed

greatly. If a farm in New England ran down when its owner took up a trade, nobody raised an eyebrow in censure; there wasn't the pride in efficient farming that was evident in the "German empire" of Pennsylvania, where neglect of fields and barns was considered sinful and where farmers applied scientific methods that New Englanders generally ignored. A third attitude prevailed in the Southern colonies, where large plantations were commercial operations managed less often by the owners than by superintendents and overseers.

Heritage and regional attitudes influenced farming as a business and so did land policies, colony by colony. By far the most progressive and democratic were those in Massachusetts, where the General Court, as the lower house of the legislature was called, created new towns of fairly uniform size, ordinarily six square miles; required the proprietors to divide the land equably and to set apart specific areas for common pasturage and woodland; virtually handpicked the prospective settlers and encouraged grass-roots government, as soon as possible, through town meetings and elected selectmen. Everything possible was done to prevent individuals from accumulating large holdings, although a few did in Rhode Island; entail and primogeniture were unknown in New England in 1775. But while the regional policies fostered homestead self-sufficiency, they effectively reduced the possibility of farming

for profit, for the average family owned only about twenty-seven acres. It seldom paid to have a slave or an indentured white servant to work so small a holding.

In the Middle Colonies, town development was less by legislative action than by groups of settlers, many of them religious congregations immigrating as bodies and preserving their close-knit mutual enthusiasm. Individual farms were considerably larger than in New England, averaging between one and two hundred acres, enough to provide for the family needs and to produce for the commercial market. Slave and indentured help was feasible, and both soil and climate were more favorable than those in New England.

An earlier policy, however, especially in New York, first under the Dutch and continued by the English, limited the increase of agriculture by sequestering large blocks of land in private holdings. What was called a manor, twenty-four square miles (more than fifteen thousand acres), could have provided adequate farms for a hundred families. Some of the patrician estates in New York, along both sides of the Hudson River between New York and Albany, were much larger. Their owners charged fees for sections they chose to rent and vigorously prosecuted squatters in their desire for eventual sale at a tremendous profit. In the meantime, they paid into the public coffers a token annual fee called a

Right: View of Boston Common, sketched for John Hancock in 1768. Encamped on the Common are members of the unwelcome Twenty-ninth Regiment, sent by England to police citizens who, since the Stamp Act, had been making life difficult for British officials. *Below:* Moravian village of Bethlehem, Pennsylvania, 1757. In center foreground is the tavern; houses, stable and barns are nearby.

"quitrent" (about four shillings a year for each hundred acres) and wielded a disproportionate power in the colony's affairs. If this system, which smacked of feudalism, had prevailed throughout the colonies, it could well be considered the general economic base; but in no colony did it preempt all the land, and with so many square miles in the colonies, there was always space for small holdings, though least in New York.

The largest landholdings were in the plantation colonies, where they averaged more than four hundred acres; but the range in size was enormous. Privilege begat greater privilege, as royal favorites increased their original grants and as plantation owners, in good years, bought up land for future use. Thomas Fairfax, Sixth Baron Fairfax (1693 to 1781), the only resident peer in the colonies, owned Virginia's "Northern Neck," between the Potomac and the Rappahannock, more than 5 million acres as confirmed by the Privy Council; Lord Granville, before his death in 1763, was the absentee owner of half of North Carolina. These were conspicuous relics of the original class of proprietors in all the colonies. The class dominant in the South in 1775, the plantation owners with no heritage of nobility but successful in their imitation of the English landed gentry, defended the quitrent system with all the political power they could wield and maintained the twin feudal archaisms of primogeniture and entail. The law of primogeniture passing ownership to the oldest son was less effective than the law of entail, which kept large estates from being broken up. As population grew and with it the demand for land to farm, these legal fossils were barriers to democratic progress and healthy competition. The small farmers, generally newcomers, had to rent from the large landholders or pay parish taxes on less fertile upland farms or settle for mountain acres as hard to cultivate as any in glaciated New England and far from any potential markets. The one advantage of remote farms was that the rents or land taxes were generally waived because the cost of collecting them was too high.

To Market, to Market

Wheat was little grown in New England, partly because the farmers there believed that the region would not favor it; but no such prejudice existed in New York or in other colonies as far south as North Carolina. Because wheat flour is the most common ingredient of bread, it bulked large in intercolonial commerce, which the British government tried to discourage but could not control. This trade between colonies employed a good many men, mostly sailors, and was a force in creating the sense of common cause in the struggle for independence.

What most discouraged New Englanders from growing wheat was black stem rust; by 1775, the farmers of the region were positive, almost to a man, that it was useless even to try. Corn was better, anyway. It was easier to plant, in hills rather than in rows and with a rotting fish in each hill as fertilizer in the Indian fashion, and it was easier to harvest. The corn could be eaten on the cob, boiled or roasted, or the kernels could be cut off and combined with beans as succotash, another Indian con-

tribution, or with other vegetables as a pickle, and surplus ears could be strung up on ceiling beams to dry for winter use or for the next year's planting. The stalks made excellent fodder for cattle, and the shucks went into mattresses. Cornmeal took the place of wheat flour in many baked foods.

But corn was almost never a money crop in New England. Neither were the other vegetables that increased in variety, though not without widespread resistance, in the eighteenth century: asparagus, beets, cabbage, carrots, cauliflower, celery, lettuce, onions, parsnips, radishes, spinach. Root vegetables kept best, stored in the cellar, but many Yankees were positive that white potatoes were unsafe to eat; like tomatoes they were shunned as poisonous, even deadly. As for fruit, apples alone found their way into commerce in any quantity; few families grew more cherries, pears, plums and crab apples than they could consume, fresh or preserved like the berries, in honey or maple syrup. Truck farmers raised cash crops for city markets; but for the great majority of New Englanders farming as an economic base was a dead end, yielding none of the income that everybody wanted.

Middle Colony farmers grew everything produced in New England and more. Wheat was no easier to plant or reap there, and in addition to stem rust there were Hessian flies; but Pennsylvanians stubbornly refused to surrender to such handicaps and earned for their area the reputation of being "the colonial breadbasket." They had discovered that winter wheat, sown in the fall before the ground froze, resisted pests and disease; and they were quick to adopt a ,wheat cradle, essentially a frame attached to a scythe to catch the grain as it was cut, when it came onto the market shortly before the Revolution. They grew enough wheat to supply other colonies and to export large quantities to the West Indies. Other exports of the region were

Fig.II.
A Bunch of Seed, enlarg'd to its natural Size.

M

hay, of a much better quality than New England could produce, potatoes and fruits, especially peaches, and livestock. The melon capital of the colonies, however, was the Long Island farmland near New York City.

But if the best farmers lived in the Middle Colonies, agriculture was hardly the exclusive base of that region's economic life. Only in the plantation South was that the case—not totally, but so very nearly so that agriculture could be called the only Southern industry. Stress on money crops was so great, moreover, that some plantations had to import their meat, vegetables and fruit from the North or go without. Tobacco was the most valuable crop of the Chesapeake region, and it was not edible. Neither was indigo, the chief export from Savannah. The only major crop for human consumption was rice, the specialty of South Carolina; Charleston shipped out every year about one hundred twenty-five thousand barrels. All three of these crops were difficult to plant, to cultivate and to harvest; the work was so tedious that nobody free to choose would do it, and it fell to slaves, who were subject to command. The net result of this concentration on money crops over a period of many years was disaster: By 1776, the large Southern planters owed £3,372,760 to London merchants. As an economic base, this kind of agriculture was ruinous.

The small farmers of the South, the few who survived near the coast and the much greater number in the backcountry, lacked the credit needed for major money crops and were wise enough to diversify, stressing wheat, oats and rye in Virginia and North Carolina; hemp, beef and vegetables in South Carolina; figs and oranges in Georgia. Livestock did well in that climate, but as in the North, most cattle and hogs were ill cared for or totally neglected. Some reverted to nature as "scrub" cattle and razorback hogs and were hunted like other game. Better care of these animals would have strengthened the farmers' position, as the Germans in Pennsylvania demonstrated. Hindsight even suggests that the aristocratic Southern planters would have fared better, and would not have been so deep in debt in 1775, if from the beginning they had adopted ranching.

"Worse Ploughing Is No Where to Be Seen"

Expert farmers could be found here and there in 1775, but most Americans who farmed at all were too preoccupied with other matters to show much interest in scientific agriculture. The rural New Englander on his self-sufficient farm carried on much as his father and grandfather had done; expansion of local trades and business increasingly absorbed his attention. A few Southerners, Jefferson among them, were interested in new crops and methods, but most plantation owners either ignored the details of the farming they depended on or used archaic methods and did not keep up with agricultural science.

One Englishman who obviously knew both agri-

culture and the colonies very well, reviewed agricultural practice from Nova Scotia to the West Indies and found it everywhere distressingly backward. Nowhere, for example, did he see proper fencing. Some farmers rotated their crops but on no scientific basis; on most farms, including Southern plantations, the same crop was grown year after year until fertility was exhausted and the plot had to be abandoned. Cattle, swine and sheep were almost universally neglected, turned loose in all seasons to find their own forage. Fertilizer was neglected, too; horse and cow dung was left in piles to rot instead of being spread on growing plots, most of which needed enrichment badly. Horses were overworked and poorly fed, and "worse ploughing is no where to be seen." Recent European improvements in farm implements were ignored; American farmers relied on old-style plows with beams too long, shares too narrow, wheels too low, and on ill-made harrows with teeth of wood instead of iron. Most farmers were indifferent to new products already well established in England—carrots, cabbages and parsnips, which could improve the diet of cattle even if people wouldn't try them, and alfalfa, then called lucern. The sheer abundance of land, the author supposed, explained the poor husbandry. He reported exceptions where he found them—the wide variety of vegetables grown in Maryland and backcountry Virginia, irrigation (by diverting brooks) in some hilly regions and the all-inclusive excellence of the Pennsylvania Ger-

mans—but the general picture as he saw it was bleak. Once he even departed from his usual objectivity to remark, concerning the treatment of cattle in New England, that "most of the farmers of this country are . . . the most negligent ignorant set of men in the world."

In what some people called the "German empire," west of Philadelphia and east of the Susquehanna River, farmers demonstrated how very good farming could be. Their first step was to choose the land carefully: Where trees were tallest, walnuts in particular, they knew there was a good lime base. But they took no chances, for they added lime to their fields regularly and fertilized with their barnyard manure. Instead of rotating fields, they rotated crops on a four-year cycle: corn, oats, wheat, hay. The Amish considered soil depletion sinful; others in the region simply called it stupid. The German-language newspapers printed numerous articles on farming. New crops and tools and methods were quickly tried; if they didn't work, like the experiments with vineyards, they were just as quickly abandoned. But most things succeeded: vegetables not yet grown commercially in other sections (lima beans, sweet potatoes, squash), new varieties of apples, pears, peaches and cherries, along with the complete range of other farm staples. Wheat was their chief money crop; the rye they grew they preferred to use for their bread and to make into whiskey. Some of their fruit ended up in the form of brandy. Not even pigeons were overlooked; squab was a regional delicacy. Livestock was well cared for; the hillside barns with hay stored above and the lower level open to horses and cattle were by far the largest in America. The English and Scotch-Irish considered such big barns a luxury; the Pennsylvania Dutch knew better. Salt, pepper, molasses, spices and coffee they had to buy; everything else for their bountiful tables they produced, in a triumphant combination of self-sufficiency and salable surplus. They proved that farming *could* be a firm and successful economic base in America. But in most of the colonial area in the Revolutionary period, it was not.

The deficiencies of American agriculture, as reported in books and articles read in England, bolstered the British contempt for everything American. People as backward and careless as most colonials were in so essential an occupation as farming must have seemed unlikely candidates for independence. The buildup of the trades was less fully reported and less a factor in British calculations. Such a nation of farmers, if their farming was any measure of their efficiency, would pose no serious threat if their rebelliousness led to all-out war. But some images are woefully incomplete, and this was among the incomplete ones.

"Tobacco Was the Villain"

E Pluribus Unum was proposed as a motto for the united colonies in 1776 by John Adams, Benjamin Franklin and Thomas Jefferson; although the Continental Congress was ready that year to declare independence, it took another six years to agree on the motto. The sectional differences were so great and their interests so divergent that political unity seemed to many colonials an impossible and foolish fancy and to others a dangerous threat. Combining to oust the British was one thing; permanent union

was quite different. Pluralism was so marked in colonial life that it would have been logical in 1775 to predict, with independence, the emergence of not one but several nation-states.

The agrarian South was the region most likely to become a separate nation—as it sought to be in the next century. Conditions prompting secession in 1860–61 already existed in the 1770s, particularly the reliance on agriculture and the sharp lines between privileged and disenfranchised classes. Every traveler noticed the difference; any perusal of

Above: Painting by Thomas Coram of Mulberry House, a plantation near Charleston that produced rice and indigo. The houses in the foreground are slave quarters. The river, beyond the main house, offered an easy way of sending crops to market. *Opposite:* Carter's Grove, near Williamsburg, one of the great plantations. Built on the James River, it had its own private docks from which its main crop, tobacco, could be shipped.

Southern legislation, plantation records and personal memoirs would make it crystal clear.

Nicholas Cresswell, visiting Virginia in the spring of 1774, noted first that Urbanna, where he landed, was a small village dominated by tobacco warehouses. En route to another tiny village, by boat, with three Negroes rowing, he admired the fine houses along the shore, each far from any town. He watched some slaves planting tobacco, making hills the size of molehills, about four thousand to the acre, poking holes with a finger or a stick and putting the plant in—a process that astonished him. Agriculture, he decided, was in a very poor state; "they know little about farming." Later he watched as men reaped the spring wheat: "The greatest slovens I ever saw, believe that one fourth part is left in the Field uncut."

Everything Cresswell reported was echoed by other observers—the insignificant communities, the isolated homes of the planters, the extravagance of the wealthy despite their lack of money, the inhuman method of executing miscreant slaves, travel by water where possible in the absence of good roads and especially the backward agricultural methods. Tobacco was the villain, historically; the great demand for it in Europe encouraged its production in Virginia to the virtual exclusion of all other occupations and was the basis for the semifeudal class structure. The dominant plantation families—Burwells and Byrds, Carters and Corbins, Fitzhughs and Harrisons, Lees and Ludwells, Nelsons and Pages and Randolphs, among others—were no longer on the make in 1776 as was the fluid recent aristocracy in South Carolina; their struggle toward the top was long past. They were as assured, as proud, as condescending to inferiors and as confident of their right to rule as the nobility anywhere in Europe. All they had to do to stay on top was to enforce the laws their ancestors had passed. Since those laws gave them control of the sixty-member House of Burgesses, the twelve-man Council of State and the administration of every county and even every parish (or vestry), the growing majority of small backcountry farmers were severely handicapped before the war—even marriage into the "gentry" was not possible as it was in other colonies. Local residents, moreover, had no vote or voice on such local issues as tax rates, road repairs, bridge construction or the licensing of taverns; nothing remotely like the New England town meeting existed in the South.

The unit of government in the Southern colonies, the parish, was so large, averaging about five hundred square miles, the farmers were so far apart, because fields had to be alternated to preserve their fertility, and trades were so underdeveloped that villages were few and small; if there *had* been parish meetings, getting to them would have been difficult. The small-scale farmers, for all their struggle for a fair share in colonial government, depended on the large plantation owners, who acted as their agents for the sale of crops and let them use their river landings for moving those crops to market. A few of the yeoman farmers had one or more slaves or indentured servants, but even so, all members of the family had to work hard, as on the self-sufficient Northern farm, to show a little profit each year. Adding to income by adopting a trade was not an option, unless a large plantation needed a cooper or blacksmith. Lacking credit, the yeoman losing ground financially had only unwelcome options: One was to abandon the farm and move to the frontier, beyond the reach of tax collectors; another was to indenture himself, and perhaps his wife and children, to a prosperous neighbor; a third, not really an option, was to drop into the wretched category of "lubbers," as poor whites were called. Yeoman farmers are usually described as a sturdy lot, and most of them had to be to survive; but some were not sturdy enough, and others were unlucky. The area that William Byrd called "Lubberland," in North Carolina just below the Virginia line that he helped survey, of all regions in the colonies came closest to being the land of the poor and the home of the cursed.

"Factories in the Field"

Food, shelter and clothing, that trio of human essentials, could all be provided in the self-sufficient pattern. It also yielded a sense of independence, of being able to survive with no help at all from neighbors or from government. "That government is best that governs least," according to Jefferson, and the words would have been welcome as a motto for rural freeholders from Maine to Georgia and doubly welcome on the outer fringes of settlement.

What self-sufficiency by itself could not provide was spendable income or the chance to rise on the economic scale. Gaining small sums by selling surplus products was hardly better than exchanging the surplus by barter. If and when a rural family did develop particular products for market sale, it was a drift from self-sufficiency to truck gardening, a form of agricultural business. The much greater shift was to the trades.

Most would-be tradesmen began as apprentices, learning by doing. Fathers who had become established in trades and looked forward to keeping them in the family took their own sons as apprentices; their willingness to take other lads depended on whether the business was expanding and on personal factors: A delicate boy was a poor risk for the village blacksmith, and clumsiness was nowhere a virtue in demand. A bright boy of twelve, well muscled and healthy, with stamina and ambition, was a potential asset in any workshop, and he could be

confident of a secure position and increasing income whether he stayed in the village or drifted to the city. Nowhere in 1775 was every adult male engaged in a trade for income, but this was increasingly the pattern, pointing away from self-sufficiency and toward today's almost total delegation of functions.

A typical sequence would begin with an outbuilding on the farm converted to a shop, with apprentices living with the family. As job orders multiplied, a new shop near the village green had obvious advantages, and as shops increased, the village grew in both size and importance. The final move was to a city, for its greater number of potential customers and the resulting increase in profit. But business remained small. Farmers-turned-tradesmen retained their pride in good work and their sturdy independence. At the same time, the increase in tradesmen transferred self-sufficiency from the homestead to the community; villages as well as cities provided services formerly done by families but now of better quality because they were the work of experts. The jack-of-all-trades farmer might know how to tan leather or weave cloth, but the local tanner or weaver could do it better. Finer work, like clockmaking or wig-styling, was beyond ordinary capacity; but with a trade himself any man had income to pay other tradesmen. Here was another kind of revolution, accelerating in the Revolutionary years and projecting self-sufficiency beyond family and community to the national level. Dependence on English skills declined as American tradesmen gained in proficiency and turned to products their fathers had to import or do without. By 1775, the suspension of transatlantic commerce was no great hardship; the chief sufferers were not the Americans but the tradesmen in England.

Of all North America's natural resources, timber was the most accessible. Its contribution to rural self-sufficiency is obvious, and its export to Europe,

where the forests were close to exhaustion, was a major source of colonial prosperity. The American forest was so vast that sea captains swore they could smell the trees, especially the pines, a hundred miles from the coast. This sounds like an exaggeration, but it would be hard to exaggerate the sheer number of native trees or their variety and utility—white pines for masts and oak for the hulls of ships, other species of pine for pitch and turpentine, willow and alder for baskets, walnut and birch and maple for furniture and utensils, locust for posts that would not rot, hemlock, or rather its bark, for the tanning of leather. One kind of maple yielded sap each spring that could be boiled down to syrup or maple sugar. Nut trees were plentiful, including chestnuts, not yet the victims of blight. Ash made the best shafts for hand tools, and beech was ideal for carved initials and intertwined hearts, as essential to courtship as the springhouse or hayloft. Almost every wood except poplar was good as fuel; housewives knew their particular qualities—relative

ease of igniting, rate of burning, aroma, degree of smokiness and such habits as throwing out sparks. Do-it-yourself home carpenters knew the values of different woods for repair and construction; some made durable sills, others were better for siding and rafters, floors and walls. Shipbuilders were particularly grateful for the available variety: Shipyards commonly had supplies of live oak from Georgia, red cedar and locust from the Chesapeake region, light pitch pine from the Carolinas, oak and white pine from northern New England. Most rural householders, wherever they lived, also welcomed the variety of trees in their own woodlots or in the town or parish stands reserved for common use. The forest provided work in many trades as well, from lumber cutting and sawing to the carving of exquisite fireplace mantels and figureheads for schooners.

Most ships were built in port cities, but some were put together in the forest and hauled overland by oxen. Small vessels, like the flat-bottomed gundalows used on creeks in upper New England, were "country-built" by farmers with products to ship to market. The recent suggestions of "factories in the field" is a reminder of the general decentralization of trades in the 1770s.

"A Country Industry"

The most refined trades, like work with gold and silver, were the pride of cities, but much of the production was in rural areas. Iron and copper mills, for example, were almost always close to the deposits of ore, in locations remote from the main road network.

Colony-planters were well aware of the importance of tradesmen. If the first passenger manifest did not list a few men skilled in basic trades, the new settlement was in grave danger of collapse. Sawyers and carpenters were most essential at the outset, but

Below: Silversmith's scale, silver filings and pieces of silver. Old silver objects and coins were brought to the silversmith, weighed and melted. The new object made by the silversmith was also weighed, and the value of the old silver deducted. *Opposite:* A vertical-sash sawmill, operated by water power, on Fort Anne Creek, north of Lake George, in 1777.

the community blacksmith emerged, soon enough, as the first full-time tradesman, and his shop rivaled the meetinghouse as a local gathering place. The village smithy, as Longfellow described it in 1841, had a peculiar fascination for children and adults alike, with its flaming forge and roaring bellows and with the well-muscled arms of the smith gleaming with sweat in the red glow as he used one or another of his many tools. Ironworking had by 1775 developed far beyond anything the average local blacksmith could do, but he was still a conspicuous and essential figure in village life.

Iron ore was found on or near the surface in most of the colonies. The commonest early form, bog-iron, was collected by scraping the beds of marshes; by the mid-eighteenth century, most of it came from rock ore, which had to be crushed and heated to a semifluid state in an oversized blacksmith shop called a "bloomery" and fueled by charcoal. Before the bloom could cool, it was hammered on large

anvils to remove most of the slag; what remained was wrought iron. Providing charcoal enough was a separate industry that employed large crews of men to cut and transport the wood and to burn it in airtight kilns.

By the 1770s there were large smelteries with mechanical bellows and fairly tall smokestacks, which, like the hearth, were carefully built of fire-resistant stone or clay. A flux of limestone or oyster shells was thrown into the hot ore to stimulate its fusing. The finished product, in the form of pig-iron bars, was sent to slitting mills, where it was ordinarily rolled at white heat into the slender rods most useful to blacksmiths in the making of nails or implements, chains or horseshoes. Heavier objects called for bulkier shapes and sizes of workable iron.

If the Board of Trade in London had been able to enforce its edicts, designed for the advantage of British industry, colonial iron-making would not have advanced beyond the stage it attained by the

1740s. The Iron Act of 1750 somewhat slowed the advance but did not halt it; what economists call benign neglect, and what stern Crown officers after 1764 viewed as unforgivable British permissiveness, operated before that year to tolerate or encourage the steady expansion of iron mills. Even the export of iron increased, from 1,130 tons in 1730 to 7,500 tons in 1770. Some steel was made as well, by the lengthy process of heating two bars of iron with charcoal in a closed furnace until the bars acquired a high carbon content, lost most of the impurities residual in iron and gained high tensile strength and hardness. Steel was not in great demand before the opening of the Revolution, but the advantage of steel ramrods in that war stimulated its production.

The New Jersey Highlands, in the northwestern corner of the colony, were particularly rich in iron ore and, by 1775, could boast of at least thirty ironworks, especially in or near Ringwood, Morristown, Charlottenberg, Long Pond and Bloom-

ingdale. One village in Morris County was named for the ore: Ironia. Bog iron was also abundant throughout New Jersey.

The most impressive example of colonial capacity in ironwork, the great chain across the Hudson River, was entirely a country product; none of the large cities had the facilities for making it. Early in the Revolution, when there was fear that British men-of-war might help cut the colonies in half by controlling the Hudson, the Continental Congress decided to block passage at West Point with a great chain, and the workmen at Peter Townsend's Sterling Iron Works near Monroe, New York, were able to forge and install it in just six weeks. It was five hundred yards long and weighed one hundred eighty tons. The links, of rod iron about three inches in diameter and weighing an average of one hundred forty pounds, were carried on muleback or in oxcarts over the hills to the riverbank, where a special furnace had been built to join them. Swivels

Top: Silver spoon made by Samuel Vernon, Newport's first great silversmith. *Left:* Silver tray, inkpot, sandbox (sand was used for drying ink), made in England. *Above:* Silver pepper or spice caster, made in Boston by Jacob Hurd. *Opposite:* Examples of ornamental grillwork made by colonial ironworkers.

were inserted at hundred-foot intervals and a clevis for every thousand-foot section. The chain worked; the British plan was thwarted.

The most familiar ironworker, the local blacksmith, found everywhere in the settled parts of the colonies, bought his iron from the mills. Even if he never tried anything fancy, like ornamental grillwork, he had to be proficient with an impressive variety of implements—the hearth with its huge bellows, pokers, rakes and water trough; the anvil with its big and little sledges, flattening hammers, cutters, chisels and tongs and the swages for bending and shaping the metal; and the shoeing box with the special hammer to drive the nails in, nails of various sizes, and, for trimming, assorted knives, rasps and files. Most blacksmiths learned their art as apprentices, and taught it in turn to boys, often their own sons, who began work at the age of ten or twelve. It took a long time to learn the three degrees of heat: the white-hot "snowball," needed for weld-

ing; "full-welding," not quite so hot, for mild steel; and "light-welding," cooler yet but requiring the greatest skill. Other processes that had to be mastered were drawing out, the repeated hammering to get rid of imperfections, doubling back to multiply thickness, punching, joining, riveting, collaring and twisting. How-to-do-it manuals were in print though scarce in the colonies; blacksmiths didn't mind, for word-of-mouth instruction preserved the secrets within their trade.

As communities grew and life became more varied, it was tempting to specialize. Some blacksmiths concentrated on making and repairing edged tools: scissors, knives, axes, adzes, hatchets, drawing knives, sickles and scythes; others turned to household gadgets including trivets, dippers, skillets, door bolts and hinges, latches and knockers and fireplace tools. It was hard work, much of it, that defied replacement by machinery until about 1930. Many blacksmiths, by 1775, had acquired other names,

merely by branching out. A nail-maker—you guessed it—specialized in nails, and a farrier in horseshoes, though he also treated the ailments of horses in those days before veterinarians. A wheelwright made not only wheels but the iron tires and hub bands that held them together. A cutler earned his name by making the swords and other edged weapons beloved by militia officers; he also made small implements, some of them from steel—corkscrews, penknives, lancets.

The iron industry, worldwide, was barely out of its infancy, but in the Revolutionary period it employed more Americans than all the other metal trades combined. Most pewter was still being imported from England; it was an advance over the old homemade wooden plates and platters and was prized in the form of mugs and pitchers, but its low melting point limited its popularity and its attraction for colonial craftsmen, especially in competition with copper and tinware.

Copper ore was plentiful in New Jersey, along the main population corridor from New York to Philadelphia, and substantial mills were built in such villages as Newark, Bound Brook and New Brunswick. The largest single copper mine, however, was near Simsbury, in Connecticut, northwest of Hartford. The going price for copper ready for manufacture was forty pounds a ton, twice that of iron, but the finished utensils were lighter in weight, more attractive in a kitchen and favored by those who could pay the difference. Coppersmiths, including Paul Revere, had to apply at least as much artistry to their products as the ironworkers commonly did, to stay in business.

Whitesmiths, as tinsmiths were then called, could ignore artistry; only one of them in the Revolutionary period, Oliver Bronson, made any attempt to create new forms or to imitate the expert japanned ware of England. The industry was barely a quarter-century old, having begun in 1750 when a

Scotch-Irish migrant, Edward Pattison, settled in Berlin, Connecticut, with a knowledge of tin-plating that he taught to neighborhood boys. Tin, in usable form, is actually thin sheet iron coated with tin to prevent rusting. Production costs were low, and the Berlin workers, who carefully guarded their trade secrets, turned out vast quantities of cheap utilitarian ware: lanterns, sconces, boxes, canisters, candle molds, measuring spoons and cups, salt shakers, mugs and dippers, all at prices almost anybody could pay. Housewives bought them eagerly from peddlers sent out from Berlin to cover the colonies. As long as an object was well made and in steady demand, why worry about art, or even about change? The chief improvements in tin-making in the Revolutionary period were in production and distribution techniques, for greater profits; but as in ironwork it was a country industry, one that closing the port cities could not seriously affect.

Wealth from the Sea

In the years just before the Revolution, about ten thousand men in New England alone made their living by catching fish in coastal waters. Cod brought the most money, followed by herring, mackerel, bluefish, salmon and shad. The largest and heaviest fish were sold in local markets; families in seacoast communities, as they always had, ate much more fish every week than most of us eat today. The best smaller fish were shipped to Europe, salted or packed in ice, and the junk fish were consigned to the West Indies, where the rich planters used them as fertilizer or as food for their slaves. The Sugar Act of 1764 set prohibitive duties on the sugar and molasses that the West Indians gave in exchange for the fish, but it was relatively easy to evade the duties, and the trade continued to flourish until, like all ocean trade, it dwindled with the British closing of the ports as a war measure.

Cod was most easily caught in the summer, but the best grade, known as "dun fish" for its color, could be caught only in the winter. It was unfit for human consumption until the next August, after fermentation, accelerated by salting, had run its course. A profitable by-product was cod-liver oil, used for currying leather. The demand for cod was so great that the fleet, composed of more than six hundred schooners weighing from twenty to fifty tons, had to go several hundred miles up the coast to the banks off Nova Scotia, making two or three trips a year. Mackerel in commercial quantities was also harder to find than in the good old days; it had once been harvested near shore, in huge nets, but by the 1770s had to be caught by hook and line in deep water. The total value of New England's commercial fisheries in that period is estimated at $2 million a year, or an average of about two hundred dollars for each fisherman, not a bad income even without other work in slack seasons.

Shellfish—crabs, lobsters, oysters, clams, scallops and shrimp—were taken, in bays and inlets, by individuals for their own consumption or for the specialty market, particularly in New York, New Jersey and Chesapeake Bay. But at Wellfleet on Cape Cod, the diminishing supply of oysters prompted one enterprising Yankee to come to nature's rescue with the first oyster "planting," in 1774. Human and industrial effluence had not yet reached such proportions as to threaten the shellfish industry; most of the coastline was blissfully empty of human beings, as it would continue to be until saltwater bathing became fashionable in the late 1800s.

The most legendary of all ocean fisheries was whaling, which began on a large scale when, with the close of the French and Indian War, new sea areas, including the Gulf of St. Lawrence, were opened for search and destruction of these largest of all mammals. In 1763, of five thousand tons of whale oil taken to England, three-fifths came from the colonies. Lord Grenville's suspension of a bounty to English whalers was a boon to their competitors; by 1764, American whaling was rapidly expanding, and its range was extending—to Baffin Bay in the far North and to the coasts of Brazil and West Africa. In addition to the sperm oil used in lamps, the white waxy substance called spermaceti, also from the whale's head, was excellent for candles, ointments and cosmetics. The bones of the whale rivaled ivory, and the grayish ambergris, from the intestines, was prized by perfume-makers because it retarded evaporation.

Not all income from the sea was pocketed by the shipowners and the sailor-fishermen they employed. When Nantucket Island, south of Cape Cod, became the world capital of the whaling industry, it was not only the home port for about half the three hundred whaling vessels in the colonies and for their crews; it was also crowded with shipwrights, sail- and rope-makers, coopers and blacksmiths and specialists in preparing the catch for reshipment. Practically all was handwork. Taking most space were the rope walks, long and narrow, where men walked back and forth twisting together strands of hemp and flax twine into a cord, then three or four cords to form a rope an inch or so in diameter and finally three or more ropes to make a cable. All told, about four thousand men earned their living, and a good one it was, on Nantucket from 1770 to 1775. For Massachusetts as a whole, it may be added, there was one seagoing vessel for every hundred people in 1775; and in Maine and New Hampshire, many more men were engaged in shipbuilding than in farming.

Thousands of colonials were regularly employed in maritime commerce, which was cheaper and faster from colony to colony than overland trade, given the generally poor roads of the period, and was of course the only means of transportation across the ocean. British naval captains, harsh and arrogant men, were heartily disliked by all American mariners; officiously detaining ships and inspecting their cargoes, they succeeded, as the current phrase went, in "annoying the coastal trade." Ports were so numerous, however, that more American ships slipped in or out without detection than the limited number of British men-of-war could keep under observation. Ships bound for British ports could be boarded and inspected on arrival; but some harbor masters in England could be persuaded, by bribes, to ignore certain American ships that dropped anchor and were unloaded in the dark. Port officials in continental Europe were even more lenient, especially if the cargo was something in particular demand—prime white pine lumber, perhaps, or beaver pelts and other furs or transshipped West Indian sugar. Whatever figure the British government gave for American ships crossing the Atlantic in any given year was well below the actual number. Governor Bernard of Massachusetts, after the passage of the Sugar Act, warned his London superiors that the restrictions would hurt England more than the colonies, and he was right; if anything, the act spurred colonial crews and captains to carry elsewhere what England needed but insisted on taxing.

Historians refer to the triangular trade, as if there were only one, from New England to Africa to the West Indies and back to New England; actually there were several in regular operation in the 1760s and 1770s, some with shapes other than triangles. One standard route was from Portsmouth or Boston, with fish or lumber, to Great Britain, then to the slave coast of Africa with textiles or metal ware, then to Jamaica or Barbados with slaves and back home with sugar and molasses for the rum-makers. Another took horses and fish to the West Indies, sugar from there to Madeira and wine back to New York or Philadelphia. American sailors plied the Atlantic in every direction, ignoring British restrictions and evading British captains assigned to control them. The importing of slaves to Boston, where they were quickly sold out of the region, began to decline in 1765, and in 1774, the four New England colonies agreed to halt the trade; but this didn't prevent good Yankees from transporting Africans to the West Indies—the price of a prime field hand had risen, to about two hundred gallons of rum.

Men who lived on farms near the sea thought nothing of doubling as sailors or fishermen, just as other men became part-time professional hunters or trappers. Such work made rural tradesmen of them, in an elementary sense, but most of the work that farmers turned to added value to raw materials by the application of acquired skills.

Spinners and Weavers

One industry that lagged before the war was textiles —perhaps because so many families made their own clothing. That the colonials could make decent clothing at all was one of the things that Englishmen doubted. Cloth made of wool, they were certain, had to be inferior because the wool itself was inferior—only seven inches in staple length compared with twenty-one-inch Leicestershire. What those British critics did not know was that the shorter staples were easier to card and, when woven, to shape into clothing or that almost every American family was able to card and spin its own wool.

Nor did the generals who fought against George Washington know that on his Mount Vernon estate he had developed an experimental weaving shop, with a manager and several slaves turning out fabrics of wool, cotton and linen. He did not advertise, but another Virginian, William Simmons, was more

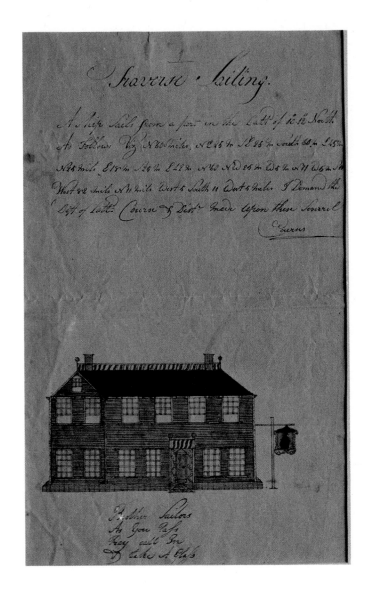

Top: Page from a navigation exercise book. *Bottom:* Bill of lading, 1749.
Opposite: Illustrations from the journals of Ashley Bowen, merchant seaman; his ships, *Success* (top) anchored and *Swift* (below) in a storm at sea.

1763

1741 October We left Gibaralter Bound for
Boston Note We took on board the Common
Sand which was as the Red Sand in Time gl...
and as we came to the westward and Lynn

forward, with a notice in the *Virginia Gazette* for January 13, 1774:

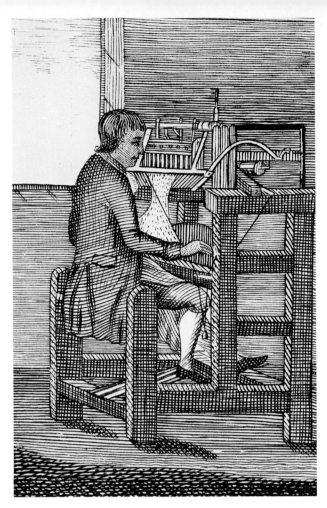

Surry County (Cabin Point), Dec. 27, 1773. This is to inform the Publick, and those Gentlemen in particular who were so kind to assist me in my Plan for executing my Fulling Mill, that it is now complete, and at Work. All persons that are disposed to encourage this laudable Undertaking I shall be obliged to for their Favours. I advise the Publick, that I have two Looms at Work that weave five Quarter Yard wide Cloth, as it is much to the Manufacturers Advantage to have their Cloth, wove of that Width. My price for Weaving is one s. a Yard, Filling, Dying, Dressing &c. ls. more, for common Cloth, but dearer for live Colours. Those Persons that dye their Cloth in Grain have it done much cheaper; all mixed Cloths require Nothing more than Filling and Dressing, which are done at a moderate Price. Some Time ago a Person of the Name of Willie set forth a small Pamphlet, which any Persons that are disposed to have Cloth made would do well to attend to; but as it may not be in the Power of every One to get them who may be desirous to have Cloth made, I shall observe to those, that it is very necessary to have the Wool sorted, taking the fine from the coarse, young Sheeps Wool from old. After this is performed, let it be well washed and greased, then carded with a Pair of coarse Cards into large Rolls or Batts. These Batts are to lie broke all to pieces by Hand, and laid in a Heap. You may break them as often as you please; the more your Wool is mixed the evener and prettier the Cloth will be when milled. After this Operation, it is in Order to be carded into Rolls for Spinning, which is to be a moderate Twist for the Warp, not too hard. The Filling is to be spun as slack as you well can spin it; so that it bear winding it is sufficient. Those who choose to weave it themselves should slay it thin, and not weave it too close. The opener the Cloth is the more beautiful it will be when fulled. All Persons that send their Yarn to me may depend on the utmost Punc-

tuality, and that their Instructions shall be duly observed. I am the Publick's most obedient Humble Servant, William Simmons.

N.B. It is observed, that I work for ready Money only: and that any Person who wants to be supplied with Wool may have it of me.

The details that Simmons must have thought it necessary to include suggest that in Virginia, at least, people knew very little about textiles. Virginians of any substance had ordered their clothing and other fabrics from England out of long habit; it was part of the general reliance on England for manufactured goods, in exchange for raw materials, that had kept the colonials colonial. But now it was different; the decade of rising tension, and the desire to live and be known as Americans, destroyed the old willingness to be colonial. Rapid development of the trades was the one way out, and the means of that development was the accelerating conversion of self-sufficient farmers to skilled tradesmen. It might have lessened the poetic tone of "Concord Hymn" to change one word, but it might be more accurate:

Here once the embattled tradesmen stood
And fired the shot heard round the world.

Above: Stocking maker at work. By 1775, the area around Germantown, Pennsylvania, boasted 150 such machines for producing woolen hosiery. *Opposite:* Engraving of machine for spinning cotton or wool, 1775.

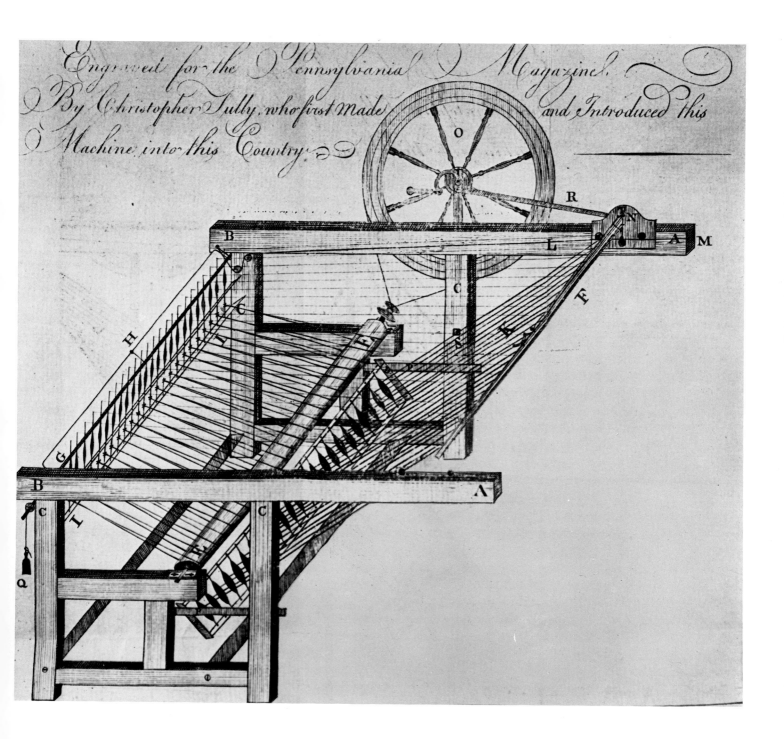

Engraved for the Pennsylvania Magazine. By Christopher Tully, who first Made and Introduced this Machine into this Country.

5

Urban Americans

If the Yankees who fought at Lexington and Concord were unsure about the other colonies, the old rural suspicion of cities prompted another question: Now that violent talk had given way to actual fighting, what help if any would the cities provide? Mob violence, of the sort reported from various cities, showed that rebel sympathy was not lacking, but it was a poor measure of willingness to serve in a formal campaign or to submit to military discipline. The rioters, moreover, were not the people who controlled the cities and would determine their course in a general war. That power was in the hands of merchants and landlords, owners of great fleets, men who set the wages of the working poor and tradesmen accumulating fortunes —in short, the kind of men who might put profit ahead of patriotism.

Boston, as the seedbed of rebellion, could reasonably be depended on; it had originated the Committees of Correspondence, and despite the British occupation, it had sent out the riders, that night in April, to alert the countryside. New York had its Sons of Liberty, who had staged their own Tea Party and were making things hot for Governor Tryon; but Loyalists outnumbered them, and the city's addiction to profits and pleasure made participation improbable. If anything, New Yorkers would join the British army. Philadelphia could also be written off if Quaker pacificism prevailed to keep that city neutral. Charleston, if it did join the rebellion, was too distant to give effective help; but it was doubtful whether the oligarchs, whose wealth depended on exports, would act to alienate their customers in London. As for lesser cities, Portsmouth seemed in too chaotic a condition to be counted on, Newport with its exposed location was at the mercy of the Royal Navy and the Southern capitals were too small to be much help to whichever side they might give their support.

How the cities acted was not, however, a matter of grave anxiety. The twenty largest accounted for only 7 percent of the colonial population, and the biggest of them all, Philadelphia, had only forty thousand residents. The process of becoming an overwhelmingly urban nation was barely under way. But any city, as the center of a trade area, had a concentration of wealth and talent that the country people could not ignore, though they might have wished to; they could neither live with the cities nor live without them.

Urbanites led different lives from those of their country cousins. They could not practice self-sufficiency; their whole livelihood depended on trades and business. One major difference was their open preference for city living. If rural Americans liked country life, close to nature but not to each other, townspeople liked compactness and shared the conviction that cities gave a nation its dignity and luster and were the natural home of science, commerce and patriotism. They equated urbanism with urbanity, a quality that they found missing in the farmers and the villagers, whom they viewed as pitifully benighted.

No two cities in 1775 were alike. All were attractively located, and almost all were important ports, but each had an undeniable individuality. They shared certain problems unknown in rural areas, and all of them were busy places, with jobs enough for everybody willing to work and eager to get ahead.

In 1774, the British government put Boston under martial law, to be lifted only when the residents agreed to pay for the tea dumped in the harbor in the famous Tea Party. As an immediate result, so many Bostonians fled from the city that the population fell from about seventeen thousand to thirty-five hundred. Later, when the Royal Navy blockaded other port cities, a similar exodus oc-

View of the north end of Boston, with Charles Town beyond, sketched about 1760 by British lieutenant Richard Byron, great uncle of the poet, Lord Byron.

curred. The resulting depopulation skews any ranking we might like to see. Some figures are quite precise, and others, as the round numbers in the following table suggest, were mere estimates. Years when the counts or estimates were made, if other than 1775 or 1776, are shown in parentheses.

Largest Cities, 1775–76

	City	Province	1775	1776
1.	Philadelphia	Pa.	40,000	21,767
2.	New York	N.Y.	(1773)	21,463
3.	Boston	Mass.	17,000	3,500
4.	Charleston	S.C.	12,000	12,000
5.	Newport	R.I.	11,000	5,299
6.	New Haven	Conn.	(1771)	8,295
7.	Norwich	Conn.	(1774)	7,032
8.	Norfolk	Va.	6,250	
9.	Baltimore	Md.	5,934	
10.	New London	Conn.	(1774)	5,366
11.	Salem	Mass.		5,337
12.	Lancaster	Pa.		5-6,000
13.	Hartford	Conn.	(1774)	4,881
14.	Middletown	Conn.	4,680	
15.	Portsmouth	N.H.	4,590	
16.	Marblehead	Mass.		4,386
17.	Providence	R.I.	(1774)	4,361
18.	Albany	N.Y.		4,000
19.	Annapolis	Md.	3,700	
20.	Savannah	Ga.	3,200	

Wealth in the Cities

The rural suspicion of cities was broadly based. A hard-working man in a village might, in the course of years, accumulate money enough to build a comfortable new house, hang in it his portrait by a respectable artist, acquire a few mortgages for additional income, dress well, send a son to college and perhaps travel modestly to one of the fashionable spas or even, in his late years, to Europe. But he would view with chagrin or envy the ease with which city men, in his own trade or profession, built even larger houses, sat for portraits by Copley or Peale, acquired numerous mortgages, sent all their sons to college and traveled frequently, all much earlier in life. Some country men built large fortunes, but cities were far more generous in opportunities for wealth.

Of the twenty largest cities, only one, Lancaster, was not a port. The others owed their origin to harbors along the coast, part of nature's benevolence, or to navigable rivers. Portsmouth, for example, could be the great outlet for the timber of New Hampshire and the home of wealthy shipowners and well-paid workers because the mouth of the Piscataqua is an excellent deepwater harbor. The shoals of the Merrimack, in contrast, kept Newburyport from growing. Massachusetts Bay, with its dozens of harbors in a great arc from Gloucester to Nantasket, was even more productive of wealth than the Piscataqua, and Boston owed its dominance in New England to deepwater channels along miles of shore.

Other harbors supported commercial activity on down the New England coast: New Bedford on Buzzards Bay; Newport and Providence and Fall River, which collectively barely tapped the potential of Narragansett Bay; and in Connecticut, Mystic, New London, Norwich, New Haven, Bridgeport, Norwalk and Stamford, the last few overshadowed by New York, the finest harbor anywhere on the Atlantic coast.

With deep water on both sides of Manhattan

Island and on the Long Island and New Jersey shores opposite, New York could be confident of never running out of harbor space whatever its population might become. The port potential extended up the Hudson as far as Albany, at the head of tidal navigation, but there were very few ports of any size along the way.

Delaware Bay was an even larger roadstead, but most of its eastern shore, in New Jersey, was too low and swampy for port development. The one great port was above the bay, on the Delaware River, where Philadelphia boasted the longest developed waterfront in the colonies. Camden and Trenton, on the New Jersey side of the river, shared some of the shipping, and so did Wilmington, in Delaware;

Oil painting by an unknown artist—view of New York, looking west, about 1760. A group of militiamen are in training, center. The ship to the left is French, possibly the prize of privateersmen.

shoreline for future development was still ample.

Not much farther south, Chesapeake Bay and the sizable rivers draining into it comprised the largest expanse of protected water in the colonies, so vast that its few ports were almost lost on the map. The one major development was near its mouth, where Hampton Roads served Norfolk and Portsmouth on one shore, Hampton and Newport News on the other. These four communities, virtually a single port, were the largest area of concentrated population in the entire South. Baltimore and Annapolis, near the head of the bay, were much smaller. Of these Chesapeake port cities, only Annapolis, with its Scottish heritage, possessed mansions like those in Northern port cities; the great

houses of the Tidewater aristocracy were on scattered plantations, but these were almost always close to navigable waters.

Nature was rather stingy with harbors along most of the remaining coast. Shoals and sandbars made navigation treacherous, even for ships of shallow draft, anywhere in North Carolina except in the Cape Fear River estuary. Wilmington, at its head, was the colony's one dependable port. In South Carolina and Georgia, the major deepwater harbors of Charleston and Savannah were on rivers, several miles inland, but the chain of sea islands and the channels between them brought navigation and agriculture as close together as anywhere in the colonies. Shifting sandbars were a problem but not a fatal handicap. For the colonies as a whole, however, few other coastlines in the world provided better facilities for ocean commerce, which was humming everywhere in 1775 and adding to colonial wealth.

Commercial shipping would alone have set the cities apart from the rural areas, as productive of greater per capita wealth, but by 1775 the skilled trades were rivaling commerce in economic importance. The trades offered a particular advantage: When the port of Boston was closed, they could move inland as shipping could not. The most highly specialized work suffered, but trades were trades, and skills used at one level could be applied, with reduced profits, at lower levels.

"Country Work, Country Pay"

The term "country work" applied to trades basic to life whether practiced in a village or a city; the blacksmith was a mainstay of country work and so were the cooper, who made containers of many sizes from wooden staves, the white cooper, who turned out sieves, firkins, grain measures and even bellows, the sawyer, joiner, mason and housewright, the workers in leather—tanner, currier and "cat whipper" (or shoemaker)—the miller, the weaver, the tailor and the chandler (or candlemaker). Tinkers, who repaired tin or pewter objects, and other itinerants were also in the category of country work, which seldom led to fortune but produced a steady income, even if much of it was in "country pay," an extension of the barter system.

Most country work was traditional, using methods long familiar in Europe before the migration began. The new element, conspicuous in the Revolutionary period, was the rapid conversion of do-it-yourself householders to specializing tradesmen—or, to put it in academic jargon, the increasing dele-

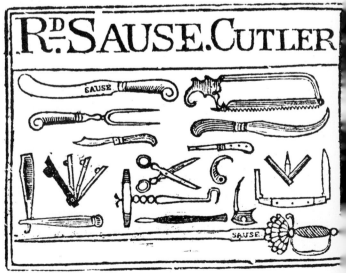

Below: Brazier at work amid some of his equipment. *Top right:* Cutler and helpers making edged instruments. *Bottom right:* Desk made in colonial Pennsylvania. *Opposite top:* Cabinetmaker at work on furniture. *Opposite bottom:* Cutler's advertisement, showing many of the products he made.

149

gation of functions. As coopers, for example, took over the production of tubs and barrels, pails and boxes, other men could lay aside the tools of that trade, if they ever owned them, and could gradually forget how to use them—the curved drawknives, the fixed jointer plane, the sun plane, the howel to bevel the chines of barrel staves, the kerfing saw and the croze.

Urban tradesmen also carried on ancient work but steadily improved their techniques to satisfy demanding customers with more money to spend than they ever had before. Barbers had to be versatile. They spent a good deal of time shaving customers— only pirates and backwoodsmen went bearded—but they also made wigs and dressed them periodically. Some men paid an annual fee to have their wigs properly cared for. Barbers could no longer practice general surgery, but they still pulled teeth and bled patients besides the more usual tonsorial chores.

Other tradesmen seldom found in rural areas included the baker, the hatter, the cutler, the tobacconist, the apothecary and the hornsmith, who flattened cows' horns, and sometimes the upper shell of hawksbill turtles, into sheets used mostly for combs but also for horn spoons, eyeglass frames, snuffboxes and buttons. Ivory carvers made billiard balls, heads for canes, toothpicks and false teeth. Some of these tradesmen made their various products on individual order—hats, for example, or eyeglasses, in what was called "bespoke work." All tradesmen at whatever level took pride in their handwork, developing a recognizable American style even if the basic design was foreign; but the highest level of artistry was in bespoke work, and most of it was urban.

The country carpenter ordinarily built in a traditional style, but a "builder," especially if he was a

Top: Drawknife weaving out a beam or plank. *Bottom:* Footwear for bad weather, forerunner of overshoes. *Opposite:* Shoemaker's bench with tools and materials—lasts or molds for shoes had no left or right shaping.

151

master builder, added individual artistry to tradition and also tried to meet the specific needs of his client. Locksmiths, most of them former blacksmiths, made all the parts by hand and fitted them into specific doors. They also made safes or strongboxes, the only good substitute for bank vaults, with two or three different keys; some were very large, weighing more than half a ton, for city or colonial treasuries.

The rural joiner, who made sturdy, durable furniture, became a cabinetmaker in the city; and some of these men eventually were as expert as any in Europe. Mass production of furniture was not even dreamed of. But other kinds of production were pointing the way to modern industry. Shipbuilding called for the skills of twenty different trades. Potteries, block printers and letterpress printers also needed sizable staffs with varying talents. In the 1770s, however, the largest factories, employing the most men and machinery, were those making paper, brass (especially bells), glass, clocks and, biggest of all, the ironworks. The great ironmasters lived and worked in remote rural locations, but most industrialists operated in the cities.

The textile industry was underdeveloped, although twenty-five hundred pounds of linen, from locally grown flax, were produced annually in New Hampshire for the retail trade, and a firm in Germantown, Pennsylvania, turned out sixty-thousand dozen pairs of stockings a year—hardly enough for all the legs in the colonies but at least a start. Duck, a durable fabric of closely woven linen and cotton, had been commercially produced in Boston as early as 1735. The sudden wartime demand for uniforms, blankets and tents gave textile-making a tremendous boost and caught the industry unprepared, although in time it was able to fill the surging orders.

The fur trade, with New York as its capital, had an annual value of a hundred fifty thousand pounds in the 1770s. Despite British demands that all furs, like most other raw materials, be sent to England for processing, many stayed in the colonies and were made into coat collars by housewives for pin money or into hats. Hat factories, liveliest in Rhode Island and New York, supplied most of the domestic demand and, despite the restrictive Hat Act of 1732, exported a good many hats to the West Indies. Those made of beaver pelts were in constant demand, at the steady price of thirty shillings. The coonskin caps of Revolutionary fame, popularized by Benjamin Franklin when he was our envoy in Paris, were usually homemade. Men who considered them undignified for social wear but who balked at the cost of beaver hats had their choice of less expensive headgear made either of cloth or of deerskin, most of it from Virginia. Deerskin was popular for other garments too, especially on the frontier, but most leather jackets and all shoes were made from the hides of domestic animals. Lynn, Massachusetts, was the center of shoe manufacturing in the colonies. Most self-sufficient farmhouses had a set of iron lasts, one for each member of the family, but making shoes was tedious and exacting work, and people bought their shoes as soon as they had income enough. The best shoes, by 1775, with the square toes, low heels, high tongues and buckles in the fashionable French style, could be made only in factories. The high work boots required for farm work, however, were almost always made by their wearers. Gloves, especially the formal kind worn at funerals, were almost all factory-made.

Other relatively small industries were solidly established in the colonies. Samuel Adams was a Boston brewer, one of several making beer and ale, not yet widely popular but consumed in some quantity in the port cities. Rum-making was more profitable because almost everybody drank rum unless they preferred hard cider or brandy, which could be

late. Candles were almost wholly of domestic make, from wicks dipped in beef tallow, beeswax or crushed bayberries. Tin molds with a variable number of cylinders reduced the labor and produced candles of uniform tapering shape. Most homes in the Revolutionary era had at least one such mold. The demand was enormous; any sizable gathering after dark needed hundreds of candles, in large chandeliers, for adequate light. Every city, whatever its size, could boast a shop that made and sold both candles and assorted candlesticks to hold them. This combination of factory and retail shop was common also for buttons, thread and twine, tinware and brass utensils, bottles and rum measures, pipes and cigars and a wide variety of other small essentials for the good life.

"With silver, style had a chance," somebody once remarked. Its scarcity in nature made it expensive, a luxury for the wealthy who could demand and get exquisite workmanship. Harder than tin or copper but not so hard to shape as to discourage patient silversmiths, silver—the relatively little of it that was for sale—has survived the disintegrating forces—rust and corrosion, for example —that have destroyed most objects made of lesser metals. One practice among the rich was to melt down silver coins and have them recast as silverware (the "coin silver" of collecting fame) as a means of keeping specie in the colonies; the silver lost no value in the process and, with a shift in exchange, could always be reconverted into coins, though British law strictly forbade it. Some silver was brought in by pirates, as part of their booty from captured Spanish galleons. As with the tinware and pewter, the form given it by American silversmiths was imitative of English standards or, in New York, of Dutch. Gold was even scarcer than silver, but a few goldsmiths in the larger cities made substantial fortunes. Silver and gold, in any event,

made at home. Glass making centered in New Jersey, where Caspar Wistar's large-scale glasshouse, built in 1739, was still flourishing in 1775, and in Pennsylvania, where Baron Stiegel, in 1767, introduced flint glass at Manheim with a brace of imported English specialists. Paper, some of it of a quality as good as any made in Europe, was made from plant fibers and rags; its supply seldom equaled the demand, but the expert printers at the Ephrata Kloster (Cloisters) in Pennsylvania made more than enough for their own fine books and sold the excess at a good profit. There were paper mills near Boston, one in Milton and two in Dorchester, which also had factories producing snuff and choco-

were at the top of colonial craftsmanship and show how very high that top could be.

Women's Work

Most women of the Revolutionary period worked as long and as hard each day as the men in their lives. Not all of them, however, accepted the role of home managers and partners in the endless struggle to break even, or get ahead, or, in the moneyed class, to keep up socially with the Byrds or DeLanceys, the Hancocks or Whartons. A few were independent, ambitious and energetic enough to enter occupations of their own. Law and tradition made women subordinate to men in many respects, including rights of inheritance, but conditions, especially in the cities, were more favorable for their independent ventures in that period than in the nineteenth century, when attitudes toward women took a strange new turn, to their disadvantage.

Most women had husbands to provide homes for them and all their financial support. But partly because Puritan theology abhorred idleness, and also because a new country needs labor, the social code barred women from only a few kinds of work they were physically able to do. As the colonies grew in maturity and wealth, moreover, the drive for upward economic mobility, coupled with a gradual decrease in menial chores in the home, prompted more and more women to work at an increasing variety of jobs.

One of the oldest trades for women, if not their oldest profession, was serving in taverns; and the woman tavern keeper, familiar in Elizabethan England, was a common phenomenon in colonial cities and large villages. She was ordinarily a woman widowed beyond the age of child-bearing, one whose children were long since married with homes of their own. Men could keep taverns, too, but women

were generally liked in this role as being better able to maintain an approximation of decorum.

Many more women turned their talents to profit by making and selling such essentials as bonnets, gowns, quilts, malts, distilled essences and baked goods to their neighbors, in a form of cottage industry, for they could do such work at home, whether in the country or in cities. Others, including some of the social elite of New York, opened shops, often on the ground floor of their homes, facing the street, with a variety of wares—cutlery and brazier products, hardware and eyeglasses, drugs and tobacco, books and the latest London newspapers less than a month old. In 1773, one Elizabeth Perkins advertised glass at her shop in Boston's King Street, and the *Boston Courier* carried other "notices" of specialty shops owned by women.

Some occupations later open to women were still wholly in the masculine world: There were no

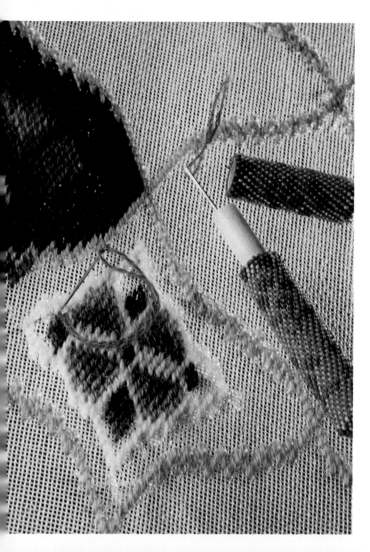

Above left: Irish or Florentine
stitch, crewel in flame design, on canvas,
with scissors and beaded needle
holder. *Above right:* Quilt-making
detail, with needle holder and
silver thimble. *Left:* Implements
for sewing—ivory stiletto, thread
holder and needle holder; the
purse being worked on is in "queen's"
stitch. At right, knitted pinball.

women lawyers or judges, or secretaries or filing clerks, or members of appointed boards or their staffs, or such local functionaries as surveyors, road tenders, hogreeves or public measurers. But some women did well in the health professions, less often as surgeon-apothecaries than as midwives and nurses. Men were not alone, moreover, in making and peddling toothache cures, all sorts of remedies for specific illnesses in the form of salves, powders and tar-water emulsions, special concoctions for scurvy and eczema and particularly for "female complaints," including sterility. The same or other women admitted their human fallibility by keeping, as a sideline, a stock of grave clothes. The fact that particular medical treatment didn't invariably help or that many patients grew worse under treatment or even died is no indictment of the female sex in this role, for most male "doctors" were no better trained and no more efficacious except in extracting their fees.

On a more respectable level, women served as lower school teachers almost as often as men, advertising for pupils and earning the title of "Madame." No woman could hope to teach in a college, for higher education was strictly a man's world. Nor did women aspire to careers in research, although Jane Colden, daughter of the lieutenant-governor of New York, earned a reputation as a botanist before her early death in 1766. The writing of prose tales and poetry was socially acceptable, however, especially if it turned on Indian captivity or thwarted love or excessive saintliness, or if, like the verse of Phillis Wheatley, it paid tribute to leading patriots.

There were also actresses, touring from city to city in dramatic troupes that put on plays old or new for audiences hungry for any theatrical fare. But like the actors, stagehands, directors and managers, they were out of work in October, 1774, when American theaters were closed for the duration. Women in religious roles were rare, although Ann Lee of Manchester arrived in 1774 and settled in Watervliet, New York, where she founded the Shakers; a minor disturbance like a war could not interfere with the organization of a religious order. But neither theater nor religion engaged the talents of as many women as real estate did. Most of these women were widows, managing the sale and rental of family land and buildings and advertising frequently in the newspapers. In 1771, for example, one Marcy Cheese advertised her willingness to sell Chopoquidic Island, east of Martha's Vineyard.

But the profession in which women made their most significant mark was printing. Eleven women owned printing presses in the colonial period, and ten of them published newspapers. When Richard Draper died in June, 1774, his widow Margaret continued to issue his *Boston Newsletter,* a Royalist mouthpiece, until the British evacuated Boston. Also in 1774, Mary Katherine Goddard took over from her brother the *Maryland Gazette* and continued its publication during the war. Isaiah Thomas, not noted for giving praise where it was not earned, described her as "an expert and correct compositor of types." She was also a postmistress, but this was hardly exceptional, for many printers doubled as postmasters in that era.

Neither Franklin in the 1780s nor Emerson in the next century offered any comment on women who held jobs outside the home. The assumption that most colonials were farmers would carry the corollary that if women worked, it was on the farm. What drew men in steadily increasing numbers from farm work to other occupations also, apparently, attracted women. The one curiosity in this matter is the relative decline after 1800 of women seeking income of their own, independently of home and husbands.

The Colonial Big Five

Three colonies—New Jersey, Delaware and North Carolina—had no cities big enough to be in the top twenty. The four New England colonies had eleven of the twenty, and Connecticut alone had five. But Boston was easily dominant, as capital of the oldest and largest colony in the region and as possessor of the best natural harbor north of New York.

Salt water made Boston almost an island; extensive landfills later expanded the city's area, but in 1775 the residents lived and worked on a small peninsula extending from Beacon Hill eastward. The streets resembled a crazy quilt that a frugal housewife might make of odd-shaped bits of material, and most Bostonians saw no reason for change. In 1766, Pudding Lane was widened and given a more dignified name, Devonshire Street, but the next ten years saw no further improvements. Most of the streets were paved but not the sidewalks, which were marked by posts that traffic was supposed to respect but seldom did. City paving in that period was of stone slabs or brick or a mixture of gravel and pitch; and streets were either crowned, with a gutter on each side, or graded down to a gutter in the middle, the practice in Boston. Traffic, with no policemen assigned to direct it, was heavy and often badly snarled. The 1765 town meeting passed a resolution urging the drivers of carts, wagons, carriages and other wheeled vehicles to keep to the right, but it was not mandatory. Charleston two years earlier had opted for driving on the left.

Bostonians were content with their city as it was; growth and change meant less to them than preservation of the old and familiar. They took special pride in their Common, by far the largest park in any colonial city and a great place for social strolling. Two men caught chopping trees there in 1773 were charged with vandalism, tried, found guilty and given stiff jail sentences. It was quite all right, however, to pasture cows on the Common.

Most of Boston's buildings were of mellow red brick. Good clays had been found throughout the colonies, and their variety explains the differing color and texture of brick buildings from city to city. Wood had been the first choice for construction, almost everywhere, but it was replaced by brick as the danger of fire increased. A disastrous fire in Boston in 1760, leveling most of the older wooden structures, prompted passage of an ordinance requiring brick walls and slate roofs. The builders welcomed the ordinance because lumber, which by then was being shipped in from Maine, cost five times as much as brick. Fire also destroyed Faneuil Hall, in 1761, but it was rebuilt in the same style after an extended argument; a few people urged a new plan, but, as might have been expected, the traditionalists had their way. In 1769, a new courthouse on Queen Street was dedicated, the last major construction before the Revolution. With little space for new housing, property for sale or rent was scarce and expensive; the population held static as workingmen's families, unable to find quarters, drifted to Salem and Marblehead and other nearby coastal communities.

Newport, the second-busiest port in New England and the fifth-largest city in the colonies, was settled only nine years after Boston but had never acquired much of a metropolitan air. Lord Howe, who bottled up the harbor in 1778, called the city "mean," and he was right; it looked like an overgrown village, with few public buildings and modest frame houses set on ample lots. Howe could not appreciate, presumably, the tasteful style of those houses and their solid construction or the exquisite interior of the synagogue completed in 1763 (the second to be built in the colonies), which Peter Harrison designed for Congregation Jeshuat Israel.

Ambrose Serle, Howe's civilian secretary, described the city as he observed it one December morning:

Walked over Newport this morning, which was fair and mild. 'Tis built almost entirely with Wood, & makes but a mean appearance. It has one long Street out of wch run several Lanes, The whole miserably paved, and, at this time, extremely dirty. The public Buildings are but ordinary; and the Style of the Town perfectly suits the Genius of the People, who for Fraud, Smuggling & Rebellion are not to be exceeded in No. America. There are some Exceptions, but too few to take off the general Stigma.

The Redwood Library, which Newporters held in great esteem, disappointed Serle; its collection, he noted, was small, ill-chosen, poorly preserved and based on "very low, illiberal Principles, but suitable enough for the Complexion of those who read there." He did admit, however, that town and harbor were pleasantly located and that the air was salubrious.

Newport's "meanness," or its resemblance to a village, was evident in various ways. The one long street and the shorter cross streets, crowned but not paved, were graded and graveled by citizens, each contributing so many days of labor per year. The money for materials was raised by lotteries. Traffic jams were rare, certainly not the daily nuisance they were in Boston. The openness, moreover, enabled householders to grow more kitchen vegetables than was possible in Boston and to keep more cows. What other food they needed came from truck farms near the city and could be bought at the Brick Market, also designed by Peter Harrison, which was completed in 1772. Rustics might have felt uneasily out of place in Boston but not when they visited Newport.

Problems in the Cities

Despite the construction boom of the Revolutionary period, population increased faster than new houses, penalizing wage earners by pushing urban rentals and purchase prices beyond their ability to pay. Men reaping profits on the Newport waterfront— as importers or exporters, shipowners or shipbuilders, drydock operators or warehouse men—had to put their money somewhere, and with no banks paying interest or corporations selling shares, local real estate was the best possibility for investment. Buying an old house, spending a little more to spruce it up and then offering it for rent or resale at an exorbitant figure proved easy for the few with the

Left: Long Wharf, Boston waterfront, by Richard Byron, 1764. *Below:* Façade of the Clark-Frankland mansion, built in 1712, one of Boston's finest colonial homes. The interior was embellished with painted decorations, inlaid floors, heavily gilded woodwork. This painting hung over one of the mantels.

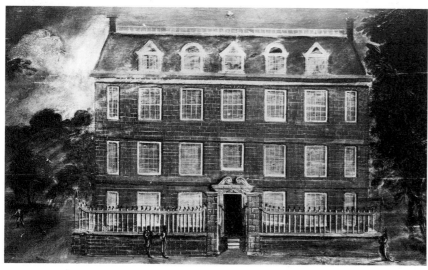

money to do it. The one visible risk was an economic recession; but what happened was worse—the British closing of the port, which destroyed the entire economy of Newport.

The housing shortage and the resulting sharp increases in rents and selling prices affected every city, although in different ways. The halt in population growth, resulting from an exodus of workingmen, was dramatic in Boston. In Philadelphia, a city much more generously planned than Boston, population increase made the rich families—Whartons and Shippens and others—steadily richer as they bought up vacant fields, had them surveyed into streets and building lots and put houses on the lots that they could easily sell or rent at a profit. The housing shortage proved a boon to the rich in New York also; a merchant with capital enough could build a house and recover its cost in rent within seven years. If the builder already owned the land, his costs were even lower and his profit greater. Working families, whose wages the same merchant class kept as low as possible, resorted to doubling up in older houses not adequately maintained; it was a process certain to produce slums. The very worst conditions anywhere prevailed in Charleston; rents were highest there in proportion to costs, and the disparity was greatest between the homes of the poor, jerry-built for quick profit, and the fine mansions and public buildings that gave Charleston its reputation as the most attractive colonial city.

Getting firewood enough was another problem growing steadily more acute as the forest receded from growing urban areas. Brick, which could be locally produced, replaced lumber for construction when the price rose too high, but fuel could not be fabricated. Woodsmen in Maine shipped cordwood as well as lumber to the Boston area, but the local distributors saw to it that the price to consumers left an ample profit. Woodlot owners in the towns near Boston also smelled profit; with cart or sledge they took in their cordwood and peddled it, like any other country produce, from door to door. Along with the profit, they earned the reputation of fleecing the urbanites by selling pieces shorter than the standard four feet. A shipload arriving from the Penobscot River could be inspected by an official measurer, but stopping every vehicle approaching Boston to look for possible infractions was hardly feasible. The 1772 town meeting adopted stringent regulations governing cordwood, but they helped very little.

Coal was not yet commonly available. A few shippers brought in British coal from Newcastle that cost a little more than good native oak but helped keep the price of cordwood from rising even higher. So did the charcoal sold in limited quantities by various ironworks. Well-to-do Newporters burned in their fireplace grates coal shipped up the coast from Virginia, and the future looked promising when coal deposits were discovered in other parts of Rhode Island. But when the Royal Navy occupied the city, the situation was soon desperate. The British, for their own heating and cooking needs, cut down all the remaining trees in the vicinity and tore down fences and vacant houses. The Newport poor resorted to ripping up old wharf timbers along the waterfront.

Surviving trees and old fences also disappeared in Boston during the British occupation. Profit-minded rustics, who hoped for a bonanza from selling cordwood to Gage, were thwarted by the siege laid down by the Continental army. The Boston poor, the few who were unable to flee from the city, overlooked their discomfort in their knowledge that the siege was effective in hurting the British.

One British regulation had for some time been a petty annoyance: Cordwood and other forest

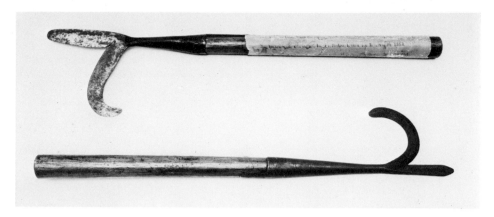

Watchmen's billhooks—the men of the Boston Watch were required to carry these.

products could not be shipped directly to Boston but had to be unloaded at Marblehead and carted the last few miles. The added cost wasn't much; it was the principle that irritated. The going retail price in Boston, despite the grafting and the British interference, was never as high before the war as it was in New York—fifty shillings a cord even though the source of supply was close by, at Queen's Village on Long Island and in the Shrewsbury region of New Jersey. If this suggests a curious economic law, that the price of cordwood varied inversely with the distance it had to be transported, the situation in Charleston tends to confirm it. Magnificent forests bordered navigable rivers just west of that city, but a handful of profiteers proved their rugged individualism by cornering the market and driving up the price from 70 shillings in 1761 to 140 ten years later. Charleston had no town meeting to adopt regulations, and the colonial assembly, dominated as it was by merchants and rich planters, refused to consider the possibility of controls. Luckily for the poor it never got very cold in Charleston, but people still needed fuel for cooking. The only sizable city with reasonable cordwood prices was Philadelphia, where charcoal and imported coal were plentiful.

Newport, with its village ways of doing things, left the lighting of streets to private citizens, but by 1773 the other principal cities had made it a municipal responsibility. New York imposed taxes to buy lamps and the whale oil they burned and to hire lamplighters, but on stormy nights the lamps went unlighted or blew out. The very novelty of lighted streets, which Philadelphia pioneered, produced a steady problem of breakage; spirited youngsters on a spree, and gangs of criminals who liked the dark, took delight in smashing the lamps. A stiff fine of twenty pounds for each lamp broken proved no deterrent but, if the culprit was caught, did

cover the replacement cost. No Northern city adopted the Charleston practice of giving a lamp breaker, black or white, his choice of the standard twenty-pound fine or thirty-nine lashes. Boston, perhaps because it lacked a large criminal element, was the last major city to install street lamps, waiting until 1774. By the outbreak of the Revolution, however, city streets throughout the colonies were better lighted at night than most streets in England.

The Oldest, the Smallest

New York was the oldest major city in the colonies, antedating even Boston by six years. It was also the smallest in area, with less than one square mile for its twenty thousand people and three thousand residences. Its compactness was not forced by geography but reflected the old Dutch habit of building with "party walls" that served adjacent houses. There where it stood on the very tip of Manhattan Island, New York would have looked, from a balloon, like a child's model of some old European city, very attractive in its setting with water on three sides and conspicuous for its neat rows of brick buildings with tiled roofs, several steepled churches, assorted wharves and warehouses and four miniature parks—elliptical Bowling Green at the foot of Broadway; Hanover Square, the heart of the city's commerce; St. George's Square; and the common in front of the new gaol (as the lockup was spelled in those days). As in Boston, the streets were highly irregular in pattern. Engrossing as the distant vista might have been, however, it would have given little idea of the diversity of life in the city or of its cosmopolitan population or of the general addiction of its citizens to good living.

Dutch for its first forty years and under English control for little more than a century by the time of the Revolution, New York was easily the most cosmopolitan colonial city. The census taken in 1773 showed 2,737 blacks and 18,726 whites. Some of the blacks were slaves, more were free, but all were subservient, as domestic help or as the lower working echelon. All were "kept in their place," moreover, by laws and common practice hardly less oppressive than in the plantation South. When times were hard, the least secure of them lost their jobs and joined the lowest class of whites as drifters and occasional criminals. What chiefly set whites and blacks apart at this bottom rung of New York's social ladder was the severity of punishment if they were caught breaking a law. White men found guilty of crimes against property were given fines or prison terms; while it sounds improbable but wasn't, black men merely accused of the same offenses—burglary, for example—were sometimes put to death without trial.

If any of the blacks conversed among themselves in African languages, it would only have added to the city's polyglot character. One scholar has stated that eighteen languages were spoken in New York in the 1770s. Older citizens were bilingual, in Dutch and English, while French and German and Hebrew were frequently heard. The mixing of European stocks was also evident in the variety of religions. Trinity, St. Paul's and St. George's served the Anglicans, and other citizens of British extraction attended the Quaker and Presbyterian meetinghouses. There were congregations, with or without their own places of worship, of Old Dutch and New Dutch Reformed, Catholics and Old Catholics, French and German Calvinists, Moravians, two kinds of Lutherans, Anabaptists and Jews, a good start toward the cosmopolitanism New York has since become known for.

Crime, not much in evidence in New England, was endemic in New York, especially the destruction of property. The have-nots, in desperation

View of John Street, New York, 1768, painted by Joseph P. Smith in 1817 from an earlier sketch, just before the demolition of Wesley's Chapel, center, first Methodist church erected in America.

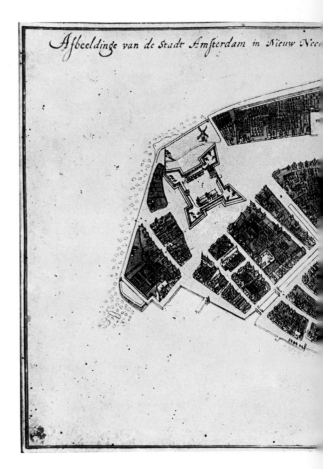

born of hunger, seem to have had a permanent grudge against the haves, who, naturally enough, were determined to protect what they had. Every able-bodied householder was enrolled in the "night watch" and took his turn patrolling the streets after dark. It could be dangerous, for a gang of ruffians known as "Night Hawks," or "Mohocks," first organized in the 1750s, loved nothing better than cornering sedate members of the night watch and clubbing them into unconsciousness. More common outlets for their antisocial exuberance were wrenching knockers from doors, absconding with signs and destroying street lamps. In 1771, the respectable citizenry, alarmed by the growing frequency of darkened streets, agreed upon a new lighting system, with lamps ten inches in diameter, ten feet above the ground, fifty feet apart and projecting four feet from the front walls of buildings. Two years later another ordinance imposed special fines for any vandalism during the three nights from December 31 through January 2, the period when spirits ran highest. An earlier act, passed in 1769, prohibited gunfire and unauthorized fireworks within the city limits. But like the perennial efforts to reduce the number of dogs running wild, it was easier to pass regulations than to enforce them. The increasingly stiff penalties did not seem to deter the lawless.

New York in 1776 extended about a mile from the fort at the lower tip of Manhattan Island to the site of the present city hall, then known as the common or the park. All to the north was open land, some of it farmed but much of it too rough for farming and better suited for strolling, which the owners called trespassing but could not prevent. Most of the city's low areas and brooks had long since been filled in and built over, and most of the original trees were gone, replaced by submissive shade trees. Lower Broadway was the most fashion-

able place to live: Here, on lots fifty feet wide and extending to the Hudson, which was closer to Broadway than at present, were the finest mansions in the city. Slightly less desirable as an address was Pearl Street. Where Pearl crossed Broad Street was Fraunces Tavern, built in 1719, patronized by the fashionable elite, and, in 1783, the scene of Washington's farewell to his officers.

The most expensive shops and the principal business firms were in Hanover Square, but some prominent merchants preferred transactions in their own homes or in adjacent structures. Houses were not numbered, but many had signs identifying the family business: a gilt mortar and pestle for a druggist, sun and breeches for a clothier, teapot or tankard for a goldsmith or silversmith, andiron and candlestick for a brass-founder. All the trades and crafts known anywhere in the colonies were represented in New York.

Business hours were short, ordinarily from ten until two; devoted as New Yorkers were to trade and profit, they also loved their leisure. The most secure, in financial terms, spent the afternoon hours in the walled gardens behind their mansions, culti-

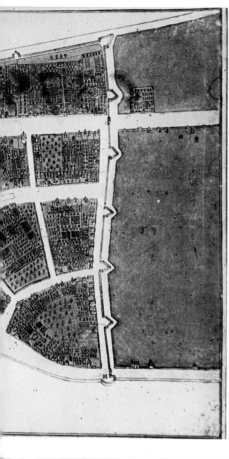

Left: New York (New Amsterdam), as it would have looked from a balloon in 1660. The north side was bounded by a wall— hence, Wall Street. Broadway runs from the fort past the wall into country beyond. *Below:* Southwest view of New York, from a painting made about 1760.

vating their trees and shrubs or simply admiring their views. The gardens, like the numerous servants, were status symbols; but in addition to wanting beauty and elegance, the solid burghers were prudent enough to grow some of their vegetables, berries and fruit. It would have been less expensive, considering the value of the land, to buy those edibles at any of the five public markets—Coenties, Old Slip, Fly, Oswego and New—where cooks and housekeepers had to go daily for meat and fish and poultry and for delicacies not indigenous to that latitude. The markets were replenished in the dark morning hours from truck farms on Long Island and from the holds of newly arrived ships. In all the colonies people ate well, whatever their economic level, but New Yorkers had the widest choice, especially of exotic foods that never graced rural tables.

What New York lacked was a dependable water supply. Wealthy families had their private dug wells, but the water they provided was little better than the less privileged had to fetch from public wells in buckets or buy from vendors with water carts (barrels on their side mounted on single axles). The best well was Tea Kettle Pump at the intersection of Chatham and Roosevelt Streets, twenty feet deep and producing, consistently, about fourteen thousand gallons a day. Few people were so very poor, however, that they had to drink the water. Beer and cider were plentiful and not expensive, rum was as popular as elsewhere in the colonies and the well-to-do consumed prodigious quantities of imported wine, especially from Madeira.

If people preferred other beverages, that was their privilege, but water was necessary for washing and cooking—and for fighting fires. The combination of limited water and buildings packed tightly together exposed New York to a perpetual danger of fire, and it was only sheer luck that the whole city wasn't burned to the ground sooner or later. The fear of just such a disaster was ever-present, however, and no doubt explains the torture and execution of thirty-odd blacks in 1741 who were accused of plotting to burn the city. Not all the buildings were of brick with tile roofs, as the Dutch preferred; after the English takeover in 1664, wood was used for at least some of the new construction, with shingles for roofing.

The Dutch element was strong enough to win political control of the city from 1768 to 1774 and to pass an ordinance forbidding further use of shingles, over the protests of builders who insisted that tile cost too much. The fire department, in the 1770s, was well organized, with four fire engines, each with a paid engineer and four assistants, and twelve citizens designated as firemen in each of the six wards. Fire engines were all the same, tanks mounted on carts, with hand pumps to throw water some distance. But Philadelphians decorated their engines handsomely. It may be noted here that in some cities a marker on the wall of a building indicated a paid-up subscription to a private fire department. If the fire department found no such marker, it might let the building burn.

Despite the risk of fire and despite the drifters and street gangs that made the night watch necessary, New York enjoyed a very high level of prosperity from retail trade and especially from ship-

To the Honourable

RIP VAN DAM, E.sq

PRESIDENT of His Majesty's Council for the PROVINCE of NEW YORK

This View of the New Dutch Church is most humbly
Dedicated by your Honours most Obedient Serv.t W.m Burgis

ping—river, coastal and ocean. The older waterfront, facing Long Island across the East River, was being challenged by new wharves on the North River, more convenient for trade with Albany and New Jersey. Ferries, rowed by squads of muscular blacks, were increasing in numbers across both rivers. Mail service was on a regular basis: monthly with England, twice a week with Boston, every weekday with Philadelphia and every Monday with Albany. Hundreds of longshoremen kept busy on the waterfront, handling not only mail but cargo from everywhere—lumber from Maine, luxury goods from Europe, tobacco from Virginia and silk from South Carolina, rum and molasses from the West Indies, ivory and slaves from Africa, daily provisions and cordwood from Long Island and New Jersey.

One reason New Yorkers put up with the crowded conditions was their custom, as soon as they had the means, of maintaining second homes in the country. Some of these, like Gracie Mansion well up the eastern side of Manhattan and the Jumel Mansion beyond the Harlem River, were magnificent, but others were more modest. As rural retreats they had the advantage of being within easy reach—most were only an hour or so away, by water or by road, northward beyond the city limits and across the Harlem by the old toll bridge, opened in 1700, or Dyckman's, which was free. These country places were usually on small plots, for the owners didn't farm while on vacation. Energy was reserved for business. The overriding goal of New Yorkers was to increase their wealth, but it was complemented by a desire to live the good life and a readiness to spend money. Croesus, not Midas, would have been their appropriate deity, but he would have shared their worship with some of the Olympians, including Bacchus, Pan, Eros and Demeter.

A detailed plan of the city of New York,
known as the "Ratzen Plan"—the engraving
was made in 1767 and published in 1776.

Not only the Livingston and Stevens mansions on Broadway, or the only slightly less imposing homes on Pearl Street, but houses of people lower on the scale of affluence were furnished with elegance. Fine furniture was still being imported from England, but local cabinetmakers could make pieces no less exquisite. John Brimmer, a 1762 immigrant, was one of the best; he could turn out Chippendale, Chinese or Gothic on demand—and the local demand held steady. Other craftsmen had been busy since 1750 replacing tapestry and wood paneling with wallpaper, which just then was very much in vogue. So were fine prints and paintings, like those John Roosevelt offered for sale at his shop in Maiden Lane, and silverware. The less wealthy had to make do with pewter, but a good pewterer, like a good silversmith, could always be sure of customers in New York and excellent pay. Talented craftsmen did well in other cities, too—Paul Revere, for example, in Boston—but only in Charleston did money flow as freely as in New York. Spending for beautiful things was a major source of pleasure.

Physically, New York in 1775 bore slight resemblance to the present sprawling metropolis, but it was the one colonial city in which moderns might feel at home—highly urbanized, cosmopolitan, profit-minded, pleasure-loving. New Yorkers in 1775 were prototypes of the future American breed, even if the interests and attitudes of most of them were hardly what was needed for a successful revolution.

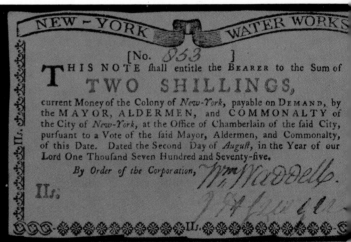

Ben Franklin's City

Ambrose Serle was a hard man to please; he found Philadelphia only a little more to his liking than Newport:

Walked early this morning about Philadelphia. It is finely laid out in a pleasant Situation upon the Banks of the Delaware. The Streets intersect each other at Right angles. There are some handsome public Buildings, and some Houses not inelegant; but the Generality of the last are rather mean Edifices, calculated more for the Reception of an industrious People in middling Circumstances, than for the Entertainment of the opulent or luxurious. There is but one market, wch is very large & built after the manner of the Fleet market at London: But I did not see one Piece of meat or a Fowl, and but very few Vegetables; all necessaries of Life being extremely dear, owing to the very small Extent of Country at this time under our Command. The Stadt-House,

Top left: Painting by William Chappel of the Tea Water Pump and Cart, New York. Spring water from the pump was known for its purity and sweet taste and was used by the colonists for making tea.
Bottom left: Note issued by New York to raise money for a waterworks. *Below:* Lamplighter on Broad Street, painted by William Chappel.

where formerly the assembly & lately the Congress held their meetings, is a large heavy Pile, & now converted into a Prison & Hospital for Rebels. This has been the Fate of some other public Buildings, wch were before employed in disseminating the Principles of Rebellion.

The Stadt-House, as Serle called it, was the Pennsylvania State House, now better known as Independence Hall because the Declaration was signed there. In the 1770s, it had a wooden steeple, which was rotting so badly that it had to be removed in 1781. Even so, it was the most imposing secular building in the colonies in 1775.

Another English visitor, Nicholas Cresswell, was more complimentary to Philadelphia and more objective. He noted in his journal for 1776 that it was "a large, rich, populous, and regular city," with streets at right angles, paved with brick and kept clean, sixty feet wide except for Market Street, which was a hundred feet. He counted three Anglican churches (Christ, St. Peter's, St. Paul's), nine meetinghouses of dissenting denominations and four of Quakers, two Catholic chapels and a Swedish church. The state house didn't "make a grand appearance," in his opinion, but he praised the new jail, the market, the brick hospital and the "Bettering House," a lockup for disorderly persons; and he concluded, "This is the most regular, neat, and convenient city I ever was in."

Dwellings in the heart of Philadelphia were one room wide and contiguous in each block, on lots about fifteen feet wide and seventy-five deep. Most were of brick, with three full stories plus cellar and garret. The ground floor, at street level or up a step or two, ordinarily had a shop or counting room in front and two parlors, one small, the other larger, toward the rear. An entry hall, at one side, led from the street to the garden, where kitchen and laundry were in a separate small structure. Above the entry

Carpenters Hall Phila in which the first U.S. Congress sat in 1775

Above: The Continental Congress first met here—Carpenter's Hall, Philadelphia.
Left: Pennsylvania State House, later renamed Independence Hall because the Declaration of Independence was adopted in this building.

hall was a passage on each upper floor, giving access to a drawing room and the bedrooms; the flights of stairs went up through these hallways.

Farther out, houses were not much larger but weren't quite so crowded together. About two hundred new ones, many of wood, were erected each year until 1770, when the annual average doubled; the city was growing fast. By 1775, an official count gave a total of 3,861 houses, or 5,957 including the near suburbs of Southwark and Northern Liberties. Ostentation was not much in evidence; the city had not yet developed an elegant town architecture. But as families acquired wealth, first in mercantile business and then in real estate, they built country homes on an ampler scale along the Schuylkill River, not for brief holidays but for warm-weather living and usually at an easy commuting distance. From their mansions, on warm Sundays, they could watch people being baptized in the Schuylkill.

Wealth prompted a shift in religion, to the Anglican; there was a saying that one could be "a Christian in any church, but could not be a gentleman outside the Church of England." A few Philadelphians betrayed the ideal of gentility, however, by acts of vulgarity and licentiousness; but any great moral lapse was condemned, like the reported action of one man, identified in the press only as "D. W.," who gave a girl fifty pounds to strip naked before him. If other proper Philadelphians cultivated vices, they did so discreetly; more of their time and energy went into cultivating their public images as patrons of the arts and as board members for hospitals, schools, libraries and charities.

The wealthy Philadelphia families, as in every colony, held the political control, but the democratic counterforce of tradesmen and artisans kept them from becoming arrogant. Nowhere else was reputation so carefully guarded—too carefully, perhaps, if Abigail Adams was a reliable judge. When the Philadelphia aristocrat Thomas Mifflin was serving as Washington's aide-de-camp in Cambridge, Mrs. Mifflin invited her to call. Afterward, in a letter to John, the future "First Lady" wrote that while she admired Major Mifflin and his delicate lady, the visit convinced her that "Philadelphia must be an unfruitful soil or it would not produce so many unfruitful women. I always conceive of these people wanting one addition to happiness."

Established Philadelphians divided mankind into three classes: "the better sort," meaning themselves; "the middling sort," tradesmen, mechanics and men like Franklin with no aristocratic connections; and "the meaner sort," unskilled laborers and others without money or the hope of getting it. The classification prompted one Philadelphian in 1776 to ask pointedly, in a letter printed in a local newspaper,

"Is not half of the property in the city of Philadelphia owned by men who wear LEATHER APRONS? Does not the other half belong to men whose fathers or grandfathers wore LEATHER APRONS?"

The classes joined ranks, however, in opposing all "aliens," meaning Germans and others in areas outside the city, some of whom had been in Pennsylvania longer than most Philadelphians. This antagonism was mutual, for the outlying counties, underrepresented in the assembly, were well aware that Philadelphians intended to maintain their control in every way possible. Everybody profited from the heavy wagon traffic between Philadelphia and the West, but Philadelphia, as the port outlet, profited the most. It was the one city in the colonies with a major trade area toward the West, through the German region and beyond it, by the Forbes

Above: Mr. and Mrs. Thomas Mifflin of
Philadelphia, painted by John Singleton Copley in
1773. *Right:* Portrait of Abigail Adams, twenty
years old when Benjamin Blythe did this pastel.

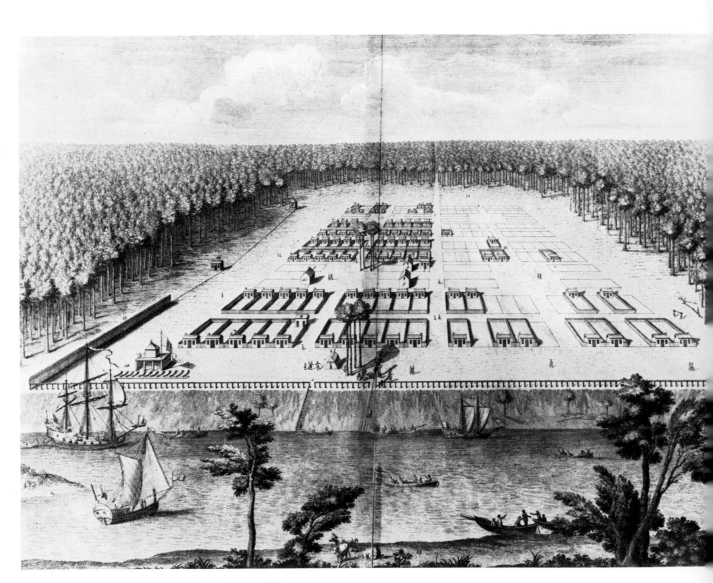

The establishment of the colony of Georgia, 1734.

Road to Pittsburgh and by the only adequate road to the Shenandoah Valley.

Cities in the South

South of Philadelphia, Annapolis and Williamsburg owed their more limited affluence to similar political control by aristocratic minorities; but without good harbors or much development of the trades, neither capital impressed visitors. William Eddis could not understand Annapolis; it struck him in 1769 as having "more the appearance of an agreeable village than the metropolis of an affluent province." Its shallow harbor, which sometimes froze solid in winter, was unfit for ocean shipping, yet a handful of wealthy residents were aristocratic in their lifestyle and lived in fine mansions on expensive shore estates. Williamsburg disappointed Josiah Quincy in 1773: "It is inferior to my expectations. Nothing of the population of the north, or the splendour of the south." (He had just been in Charleston.) The neglect of the major buildings startled him; the college (William and Mary) was "in a very declining state." But the courts were worse, in his opinion: "The constitution of the courts of justice and equity in this province is amazingly defective, inconvenient, and dangerous, not to say absurd and mischievous." He couldn't see how the people stood it. In sober fact they couldn't; but "the people," meaning the great majority of Virginians, had yet to find the means of reducing the political and economic privileges that Williamsburg symbolized. The few who enjoyed those privileges might have endorsed Quincy's conclusion as precisely what they intended: "An aristocratical spirit and principle are very prevalent in the laws and policy of this province."

Charleston was the great exception among Southern cities. Quincy could hardly approve of the vast inequities between rich and poor, but the genial social life, the generous support of the arts and the willingness to spend freely on comfortable homes and entertainment impressed him deeply. Elsewhere in the Southern colonies, large planters spent most of the time on their plantations, visiting cities rarely, but the Carolina aristocrats maintained town houses in Charleston and lived there for long periods each year; some were there permanently, making only rare visits to their plantations.

The city was laid out, like Philadelphia, with streets at right angles and with several squares; the main thoroughfares ran east and west between the Ashley and Cooper rivers, which provided cooling breezes. Low lying as Charleston was, dikes were a necessity, but they were also an attraction as a place for promenading. Most of the twelve hundred houses were of brick, three stories high; one peculiarity was that the houses were faced toward their gardens, with no main doorways on the street. The public buildings showed good taste—the exchange, the armory, the state house and the numerous churches and meetinghouses.

One British observer in the latter 1770s remarked that Charleston had few old people; the climate, he thought, was not conducive to long life. He also noted that

there are no boys or girls in the province, for from childhood they are introduced into company, and assume the air and behaviour of men and women. Many of [the people] have an happy and natural quickness of apprehension, especially in the common affairs of life, and manage business with ease and discretion; but want that steadiness, application and perseverance necessary to the highest improvements in the arts and sciences.

The art (or science) most developed, other visitors agreed, was social grace; even Josiah Quincy suc-

cumbed to it, at lavish dinners forgetting his stiff Bostonian principles and learning to appreciate the openness of such men as Miles Brewton, whose home he frequently visited. He could hardly fail to notice, however, the indifference of the assembly, a virtual private club of plantation owners, to both the civic needs of Charleston and the plight of the backcountry poor. Aristocrats never penetrated into the interior, for the resentment of the disenfranchised and the high incidence of lawlessness made travel there dangerous. As in North Carolina, the virtual absence of authorized law and order had encouraged extralegal vigilante groups, known as Regulators, who cooperated with the white overlords in Charleston only in keeping the blacks "in their place." South Carolina was the one colony in which blacks outnumbered whites—by more than two to one. It led all the colonies also in the generosity of its land grants; the aristocrats could still add thousands of fertile acres to their inherited holdings by perfectly legal means and thereby further tighten their economic–political stranglehold. Land was the base, indeed, of what could be called "instant aristocracy," a Carolina phenomenon. Charleston was the chief beneficiary, with its high proportion, far greater than in any other city, of

families with large fortunes. So much wealth in such concentration enabled other men, traders and lawyers and even skilled tradesmen, to rise quickly on the social ladder. No other city in the colonies was at all like Charleston, which was at its very peak just before the Revolution.

That peak was lofty indeed. In 1775, Charleston was, in Josiah Quincy's words, "as elegant and urbane as the best society in the Old World." Gadsden's Wharf, recently completed, was the finest on the continent, the New Assembly Room and the new theater on Dock Street were monuments of cultural progress and several new academies proved the commitment to education. Not even the war hurt Charleston badly; it was the one major city that lost no population during the war. With everything there that a civilized man could ask for, where would any Charlestonian have chosen to go?

Writers and Their Readers

Rural critics of the cities had much with which to find fault, but they could not deny that culture, in its higher forms, was an urban monopoly, or very close to it. That it existed at all was of course rejected by the average Englishman, whose low opin-

Top: A view of Charleston about 1773, painted by Thomas Leitch. Large edifice, right center, is the Exchange Building. *Bottom:* Baltimore in 1752, showing tobacco fields at right, St. Paul's Church on the hill, center.

Box in which readers could place requests for books, maintained by the Library Company of Philadelphia.

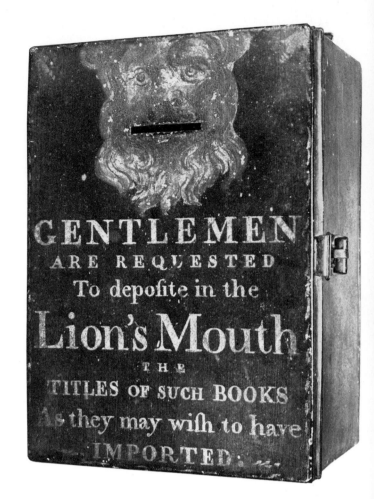

ion of the colonies survived the Revolution. As late as 1820, the Rev. Sydney Smith wrote, for the *Edinburgh Review,* what may be the most fatuous set of questions ever assembled: "In the four quarters of the globe, who reads an American book? or goes to an American play? or looks at an American picture or statue?" We must let 1820 take care of itself and consider the implications for 1775. Who *was* reading an American book, and what kind of literature was there?

Nobody, to start with, was reading novels written in the colonies; not until 1789 was the first one published. But poets were active, in what we look back on as the first real flowering of poetry in America. Philip Freneau, a New Yorker of Huguenot ancestry and a Princeton graduate, stands comparison with his pre-Romantic English contemporaries, turning out numerous pieces of high quality: "The Wild Honey Suckle," "To a Caty-did," "The Beauties of Santa Cruz," "The House of Night." His chief rival was John Trumbull of Hartford and New Haven, best of the group known as "The Connecticut Wits," whose amusing *Progress of Dulness* (1772–73) traced the futile education and subsequent misadventures of three contemptible young Americans, Tom Brainless, Dick Hairbrain and Harriet Simper.

Both Freneau and Trumbull used the standard poetic forms and devices of English convention, even when abusing the British; no American poet for another sixty years would think of breaking out of the mold. Both men, however, used native subject matter, to their credit, and neither was as obviously derivative as the great poetic sensation of the period, Phillis Wheatley. Her verse was wretched, earning Jefferson's comment that it was beneath the dignity of criticism, but her *Poems on Various Subjects,* when it was issued in 1773, sold well for one simple reason: She was a slave in a Boston house-

hold, and blacks were universally considered incapable of anything at all intellectual.

What most interested American readers of the Revolutionary period, understandably, was the political situation. From the time of the Stamp Act until the war began, and even later, printers turned out thousands of pamphlets attacking and defending British policy, and the best of these deserved the label of literature. The ablest champion of the resistance movement was John Dickinson, who signed himself "A Farmer in Pennsylvania," but at least two Loyalists answered on the same high literary level: Samuel Seabury of New York, using the pen name "A Westchester Farmer," and Joseph Galloway of Philadelphia. Like others who tried to be neutral, both Seabury and Galloway suffered for proposing a negotiated settlement, a position that ardent rebels seemed unable, in 1774 and 1775, to distinguish from total subservience to the Crown; and both men were forced into the Loyalist camp.

The political writing of the Revolutionary period could condition a generation to a war for independence, but it could not wean readers from their liking for English books and authors. In the decade from 1760 to 1770, only one American work sold well enough to be considered a best seller, John Dickinson's *Letters from a Farmer in Pennsylvania* in 1768, and from 1771 until the peace treaty was signed in 1783, only two—Paine's *Common Sense* in 1776 and the last canto of Trumbull's *M'Fingal*. All the other best sellers were British: Oliver Goldsmith's *The Vicar of Wakefield* in 1772, Laurence Sterne's *Tristram Shandy* in 1774, and three the next year—*Robinson Crusoe*, first issued in 1719, Lord Chesterfield's *Letters to His Son*, just out in London, and *A Father's Legacy to His Daughters* by Dr. John Gregory, a professor of physics at the University of Edinburgh.

How many people made up the book-buying, book-reading public would be hard to estimate, but there were enough of them to keep more than fifty bona fide bookshops in business—seventeen in Boston, twenty-one in Philadelphia, four in New York, three each in New Haven and Charleston and one each in Newburyport and Salem, Newport and Providence, Hartford, Lancaster and Germantown, Wilmington, Annapolis and Savannah. New Hampshire had "no bookstore of any note," as Isaiah Thomas observed in his monumental *History of Printing* (1812); nor did he list any for 1755 in New Jersey, North Carolina or Virginia.

Booksellers might have prospered without offering the gems of English literature, for their stock included Bibles and prayer books, almanacs and dictionaries, music and cookbooks and stationery. No bookseller can ignore what buyers want, and what they wanted in the 1770s was a broad assortment. *The Farmer's Companion* and *Pilgrim's Progress* shared shelf space with Voltaire's *Candide*, Locke's *Essay Concerning Human Understanding*, standard histories and such Greek and Latin classics as the *Odyssey*, Cicero's orations and Ovid's *Metamorphoses*. Shakespeare and Bacon were in momen-

tary eclipse, less popular than Dryden and Milton.

Pamela, which pioneered the English novel in 1740, was steadily popular in America, which suggests a hearty appetite for seduction in fiction. The authors of all seduction novels insisted, tongue in cheek, that their purpose was to instruct young ladies in how not to behave. Advice and admonition were popular in nonfiction as well; *A Father's Legacy* owed its "best seller" standing in 1775, no doubt, to the wide approval of its ideas among "persons of refinement and sensibility." Man falls in love, woman never, the author asserted. A woman marries a man because she esteems him, and if she does happen to love him, she never reveals the fact to him. The man, for his part, asks for no greater proof of her affection than her willingness to be his wife. Such lofty treatment of love and sex was balanced by the earthy frankness of Lord Chesterfield in his *Letters to His Son;* which of the two books was closer to colonial morality we can only surmise.

Bookstores flourished as they did because libraries were very scarce and not open to everybody. Gentlemen, by one definition, were men who bought books and read them; especially among the plantation aristocrats, one outward proof of being "gentle" was the private book collection and another was the ability, in assembly debates, to quote from memory one passage or another from a Greek or Latin classic or from a more modern authority. As with the Latin orations at Harvard commencements, auditors had to pretend that they understood; the alternative was admission of inadequate "culture."

This may be unfair, for Virginia aristocrats seem to have developed, and passed along to their sons, a genuine fondness for great literature. For the less affluent masses, who had to scrape the pennies together to buy an occasional book, fine private libraries were as far out of reach as great mansions; and a public library was a godsend. No library in

1776 was public, however, in the modern sense; would-be users had to pay an annual subscription fee. Boston opened the first library in 1653, but readers could not take books or magazines out of that or any other library until the Library Company of Philadelphia, at Franklin's prompting, introduced in 1732 the radical idea of circulation. Charleston tried a free public library, but it quickly expired in 1720. But not even Franklin urged that libraries be maintained out of public taxes.

Most cities had subscription libraries by the 1770s. Charleston redeemed its earlier failure when seventeen wealthy citizens founded the Charleston Library Society in 1748. Its motto *Et artes trans mare currunt* reflects the general colonial view that Europe was the source of all culture. A 1771 bequest of a private library, a balanced collection of more than eight hundred volumes, made the Charleston library the best in the South, except for a very few individually held in great mansions. Charlestonians had the wealth for such gestures, and besides, they were proud of their culture; they even paid their librarian a living wage, as very few libraries elsewhere saw fit to do. Colleges were notoriously stingy, assigning the library to a professor as an added job when they could or, when they couldn't, hiring an untrained person and paying him next to nothing. But college libraries, exclusively for faculty members and students, were not intended to promote the general welfare. Even more than the subscription libraries, they concentrated on serious works. Books for leisure reading, like *Pamela* or *Robinson Crusoe*, ordinarily were not available in any library but had to be bought or borrowed from trusting friends.

Master Builders

A merchant prince or Virginia aristocrat, when his book collection outgrew the library in his mansion, could simply expand into another room or add a new wing. Most colonials never owned books enough to make that necessary. The subscription libraries seldom had quarters of their own, being housed in odd corners of available buildings—meetinghouses in New England towns, churches or private homes elsewhere. One notable exception was the Redwood Library in Newport, designed by Peter Harrison, a onetime sea captain who settled in Newport, practiced scientific farming and gradually emerged as the foremost architect of the Revolutionary era. The building was ready for use in 1767. Its fame rests on its priority rather than on its adequacy for library purposes. No longer standing, we know how it looked—"serenely Doric"—from a sketch by du Simitière.

To call Peter Harrison the first American architect is to slight the gifted master builders of his time and earlier, whose designs showed considerable merit, as is still evident in surviving examples of their work. No ordinary carpenter, certainly, could have produced mansions like Unkity Hall, Governor Hutchinson's country seat on the Neponset River or the elegant town houses on Beacon Hill or the manor houses of New York aristocrats or the home of Samuel Powel, mayor of Philadelphia, or the palaces crowning the great plantations in Virginia and South Carolina. From Maine to Georgia, fine dwellings, churches, college and public buildings erected in the Revolutionary period are enduring proof of architectural talent as sophisticated as any in Europe.

Travelers noted, however, that the same style —Georgian, with strong hints of the great Italian designer of the sixteenth century, Andrea Palladio —dominated everywhere. Harrison's Redwood Library almost exactly follows a building in the fourth volume of Palladio's 1570 work, *Four Books*

Above: Painting of the Adams family farm in Quincy, Massachusetts. John Adams was born in the house at right, and his son, John Quincy, in the saltbox at left. *Left:* The Redwood Library, Newport, Rhode Island, designed by Peter Harrison.

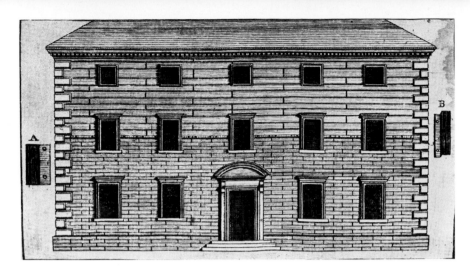

of Architecture, which had an English translation in 1716. Sir Christopher Wren, an earlier disciple of Palladio, never visited the colonies but did provide designs for a number of colonial churches and influenced the builders of many others. In the eighteenth century, moreover, a number of English experts published volumes that American builders studied and followed, sometimes slavishly; James Gibbs's *Book of Architecture* (1728) was the best known.

The most talented American builders added individual touches, but none of them, not even Peter Harrison, strayed very far from the models except in their extensive use of wood. None of them felt any need to develop an original "American style." The humbler builders, adapting European models to American climate and materials in the houses of ordinary people, did more, actually, to produce architectural forms that were recognizably new and different—especially the saltbox dwelling we associate with Cape Cod. The thick walls and large chimneys of small colonial houses in the North and the large windows and welcome openness of dwellings in the hot South stand as better examples of native ingenuity than mansions copied, with few changes, from homes of English noblemen or from designs in the architectural textbooks.

Some of the great mansions and public buildings were planned and built by English architects imported for just that purpose. The most industrious of these was William Buckland, who spent nineteen years in the colonies, first in Virginia, where Gunston Hall attests to his genius, and after 1765 in Annapolis, where he designed several of the town houses that gave luster to that small city. His masterpiece, the Hammond-Harwood mansion, observed Palladio's principles with its perfect balance—central block and symmetrical wings. Most large mansions of the Revolutionary period were not strictly

Palladian but Palladio modified by Wren, for example the Wentworth-Gardner house in Portsmouth. The First Baptist Meeting House in Providence, completed in 1775, set the standard for subsequent steeples and was one of the prime examples of "colonial Georgian," the term most appropriate for the period. For large structures, indigenous architecture was still more than a century away. But master builders in America could accomplish anything their British contemporaries could accomplish, and as well.

In one respect, at least, they did better. European builders no longer built large structures of wood, but some of our surviving mansions, wooden throughout, show that colonial builders were as much at home with wood as were the master shipbuilders and could create homes we still admire for their beauty, their soundness and their reflection of Georgian principles. Mount Vernon is the best-known mansion of the period, and it is of wood. So is the John Vassal house in Cambridge, known today as Craigie House and as the final home of Henry Wadsworth Longfellow. It was built in 1759. The Royall house in Medford is somewhat older, dating from 1733. The Miles Brewton house in Charleston and the Jumel Mansion in New York are other monuments in wood, but there are scores of others, all recognizably Georgian. Lumber, of course, was plentiful. But builders were everywhere inclined to use whatever material was available. Rubble masonry, or unhewn stone, was used for the Van Cortlandt Manor House in New York, built in 1748, and for Governor Hutchinson's mansion in Boston, which was gutted in a Stamp Act riot in 1765. Brick was used in all the colonies. Hewn stone was common only in Pennsylvania, where good limestone was plentiful.

Perhaps the finest house in New England was the Boston mansion of John Hancock, built by his

Left: Design for a house
built of wood but
intended to resemble
stone. *Below:* A Newport
desk with shell
design on door, English
brass candlestick,
desk set, wick trimmer,
account book and
unsigned portrait,
all ca. 1750.

uncle in 1737; it was granite with brown sandstone trim. The Hancock house, now gone, had two wings; one was a ballroom, the other housed the kitchen and other work areas. In Northern regions, such wings were built against the main house instead of separately as they were in warmer sections of the country. Cliveden, built of limestone between 1763 and 1767, has separate dependencies in the rear, forming a court; in 1777, it served briefly as a British fortress when George Washington, after the Battle of Brandywine, tried unsuccessfully to retake Philadelphia Whether of wood or brick, rubble or cut stone, these survivors in three dimensions are the most tangible links to the Revolution, the largest artifacts from that time of crisis and significant change.

"Everyday Objects of Grace and Beauty"

If the old mansions remind us of our patriotic past, so do a great many smaller objects—like chairs and beds and tables. Every colonial city had a number of skilled joiners, who preferred, as their reputations grew, to be known as cabinetmakers, the equivalent British term. Carl Bridenbaugh, writing about Philadelphia, suggests that the cabinetmakers of that city were tops in the colonies—William Savery, famous for his Chippendale pieces, James Gillingham and Benjamin Randolph, known for their masterpieces in mahogany, and Thomas Tufts, who specialized in humbler furniture. But Newport sang the praises of John Goddard, known for his stately block-front secretaries surmounted by exquisite carvings with a shell motif; and satisfied patrons of other cities—Boston, New York, Charleston— were confident that their own local cabinetmakers were the best. Virginia aristocrats offered the names of no contenders for priority; by long custom they imported a great deal of furniture from England.

By the time of the Revolution, in any event, the leading colonial cabinetmakers could stand comparison with the best in England, partly because some of those best had moved to the colonies. All of them worked in the established forms of the time— Queen Anne, Chippendale with its Chinese touches, early Sheraton—but as individuals, long before the advent of mass production, each "signed" his work by some slight deviation that modern collectors can readily notice. One major difference is that Americans tried native woods—pine, maple, cherry and later walnut and mahogany. No culture can become distinctive, admittedly, by adopting the forms of an-

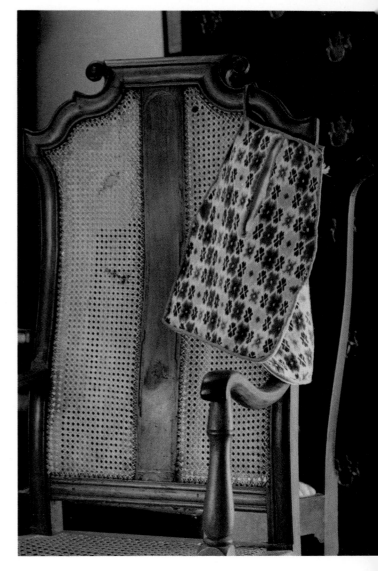

other culture, and all the American cabinetmakers could do, with their highly developed skills, was to expand English culture in the colonies. Such advance in craftsmanship, however, deserves applause in a country so new and still trying to catch up, culturally, with countries much older.

The best American furniture brought high prices and found its place only in the homes of the wealthy; but because the colonial economy was expanding and producing more wealth each year, more and more interiors were gracefully furnished. The bodily transfer of period rooms to large museums, notably the Winterthur Museum in Delaware, provides the visual evidence of how the Revolutionary generation lived, whether in humble, moderate or wealthy circumstances. All are fasci-

nating, but the rich furnishings of mansions in various sections are overwhelming evidence of how much wealth had actually been accumulated by the time of the Revolution. Pier mirrors, costly draperies, fine rugs, solid paneling, scenic wallpaper, exquisitely carved stair rails and fireplaces, ornamented ceilings, paintings and *objets d'art*—not all these were ever combined in single rooms, but all were within the means of the well-to-do and most were available from local craftsmen.

Painters and Their Patrons

Artists at work in 1775 could have done us a favor by painting landscapes and street scenes, interiors and ordinary people at work or relaxing. But pa-

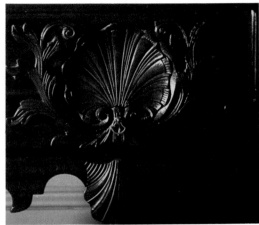

Opposite left: Label used on furniture by William Savery, a Philadelphia joiner. *Opposite right:* Philadelphia-area chair, modified Chippendale; two pockets—worn beneath a woman's outer skirt—in Irish stitch on canvas. *Above:* Drawer from a mahogany dressing table, carved in a shell design. *Left:* Unusual chair from Philadelphia area, showing Chinese influence.

trons called the tune, and the name of the song was "Portraits." It was probably inevitable, for families that acquired dignity along with wealth wanted posterity to know what they looked like, and besides, without a life-size portrait or two, the new or remodeled mansion was somehow incomplete. Old families of wealth in England always had paintings of illustrious forebears; a newly rich merchant in Charleston or Boston could create for his heirs, through portraits, the illusion of distinguished ancestry. All it took was money.

Isaac Royall of Medford, Massachusetts, was typical. He was of the fourth generation. The first Royall in America was a cooper, the second a carpenter and the third a merchant who amassed a fortune from trade in rum and slaves and spent much of his time on Antigua. Our man, with income assured, enlarged and remodeled the family dwelling in Medford and hung in it older family portraits by Robert Feke and the more recent painting of his daughters, Mary and Elizabeth, that John Singleton Copley did in 1774. As a staunch Tory, Royall moved his family and their dozen slaves to Halifax, Nova Scotia, before the war began and died in England in 1781.

Today, thanks to generous collectors and museums, we can see all the colonial portraits we care to. The Revolutionary generation could not, for the portraits were individually owned and housed and were seen only by the family, the household slaves or servants and guests. This kind of art was private, never intended for public display.

Skillful as some of the earlier painters were, especially John Smibert (from Scotland) and Gustavas Heselius (from Sweden), the "big four" of the Revolutionary period were far superior in technique and sensitivity and won greater European acclaim than the practitioners in any other art. Who looked at an American picture? Large numbers of admiring

Londoners if the painter was Benjamin West. Born in Swarthmore, near Philadelphia, he went abroad in 1760, gained the patronage of the royal family, helped found the Royal Academy of Arts and, in 1792, succeeded Sir Joshua Reynolds as its president. He scorned portraits as such, insisting that his sitters be individuals of real significance, not just people with money and family pride. One portrait he agreed to paint was of the wealthy Charleston planter (and signer of the Declaration) Arthur Middleton, his wife and their son; but his interest turned to immense canvasses of great events in history, like *The Death of Wolfe* (1771) and *William Penn's Treaty with the Indians* (1772). When he died in 1820, he had been away from America for sixty years—our first famous expatriate in the arts—but nobody challenged his status as an American.

John Singleton Copley, born the same year as West, 1738, followed him to England in 1774 when his native Boston seemed too intent on rebellion to suit his conservative nature. Portraits preoccupied him; among his best were those of Isaac Royall's daughters, Col. Epes Sargent, Mrs. Sylvanus Bourne and Mr. and Mrs. Thomas Mifflin, all people of distinction and wealth. But the painting that established his reputation was *Boy with a Squirrel* in 1766; the boy was his half-brother. By 1772, he was so famous and so much in demand for portraits that he could forget that his mother, born in Ireland, kept a tobacco shop on Boston's Long Wharf. The future painter John Trumbull, as a student at Harvard, was rather dazzled by Copley, finding him "an elegant-looking man, dressed in a fine maroon cloth, with gilt buttons." The move to England produced a curious sea change, however, for Copley's first important work in London was not a portrait but *A Youth Rescued from a Shark* (1778), sometimes called, improperly, *Watson and the Shark*. Like West, he went on to historical subjects, including the death scene of William Pitt, first earl of Chatham, a firm supporter of the colonies.

Charles Wilson Peale, whose devotion to art may be judged by the names he gave four of his sons—Raphaelle, Titian, Rubens and Rembrandt—made the usual trip to England to pay homage to West, the acknowledged king, but resisted his influence and returned home in 1769 to become America's leading portrait painter. He settled in Philadelphia in 1774, served briefly in the war as a private and was elected to the new state legislature in 1777. By 1784, he had immortalized on canvas no fewer than forty-four Revolutionary leaders. The same patriotic impulse moved Gilbert Stuart, who preferred Boston as a place to live, to concentrate on George Washington, whose likeness he painted at least 124 times. But he spent the war years in London, where he painted fellow artists, including West and Copley, Sir Joshua Reynolds and Thomas Gainsborough. His lifetime total of more than a thousand portraits must be a record. Just a fraction of that talented energy diverted to bustling waterfronts, Sunday horse races, crowded taverns or slave auctions would have preserved the flavor of colonial life better than words can describe it.

Lesser artists, many of them migrants from Europe, were numerous in urban America. A few with no great talent wandered through the countryside, exchanging crude if not primitive portraits of rural people for board and bed for as long as it took them to complete the work; but for anyone with any skill, there was always work, and good income, in the cities. Houses being built or improved by the wealthy needed decorating as well as portraits; a

Left: Benjamin West's painting of William Penn's treaty with the Indians. *Below:* Copley painting, known as *Watson and the Shark,* 1778. *Opposite top:* Mary and Elizabeth Royall, painted by Copley. *Opposite bottom:* Portrait of Jeremiah Wadsworth, Hartford merchant, and his son, by John Trumbull, 1784.

man able to copy a famous painting, restore an old one, produce a miniature or paint cupids on a plaster ceiling could prosper. In Charleston, famous for its private gardens walled in from public view, artists or skilled artisans created special effects with statues and urns and obelisks; one man, John Barnes, was conspicuously successful in making grottoes, cascades and fountains. Others advertised instruction in various art forms. Most of the artists in Charleston were foreign, attracted by the city's reputation for liberality.

Philadelphia, equally prosperous if not with such a high proportion of very wealthy people, had the advantage over Charleston in having had a longer period to develop taste. Prints were in particular demand in the 1770s. One shop opened in 1770 and offered prints exclusively—copies of famous paintings and scenes depicting horses and racing, castles and cathedrals, battles, ships, picturesque regimental garb and much more. Miniature paintings were also well regarded; the best miniaturists were Letitia Sage, Richard Collins and the inimitable Pierre Eugène du Simitière, recently from Switzerland. Francis Hopkinson, also a writer, musician and politician, worked in pastels, while Henry Bembridge, remembered for his Franklin, and John Meng of neighboring Germantown handled the portrait business before Peale arrived in 1774.

New York was less attractive for artists. Copley was there briefly, painting another "boy with a squirrel," which was called *Daniel Crommelin Verplanck,* in 1771, but he soon moved away. The best-known painting of New Yorkers in the Revolutionary period was John Durand's *Rapalje Children,* 1776. Most artists, in order to make a living in New York, had to offer varied services—Gerardus Duyckinck II, for example, who carried on his father's glazing business, taught painting and worked at japanning, gilding and silvering mirrors. This need for versatility, in most colonial cities, is well illustrated by a notice in the *Maryland Gazette* (Annapolis) on January 6, 1774:

Joseph Horatio Anderson (Architect)—

To the Ladies and Gentlemen, Samuel Rusbatch, late pupil to Robert Maberly, Esquire, coach and herald painter; and varnisher to their Majesties and the Royal Family; proposeth (under the direction of Joseph Horatio Anderson, architect in Annapolis) to carry on all the various branches of coach and herald painting, varnishing and guilding; as well plain as in the most decorated taste. Also painting in fresco, cire-obscure, decorated ceilings for halls, vestibules, and saloons, either in festoons of fruits, flowers, figures, or trophies. Carved ornaments in deception, guilding, and burnishing in the neatest manner, as well house-painting, in distemper as dead whites, as in the common colours, etc. Those ladies and gentlemen who please to favor him with their commands, may depend on his speedy execution; which he flatters himself will soon recommend him to the favor of the public. . . .

The best art of the Revolutionary period was admirable; what survives of it, in museums and galleries, dispels any lingering notion of colonial rawness and crudity. Dependence on English standards was logical enough, among people who viewed themselves, to the last possible moment, as British subjects and who could not suddenly create a new national form in art. Part of the tradition was art for private enjoyment, not for the masses, who, as always, preferred their own earthy culture anyway. Hope for an indigenous art lay within that popular unconscious culture, to be drawn out and up, gradually, over many years. The two levels are not really as distinct as art-conscious individuals believe; what was needed was recognition of the artistic potential in genre sketches, German *fractur*, humble design of furniture and fabrics, decorated powder horns and rifle stacks and carved wooden figureheads.

The Stage, the Players

On April 20, 1767, several hundred Philadelphians attended the opening of a theater on Cedar Street in Southwark, just south of the city limits. It was an event to remember, for the theater had been built for the first American acting company and the production was the premiere of *The Prince of Parthia,* written by a Philadelphian and the first play by an American to be professionally staged. The city's culture enthusiasts could hardly have been more excited if Benjamin West had returned to stay in Philadelphia for the rest of his life.

The conservative element, strong enough to bar theatricals from Philadelphia itself, called the theater "the Temple of Satan." Southwark was no great distance; most Philadelphians could walk there in a few minutes, although the wealthy rode in their carriages, having sent servants ahead to hold good seats for them until the seven o'clock curtain. The author, Thomas Godfrey, was not present on opening night; he had written his play in 1759 and had published it in 1763, but in that year he died at the age of twenty-seven. The decision to produce it two years later suggests a wish to capitalize on the nationalistic spirit on the rise since the Stamp Act, for as a play *The Prince of Parthia* had little value. Seasoned theatergoers might have had trouble following its plot of palace intrigue, but they would easily have spotted the numerous imitations of Shakespeare and other English playwrights.

Most plays that pre-Revolutionary Americans attended were staged by touring English groups, and it was one of these, Lewis Hallam and Company, that

Top: Southwark Theatre, in a Philadelphia suburb, where first play by an American was produced in 1767. *Bottom:* It was not until 1787 that the first comedy was written by an American; here is the last scene from Royall Tyler's *The Contrast.*

193

Right: Mr. and Mrs. Lewis Hallam, Jr., who carried on the traditions set by his mother, the first lady of the colonial stage, and his father, founder of the first American theatrical company. *Below:* Douglass's John Street Theatre performance.

David Douglass reorganized after Hallam's death and named the American Company. Its circuit included New York, Boston, Newport, Providence, Charleston and Annapolis in addition to Southwark; the company stayed in a city for an extended period, offering a wide repertory—nine plays by Shakespeare, two by Goldsmith (*The Goodnatured Man* and the recently written *She Stoops to Conquer*) and others by Otway, Dryden, Addison, Sheridan, Farquhar, Congreve and Cibber. But in February, 1775, as the skies darkened before the coming storm, Douglass moved his company to Jamaica for the duration. Visiting troupes from England had found it discreet to go home earlier. Except for the farces that the British were free to produce, theater was nonexistent for the next decade, reviving only in 1785.

Douglass had opened the door, even if his American actors presented only English plays. A good summary evaluation comes from a historian of Charleston, a city that was always very appreciative of Douglass: "The whole gamut of English drama from somber tragedy to the gayest farce, from Marlowe's *Tamerlane* to the latest London comedy, all fell within the scope of the versatile David Douglass and his American Company." Unlike painting with its very restricted clientele, theater was an art widely appreciated by colonial Americans.

The Moral Opera

For all its achievements in drama, the American Company was just as successful with opera, which had a peculiar advantage that Douglass, as a shrewd impresario, was quick to exploit: It was exempt from the widespread antagonism to plays, as somehow immoral, that had led to the wrecking of his New York Theatre by a mob in 1764. Some of the English plays he produced, especially from the Restoration period, did lean toward the licentious, and Shakespeare was often bawdy; in fact, the operas Douglass offered were not simon-pure. *The Beggar's Opera*, with its assorted loose women, Newgate criminals and, as male principal, a highwayman with a long record of seductions, was so well received that Douglass gave it again and again. In England, it had made Gay (the author) rich, and Rich (the producer) gay, as was popularly remarked at the time, and in America, later, it made opera fans happy. But a brand new comic opera, *The Padlock* by Isaac Bickerstaffe, roused no less enthusiasm and was, in its way, hardly less immoral. Leonora, young ward of elderly Don Diego, who intends to marry her, receives her young lover, Leander, despite a large padlock on the door; the servants prove susceptible to cajolery and bribes. The don, returning sooner than expected, catches the pair but accepts his defeat and gives the girl a generous dowry. Setting such a plot to music apparently immunized it from censure. *The Padlock* opened at Drury Lane in October, 1768, and had a run of fifty-three nights; Douglass had it on the boards in New York's John Street Theatre by the next May.

Some of the first operas produced in the colonial eighteenth century were little more than popular ballads set to music; the dialogue was often not sung but spoken, which yielded an effect hardly different from a play. By the time Douglass entered the picture, English opera was considerably more mature, with interesting plots and singing. It was sometimes necessary, as in Newport, to quiet suspicion by calling both plays and operas "Moral Dialogues" or "Musical Entertainments." Another device was to fill the intervals between acts with instrumental music. But the colonial public, in general, seems to have gained in sophistication; by the 1770s, the moral opposition had declined, only to be replaced by another problem. In the 1772–73 season in both Philadelphia and New York, unruly elements in the gallery interrupted the action, insulted the performers and injured people in the pit. Douglass denounced the rudeness in a "card" published in the *New York Mercury*, but it did little good; his English birth was held against him. The score was evened when a "card" in the *Pennsylvania Gazette*, signed "Philadelphus," alluded to "those strolling comedians . . . propagating vice and immorality." By June, 1773, Douglass had crossed New York and Philadelphia off his list temporarily. Smaller cities gave less trouble—Charleston, Annapolis and Williamsburg, where the patrician audience sometimes included George Washington.

The Honest Yorkshiremen, The Virgin Unmasked, The Harlequin Collector, The Devil to Pay, The Mock Doctor—such was the bread-and-butter fare Douglass knew would draw almost as well as *The Beggar's Opera* or *The Padlock*. More and more light operas crossed the Atlantic; their librettos were increasingly popular in the bookstores. There was even an American entry, *The Disappointment, or The Force of Credulity*, in 1767; it was announced for production and rehearsed only to be withdrawn because it contained personal reflections thought to be libelous. The libretto was soon for sale, however, and quite popular, perhaps because its wit was laced with coarseness and even obscenity.

How far opera might have gone if, like plays, it had not been discouraged by the Continental Congress, nobody can say. Both forms were rapidly developing in the early Revolutionary period, but both had serious problems. The growing unruliness of audiences in the largest cities was no doubt one reason why Congress acted; any sizable gathering could be dangerous when partisan conflict grew by the week and when the play, or the opera, was no longer the thing.

Music Everywhere

On April 2, 1765, George Washington noted in his ledger that it cost him three shillings ninepence "to hear the Armonica." This instrument, the glass harmonica, was one of Franklin's miscellaneous inventions, currently very popular in both Europe and America. It was a set of glass hemispheres fastened to an axis, kept wet by being revolved through a trough of water and yielding strangely sweet tunes when rubbed with a finger. As a public attraction it rivaled such other marvels as the Rittenhouse orrery, waxwork notables and scale models of historic cities; but it was more widely known in the colonies by being played at concerts, usually as the concluding feature, well into the 1790s. One entrepreneur in Annapolis advertised an armonica exhibit during October, 1774, daily from three to six, admission fifty cents in provincial currency.

Any new gadget attracts the curious, but the Revolutionary generation was genuinely interested in music at all levels and had more opportunities to hear music performed than to see plays. Almost nobody, moreover, opposed music on moral or any other grounds, although a few blue laws forbade the playing of an instrument on Sunday. Church organs were exempted, and most churches of any consequence had organs by 1775; the Quakers alone forswore music. Tuneful arias from operas were hummed or whistled at work or on the streets; people who never attended operas knew them from the widely sold scores and librettos. Every city had at least one singing school and instrumental teacher, while music textbooks were numerous, inexpensive and in steady demand. Communities too small ever to attract a dramatic company, moreover, developed their own musical life, sometimes very rich, as in the Moravian town of Bethlehem.

The German sects in Pennsylvania, despite their wide differences in dogma and ritual, all approved of music. The semimonastic Ephrata Kloster was past its prime by 1770, but earlier it had produced more than a thousand new hymns and was famous for its choir. Conrad Beissel, founder of the order and its absolute ruler, was a musical genius, although somewhat peculiar: He accepted for his choir only Solitary Brethren and Spiritual Virgins on the grounds that sexual intercourse injured the singing voice.

Of more enduring influence was the Moravian music at Bethlehem; its orchestra, organized in 1743, just two years after the town was established, was by 1771 as large as any in Europe, with pairs of first violins, second violins, violas, flutes, trumpets, hautbois (oboes), bassoons and French horns along with a cello, a double bass, a clarinet and kettle drums. It practiced an hour every evening. There were also two choruses in Bethlehem, from 1768 on, one for men and one for women. The chapel had one of the largest organs in America, installed in 1751; its organist, John Frederick Peter, was one of two competent Bethlehem composers, the other being John Antes, some of whose works Haydn liked well enough to perform in Europe. One special group, formed in 1754, was the Moravian Trombone Choir; and a special annual event was the *Singstunde*, dating from 1744, a church service devoted entirely to hymn singing. Training in music was provided by the Collegium Musicum, founded in 1744. No other community in the colonies, regardless of size, was so devoted to music or performed it with such mastery. The many out-of-towners who attended the Bethlehem concerts, especially those featuring works by Bach, were invariably impressed; three who said so, in their diaries, were Franklin, Washington and Sam Adams. The name of Bach is a reminder that music in the colonies was international, the only art not heavily dependent on British form and tradition.

In most places a typical evening's concert was something of a variety show, with selections for violin, trumpet and woodwind choirs, vocal solos or choruses and, if the audience was lucky, a concluding performance on the armonica. For the 120 subscribing members of Charleston's St. Cecilia Society, founded in 1762, a concert was a gala social occasion, as Josiah Quincy discovered on his visit in the winter of 1773. The ladies were not unlike those in Boston, he noted, but "The gentlemen many of them dressed with richness and elegance, uncommon among us: many with swords on. We had two macaronis present, just arrived from London. . . . 'See the macaroni!' was a common phrase in the hall." What music was played Quincy did not record; he was more observant of the flirtations and gallantry that went on after the program, when the dancing began.

He was more impressed by the music at a dinner given him by the Sons of St. Patrick, on St. Patrick's Day. During the meal an orchestra of "six violins, two hautboys, etc." played steadily, and "after dinner six French horns in concert:—most surprising music. Two solos on the French horn, by one who is said to blow the finest horn in the world. He has fifty guineas for the season from the St. Cecilia Society."

The society, typically Charlestonian, had plenty of money and no aversion to spending it to ensure quality; it advertised in the *Boston Evening Post*, June 17, 1771, for a first and second violinist, two hautbois players and a bassoonist, and it promised three-year contracts. The certainty of good pay also attracted foreign talent; late in 1774, there were concerts featuring the French violinist Abercrombie and Signora Castella, a singer from Italy. Somewhat less expensive talent provided the general public with music at the Orange Gardens and at the Vauxhall Concerts given by Bohrer, Morgan & Company, who reproduced as well as they could the famous Vauxhall Gardens of London.

Charleston was not America's first music center, though some citizens thought it was; Bethlehem had a twenty-year advantage in "quality music," and Philadelphia was well served by musicians by 1750 and more so by the 1760s—annual subscription concerts, one dating from 1768, and others given as benefits; chamber music, especially on the harpsichord, at intimate gatherings; numerous music schools and teachers; competent local singers and instrumentalists and, by 1764, three professional composers. Many of the concerts resembled the one Quincy attended in Charleston, with a variety program followed by a ball and refreshments; but they differed in that they were open to anyone who could pay the admission fee, ten shillings, perhaps, or one dollar in provincial currency (and half price after a certain hour).

The first Philadelphia composer of any consequence was James Bremner, a Scot. His most famous pupil was Francis Hopkinson, the first grad-

The glass armonica, a musical instrument, that was the property of Benjamin Franklin.

uate of the College of Philadelphia, who took to music as readily as he did to poetry, painting and politics. The soirees at his home were famous: The socialite guests could count on hearing some of his secular salon music, composed for one or two voices, with the harpsichord accompaniment provided by Hopkinson himself. He also composed songs to be sung, some in four-part harmony. His music for *Alfred, A Masque,* produced in Philadelphia in 1759, antedated his lessons from Bremmer; a similar work was *The Temple of Minerva,* a "dramatic allegorical cantata," which he composed in 1781 to celebrate the alliance with France. He loved to conduct; on October 2, 1772, he conducted a concert at

Christ Church that concluded with the grand chorus from *The Messiah.* He did all he could to bring music to the people and to extend their participation in it.

Philadelphians did not wait, however, for prodding by Hopkinson; they were already a singing people. John Adams, while serving as a delegate to the Continental Congress, wrote home glowingly of various church choirs and excellent singing by the congregations. He may have noticed the thriving music stores in the city, the best of them owned by Michael Hillegas, who in 1774 carried a large stock of organs, pianos, clarinets and stringed instruments, and his rival Martin Fay, who had Cremona violins for sale. The music shops stimulated the growth of small orchestras and bands, some of which developed professional competence. One band traveled to Princeton in 1773 to play at Nassau Hall's commencement exercises; others were hired for *entr'acte* diversion at the theater in Southwark. Musical interest filtered down to the humblest workers, who sang to the strains of a fiddle and, in time, developed catchy tunes like "Yankee Doodle" that worked their way upward to the level of professional composers. No Philadelphian was astonished that Hopkinson the musician was also an ardent patriot or that Thomas Paine, a political propagandist, composed "The Death of General Wolfe," a song rivaling the numerous patriotic ballads in popularity.

The Learned Professions

A tutor in one of the older colleges was commonly a young man preparing for a career in law or the ministry or politics on a haphazard basis, as a special kind of apprentice to a professor; no such thing as a graduate school or a professional school existed in 1775. The tutors at least had frequent contact with the professors, as the undergraduates seldom did—except in the newest, smallest, least affluent colleges where the faculty consisted of the president and two or three other clergymen, who had no time for the individual direction of postgraduates.

The learned professions suffered under such conditions and would have suffered more without the great number of imported books on professional subjects that bookshops stocked. Such books seldom found their way into college libraries, which used the munificent gifts of donors, mostly English, to build up the classical and theological collections. Undergraduates could use the libraries only under strict regulations, but freer use would not have

Top: Face of a clock made by Benjamin Rittenhouse of Philadelphia early in his career. *Bottom:* Top view of the orrery made for Princeton by Rittenhouse.

Electrostatic generator, one of
Benjamin Franklin's many inventions.

helped them much for their future careers.

But the picture was not entirely dark. The most distinguished man at Harvard was a scientist, John Winthrop IV, appointed Hollis Professor of Mathematics and Natural Philosophy (now called physical science) in 1738, at the age of twenty-four. His studies of earthquakes earned him the reputation of "the father of seismology," but he was also an expert on sunspots and electricity. A fire in 1764 destroyed much of the apparatus—a remarkable collection—that Winthrop used; but most of it was replaced by 1775. There were telescopes and orreries, pumps and electrostatic machines, solar and lucernal microscopes, a camera obscura, a large model of the human eye and a variation compass together with such collections as the Bowdoin marbles and Peck fishes.

Winthrop introduced the calculus at Harvard, set up the first American laboratory of experimental physics and led the only college expedition to Newfoundland to observe the 1769 transit of Venus. Other colleges were aware of its importance but didn't go to the trouble and expense; but no other college had any scientist of Winthrop's stature. Most scientific research was by nonacademics—men like John and William Bartram in botany; Arthur Lee of Virginia, who proved by twenty scientific experiments that quinine cures malaria; Alexander Garden of South Carolina, who started the botanical gardens in Charleston and did important work in classification; Jacob Bigelow, who compiled an American pharmacopoeia; and Benjamin Franklin. The single most valued piece of "philosophical apparatus" was the orrery constructed in 1771 by a surveyor-astronomer named David Rittenhouse, who sold it to the College of New Jersey (for £220) and then, because he was criticized for not keeping it in his native Pennsylvania, built another for the College of Philadelphia. Revolved by a crank, his orreries excelled earlier models and provided the same moving visualization of heavenly bodies that may be observed in modern planetariums.

Enough men were interested in science to organize for its advancement. The American Philosophical Society, an outgrowth of Franklin's Junto, collapsed in its first year, 1743, but revived in 1767, sent an expedition to observe the transit of Venus and, in 1771, started publishing its *Transactions*, still being issued. A journal that would accept learned articles was a stimulus to research, encouraging pioneering work in meteorology, archeological excavations of Indian mounds near Taunton, Massachusetts, in 1768 and 1774, and applications of theory to agriculture and other practical subjects. Its growth was steady; not even the war slowed it down; as a matter of fact, the war stimulated the search for useful knowledge and gave the APS a particular value because contact with the Royal Society and European scientists in general was greatly reduced.

The greatest single advance in science and technology during the Revolutionary period was in medicine in Philadelphia, which built the first teaching hospital in 1752 and opened the first medical school in 1765, at the College of Philadelphia. In the quarter-century from 1752 to 1777, about nine thousand medical and surgical clinical observations were conducted at the hospital, giving medical students opportunities never available earlier. Dr. Thomas Bond was the prime mover. One of the great speeches in the field was one he gave at his home in 1766 to a gathering that included managers of the hospital, professors at the new medical school, leading citizens and some thirty students. His topic was "The Utility of Clinical Lectures." Fine though the faculty was, he observed, it would not be complete without a clinical professor. Much more study was needed of actual cases, by the clinical method, especially in the fevers that were a summer commonplace in southern regions. Reviewing some of the treatments used for yellow fever, he made a strong case for needed study of its causes and methods of prevention. Dr. Bond had already announced his intention to give the clinical lectures he was advocating; what he was seeking was enthusiastic support. One prompt result was "An Essay on Fevers" by a physician in Charleston; it was published in the *Pennsylvania Chronicle* in 1768 and as a book in Philadelphia in 1769 that was reissued in London in 1776. This chronology is important; most such books were published first in London and only later in America.

The faculty of the medical school was as distinguished, for its size, as any to date in America. Besides Bond himself, there were William Shippen in anatomy, surgery and midwifery, Benjamin Rush in chemistry and John Morgan in theory and practice of medicine. Rush was later the most eminent of them all, but in 1765, Morgan was the most highly regarded and was chosen to deliver the dis-

course at the first commencement. It was time, he said, to regulate the practice of physic, to separate it from surgery and pharmacy, to know medicines thoroughly and to realize that anatomy cannot be learned by listening to a lecture and reading about it in a book. Medical education, based on these assumptions, would necessarily be expensive—a prediction that holds true today. Any present-day layman can understand and endorse Morgan's points; what is not so easy to grasp is their radical nature in 1765 or the breakthrough in medicine that the Philadelphia faculty made in the Revolutionary period.

It would have been better, in view of the wretched state of medicine in the colonies, if the breakthrough had been widespread, not limited to Philadelphia. But the fact that it happened at all before the Revolution is important; no primitive culture could have produced it. Better evidence of the generally advanced culture of the colonies might be in industrial technology, which was not limited to one city or colony, or in the arts, music in particular. Even where the artists were derivative, as in painting and literature, they proved that American birth was no handicap to individual excellence; and if buildings and furniture imitated those in Britain, nobody can fault their soundness or beauty.

The culture had come far in the short time since the crude first settlements—so far, indeed, that Europeans refused to admit it. Learned men abroad understood and gave due honor by electing American scientists to such groups as the Royal Society; but learned men are always a minority and cannot control governmental policy or public opinion. The common British failure to understand American progress or the pride colonials took in their culture was a major aggravation, building up tension toward the point of explosion.

6

Spreading the Word

Paul Revere's ride wasn't quite as Longfellow described it, for it ended ignominiously, well short of Concord, when Paul ran afoul of a British patrol. But his reputation as a rider was already secure, based on five trips to New York and Philadelphia as a special courier for the Boston Committee of Correspondence. The first was late in 1773, not long before the Boston Tea Party, to alert other seaports that tea ships might soon be arriving, as the *Dartmouth* already had at Boston. Sleepless after a night of standing guard over the *Dartmouth,* to prevent its unloading, and a day of discussing strategy with other rebel leaders, he ignored his wife's protests and rode off into the early darkness of the last afternoon of November. The other four trips, during 1774, were related to less dramatic but equally important developments. He averaged eleven days for the round trip, about sixty-three miles a day, a good deal faster than the scheduled stagecoaches or even the postriders.

Getting from Here to There

On those five rides, Revere probably followed the Old Boston Post Road, sometimes called the Upper Road because it was farthest inland. It led almost due west from Boston to Worcester and Springfield, then south through Hartford to New Haven for the final run to New York beside Long Island Sound. The Middle Road, a little shorter, passed through no important places until it joined the Upper Road at Hartford. A third route, through Providence and New London, was longer. All three were parts of a network that linked Falmouth in Maine to Savannah in Georgia, with important spurs to cities off the main line. Across New Jersey two major roads competed for traffic; Robert Honyman, the Scottish physician who settled in Virginia in 1771, crossed the Delaware at Burlington, and other travelers reported crossing at Camden. Beyond Philadelphia, a fairly good road led to Baltimore, Annapolis, Williamsburg and Norfolk, but there the trouble began: In North Carolina the roads were poor and had an infuriating habit of petering out, forcing strangers to retrace their routes to the last junction; and with relatively little local travel the road surface got scanty attention. Not that any colonial road was really good: Travelers of the period described them with adjectives ranging from *poor* through *wretched* and *miserable* to *worst in the world.* The Great Philadelphia Wagon Road, through Lancaster and Harper's Ferry to the Shenandoah Valley, though heavily traveled, was so neglected beyond Lancaster that it was commonly called "the bad road." Branch roads were seldom merely bad, while roads serving isolated farms and villages were hardly an improvement over the Indian trails that were the nucleus of the entire road system. There was no real planning; routing, construction and maintenance were all left to local initiative, which varied widely.

The best surface anywhere—crushed stone, needed to support the large and heavily loaded freight wagons of the region—was between Philadelphia and Lancaster. Elsewhere, for both passengers and freight, it was prudent to use the lightest vehicles possible. On high, well-drained terrain a dirt surface wasn't bad in good weather, but any hard rain left mudholes and furrows while long periods without showers produced choking dust; in heavily glaciated regions it was impossible to eliminate all the boulders. Honyman said of the stretch from Providence to Newport, "I never saw a Country so full of rocks and stones." Low marshy places posed other problems, although by 1775, the so-called corduroy road—constructed with poles ten or twelve feet long laid side by side on the roadway and held fixed with mud—helped a little. Such a road was actually a causeway and was most frequently found in Virginia. With no solid foundation, there were frequent dips, and the tendency of the logs to sink at one end forced coach passengers to be adept at leaning in unison to preserve the balance. Lurching was common even on higher ground. One familiar anecdote of the period had the passengers refusing to get out and walk past a formidable mudhole, insisting that they had paid their fares to *ride*, whereupon the driver sat down beside the road and, when asked what he was doing, calmly answered, "Waiting for the mud to dry."

Lone travelers, if not on horseback, favored the two-wheeled chaise drawn by a single horse; it was fast, it could be maneuvered easily on narrow or rock-strewn roads and it could double as a racing rig if another rider offered a challenge. Lightness was a virtue in horses, too; the Narragansett pacer and other breeds of only slightly less fame developed in eastern Massachusetts were quite small, seldom more than fourteen hands tall compared with the European average of sixteen. Horses brought over by British officers during the war seemed gigantic. Contemporary painters, indifferent to realism, have misled us by picturing our heroes astride majestic horses of black or white; the actuality was a plain, surefooted little sorrel. The Conestoga, developed in Pennsylvania to haul heavy freight, was a horse of another color, dapple gray, and much heavier and stronger. Freight traffic, everywhere, was anathema to coach passengers because it was much harder on the roads than the coaches were and because the wagon drivers hogged the right of way.

"Six Days, Boston to New York"

Four-wheel carriages always had at least two horses, but anything as large as a coach carrying passengers had four while freight wagons had six or more. The stagecoach was an elongated version of a family coach; properly it should be referred to by the contemporary term *coachee,* but we can dispense with this technicality. It was open in front except for a roof over the driver. The passengers inside sat on two seats, hardly better than benches, both facing front. The side walls rose only part way to the roof, leaving an open space that could be enclosed in bad weather by curtains let down and buttoned on the outside. Springs were crude, comfort was minimal. When axles needed grease, which was often, the squeaking wheels made conversation impossible. Luggage space on the roof was limited, which explains the tiny travel trunks of the period, covered with pigskin or deerskin to withstand the elements. If the coach was full, a passenger was limited to one such trunk and one piece of hand luggage, usually a leather sack; if there were empty seats, he could take more but had to pay for the extras.

Passenger transportation was quite new; earlier, the only land travel was afoot, on horseback or in privately owned vehicles of various builds, some with odd names. The one-horse chaise, or shay, was called a chair if it lacked a top. A two-horse chaise was called a curricle. A landau was a large carriage with seats facing each other and a top that could be raised or lowered. The aristocrat of wheeled vehicles was the chariot; it was decorated with paint and carving, the inner panels were lined with cloth, the cloth covering the seats was embroidered, there was a glass pane in front and even a silk fringe on top. The most fabulous of these chariots was probably John Hancock's, custom-made in England; the doors had double slides, one of canvas, one of glass, and bore the family crest; for travel on snow the wheels could be replaced by runners.

Stagecoaches of the 1770s had no such embellishments, although a line connecting Boston and Marblehead advertised its "stage-chariot" in 1772 to suggest luxury and comfort. The term *flying machine* attracted more favorable attention: Nobody expected the ride to be comfortable, but everybody hoped it would be fast. Where there were competing lines, advertisements attracted passengers, like one in *Rivington's New York Gazetteer* in May, 1775:

The Flying Machine

That used to ply between Hackensack and Powles-Hook, will, for the sake of a better and shorter road, begin on Saturday, the 13th day of May, and thenceforth, continue to drive from Hackensack to Hoebuck. It will set off from Hackensack every Monday, Tuesday and Saturday, at six o'clock in the morning, and return from Hoebuck at two o'clock in the afternoon of the same days. As the subscriber in this alteration has consulted the convenience and benefit of the public, has furnished himself with four good horses and provided a new and very commodious machine for the better accommodation of passengers, he hopes for the countenance and encouragement of the public, and shall endeavour to merit their favour, by care and attention. The price is 2s. 6d. for each passenger, and baggage at a reasonable rate.

Abraham Van Buskirk

Speed is of course relative; fast time in 1775 was six days from Boston to New York and two more to Philadelphia. The time would have been shorter without the frequent interruptions, especially at ferries, for only the smaller streams were bridged. Horses had to be changed fairly often, at fixed stations or stages, and the noon meal at a tavern took time. Any accident, like breaking a wheel or miring down in the mud, could add hours to the trip.

The meal stop was seldom an adventure in good eating. Some tavern keepers earned the reputation of inordinate greed among travelers, serving wretched food at outrageous prices. One of them, as a story then popular went, took down the orders, insisted on prepayment and then did not serve the customers before the coach driver announced departure. One man calmly kept his seat at the table as the others indignantly left, ate his dinner when it finally came and asked for dessert, at the same time pointing out that he lacked a spoon. When not a single spoon could be found, our hero remarked casually that people who had paid for meals they could not eat would want something for their money and hinted that he knew which passenger was responsible. A rider went galloping after the coach, and the driver turned back. Asked to identify the culprit, the well-fed man smiled, climbed aboard the coach and said over his shoulder, "Myself. You'll find the spoons in the punch bowl."

The taverns most familiar to colonials were hometown institutions, serving, like the pubs in England, as neighborhood clubhouses and for special occasions such as wedding receptions, ordination dinners, lottery drawings and political committee meetings. Travelers visiting major cities, if they did not stay with friends and relatives, commonly put up at ordinaries, so named because of their boardinghouse meals, which offered no choice at all. Good country inns were rare, but New England had several that made a business of putting up guests for the night. The Red Lion Inn in Sudbury, later made famous by Longfellow in his *Tales of a Wayside Inn,* was reputedly the best in all the colonies. On the coach routes, overnight stops, where possible, were in communities large enough to have competing inns, which kept the prices moderate. Not all New England inns, however, were of top quality. The Jenks Tavern at Spencer, between Worcester and Springfield on the Upper Road, had neat chambers, good beds and clean linen, but the

To the PUBLIC.

THAT the Stage Waggons, kept by John Barnhill, in Elm Street, in Philadelphia, and John Mercereau, at the New Blazing-Star, near New-York, continues their Stages in two Days, from Powles-Hook Ferry, opposite New-York, to Philadelphia; returns from Philadelphia to Powles-Hook in two Days also: They will endeavour to oblige the Publick by keeping the best of Waggons and sober Drivers, and sets out from Powles-Hook and Philadelphia, on Mondays and Thursdays, punctually at Sun-rise, and meet at Prince-Town the same Night, to exchange Passengers, and each return the Day after: those who are kind enough to encourage the Undertaking, are desired to cross Powles-Hook Ferry the Evening before, as they must set off early. The Price for each Passenger is Ten Shillings to Prince-Town, and from thence to Philadelphia, Ten Shillings more, Ferriage free. There will be but two Waggons, but four Setts of fresh Horses; so it will be very safe for any Person to send Goods, as there are but two Drivers, they may exchange their Goods without any Mistake. Persons may now go from New-York to Philadelphia, and back again in five Days, and remain in Philadelphia two Nights and one Day to do their Business in. The Publick may be assured, that this Road is much the shortest, than ony other to Philadelphia, and regular Stages will be kept by the Publick's obliged humble Servants,
JOHN MERCEREAU, and
JOHN BARNHILL.

One of numerous colonial advertisements for competing stagecoach companies.

food was only passable; George Washington, as he was leaving, told Mrs. Jenks that her bread was "very beautiful," the only praise that he could honestly offer.

But in some parts of the country, especially in Virginia and North Carolina with their very few towns, public houses were far apart. Nicholas Cresswell saw only one between Alexandria and Leesburg, a distance of something like forty miles through dense woods.

One inn was known, and liked, for its very low prices: Fourteen pence bought supper with tea, cider and punch, a bed for the night and breakfast the next morning. Fourteen pence, a little more than a shilling, was about the average, at most inns, for bed and breakfast alone; it was also what a pound of butter cost or two dozen eggs or a pair of work shoes or two ounces of good thread. Coach fares were steep in comparison: The two-day trip from Boston to Portsmouth cost, on one line at least, thirteen shillings sixpence—about three dollars in paper currency—the price Cresswell reported of an acre of Virginia land. One source of irritation was the custom of charging extra if the coach was not full—commonly half again as much.

Travel by coach was uncomfortable and expensive, but highway robbery was not one of the risks as it was in England, since American travelers seldom carried cash, gold coins or bank notes. Horse thieves were plentiful, however. One named George White was well known for his system: He would steal a horse, sell it some distance away, steal and sell it again the next day and then steal and return it to its usual pasture, where it may never have been missed. White and others of his fraternity were as adept at altering as automobile thieves are today; cutting a mane or covering light spots with dye was effective, and selling the horse back to its owner was a trick widely reported and as widely appreciated by travelers if the horse belonged to the only "highway robber" they knew about, a tavern keeper.

Jolting rides, delays at inlets and rivers, overpriced meals and meager lodging were all spared people who went by sea. They missed all the flavor of crude tavern stops and the ever-changing contacts with townspeople and fellow travelers; but if such things bored them, a sloop or packet was an attractive alternate. Robert Honyman alternated between land and sea travel on a trip north in the spring of 1775. But if coaches had their drawbacks, so did ships; on the packet from Newport, the only other voyager, a Princeton student named Hazard, got beastly drunk and then very seasick. On the way home, however, not one but five Princeton students shared Honyman's stagecoach across New Jersey.

Honyman was spared the worst hazard of sea travel—storms. Josiah Quincy, sailing from Boston to Charleston to recover from an illness, suffered so greatly from a violent storm en route that he fully expected to die and prudently made the trip home entirely by land. In good weather, ship passage was considerably faster than travel by land; but even without storms, the winds could fail or blow the wrong way. Ambrose Serle left Newport by ship for New York, expecting to spend only one night in a berth, but strong winds drove the ship almost to Chesapeake Bay, requiring four or five extra days to work back. Such misadventures were common enough to persuade many Americans in the stagecoach age to stay as far from salt spray as possible; the dismal toll of lives lost at sea every year was even more persuasive. Almost nobody ever died in a stagecoach accident. But really prudent people, averse to both stagecoaches and packets, preferred to stay at home.

Not everybody, fortunately, let prudence dictate behavior; potential profit, for ambitious businessmen, was a stronger motive. Conveying passengers

by coach was itself a business, and a new one, dating only from about 1760. Whether it met a demand or created the demand, it certainly increased travel from city to city, colony to colony, breaking down the former isolation, forging new links of mutual interest and helping to develop the awareness of continental unity. Even if the business purpose of a trip failed, contacts made on the coaches and in taverns along the way were instructive: Not only back home but hundreds of miles away, people were changing their notion of themselves—from colonials to Americans.

"Their Appointed Rounds"

Sending special messages by courier instead of by the regular mail saved time and, if the courier was of the caliber of Paul Revere, tightened security. The method had particular value after the fighting began, for the war disrupted the postal service as rebels and redcoats pursued each other and as territory changed hands with unpredictable suddenness. Even so, for more than two decades before the war, the Northern colonies had what may have been the world's finest postal system, thanks to the organizing genius of Benjamin Franklin.

In 1753, the postmaster general, in London, appointed two deputies for the American colonies, at a salary of £300 a year to be paid out of profits. The man chosen for the Southern district, below Suffolk, North Carolina, did little to improve the service; the postriders who set out each fortnight on the 433-mile trip between Suffolk and Charleston spent forty-three days en route, much of the time waiting at exchange points for even slower riders. Ocean packets, under favoring winds, could do much better, but a ship couldn't pick up and deliver mail at a series of inland communities. Southerners expecting mail had to resign themselves

to longer delays than the business-minded Northern man would stand for.

Franklin, who had served for sixteen years as deputy postmaster for Philadelphia, lived up to his reputation for energy and inventiveness by completely overhauling his Northern division. Within a year, what had been a steadily growing deficit yielded to a surplus of £494, which he sent to the London headquarters—the first such remittance ever received there. Each year thereafter he was able to send a comparable amount. If officials in England, who had contributed nothing to the colonial postal service since 1721, were dumbfounded, what mattered more was that the Northern colonies were much better served than ever before. One helpful change was the synchronization of schedules, which called for dispatching some riders at night as well as by day. Letters did not rest at exchange points for weeks at a time, and as one result the

time required for a Philadelphian to send a letter to Boston and receive a reply, formerly six weeks, was cut in half. Franklin also helped streamline the ocean mail service by instituting packet service direct from major Northern ports to the West Indies instead of using the older indirect route by way of England.

In 1773–74, Hugh Finlay, surveyor of the Post Roads of the Continent of North America, made an inspection trip from Falmouth in Maine to Savannah. The highly unfavorable nature of his report suggests that the British government hoped to discredit Franklin, who was in London at the time as agent for several of the colonies; but even if Finlay exaggerated, many of the details were true. Postmasters, he found, often had no offices, using rooms in private houses instead or even tavern taprooms and carelessly leaving letters about for anyone to look at until claimed by the addressee. What was worse, the law forbidding private mail delivery was widely ignored; any wagoner, ship captain or casual traveler could convey letters or parcels to his own profit. The postriders, moreover, engaged in transactions of their own along their routes. The rider between New York and Saybrook, Connecticut, who had been in the postal service for forty-six years, carried on a profitable business in money-changing; when Finlay saw him, he was waiting for a team of oxen that he'd agreed to deliver, for a fee, to their new owner. Finlay also learned of the special dispatch riders, and he accused the colonial governments of flagrantly undercutting the Royal mails. He did not see fit to report certain improvements made by Franklin, such as the milestones on the post roads, their location having been determined by an odometer he invented for the purpose, and perhaps he was unaware of the surplus Franklin sent each year to London.

If Finlay's assignment actually had the purpose of dislodging Franklin, it proved unnecessary, for by the time the final report was submitted, Franklin had been dismissed for another reason. Finlay replaced him—but not for long. Plans for an independent postal system, conducted jointly by the colonies, matured in the summer of 1775, when the Continental Congress appointed Franklin postmaster general. By that time the royal mail service he had served so long and so well was disintegrating, and on Christmas Day it expired. Finlay spoke bitterly about rebel interference with his duties and of official letters being intercepted and opened; but even if the competing services had continued, the great energy of Franklin and his staff, including his son-in-law Richard Bache, would soon have forced the British service to give up. The British did, however, maintain mail service by warship, throughout the war, to the port cities that they controlled.

As a printer who published a newspaper, Franklin had wanted the postal assignment as a means of increasing his newspaper's circulation. It was, curiously enough, contrary to British law to send newspapers through the mails, but printer-postmasters commonly did so. Soon after his appointment, however, his sense of public duty overcame his desire for profit; he ordered postriders to carry *all* newspapers and set uniform rates for the service: nine pence for every fifty miles, to be paid by the subscriber upon delivery.

Freedom of the Press

The intensifying conflict polarized journalism. Rival papers in the major cities waged a bitter verbal war, but the spirit of fair play eroded in time and Tory editors lost readers and revenues if they were lucky enough not to have their presses broken by angry mobs. Two pro-British papers in Boston were

casualties: the *Chronicle* was so unpopular that it was discontinued in 1770, when its editor fled to England, and the *News-Letter,* the oldest newspaper in the colonies, died early in 1776 at the age of seventy-two. Neutrality was no guarantee of safety; in their increasingly ugly mood, newspaper readers accused neutral editors of insufficient patriotism and forced most of them to quit. The *Boston Evening-Post,* founded in 1735 and notable for its lively style and readability, defended its practice of printing both sides of current issues but had to suspend publication the week after Lexington–Concord because feelings were running so high. The *Massachusetts Spy,* a small, low-priced triweekly issued in Boston by the prominent printer Isaiah Thomas, also sought to be impartial but quickly shifted to bold advocacy of the rebel program; when the war began, Thomas moved the paper to Worcester. The removal to the interior paralleled, in some colonies, the bodily transfer of assemblies—to Concord in Massachusetts, to Lancaster in Pennsylvania. Stern British orders to disband these assemblies had as much effect as equally stern orders to suspend rebel newspapers.

A few editors rode out the storm by changing their politics. John Gaine moved his *New York Mercury* to Newark when the British took the city but had second thoughts and moved it back, giving it a new title, *Gazette and Weekly Mercury,* and a firm Loyalist bias. Another New York paper, James Rivington's *Gazetteer,* began in 1773 as a neutral, was mobbed twice for printing Tory articles, suspended publication but resumed in 1777, during Howe's occupation, as the *Royal Gazette.* Patriots throughout the colonies referred to it as "Rivington's Lying Gazette" because of its warped accounts of battles, its slanderous charges of immorality among the rebel leaders and its reports of the financial collapse of the Continental Congress. Philadelphia, when the British controlled that city, had three Tory papers; but one of them that had earlier been prorebel, the *Evening Post,* turned rebel again when the British pulled out. It did not prosper, however; few people like a turncoat. President Witherspoon of Princeton suggested a recantation to regain public favor, but Benjamin Towne, the editor, balked because it included the statement that "instead of being suffered to print, I ought to be hanged as a traitor to my country."

So it went in other port cities before and during the war. To the extent that newspapers influenced readers, editors fought the war in their columns, using the commonest form of printed communication. This warfare reached its peak in Philadel-

Opposite: Letters cast from type matrices used by Franklin in Philadelphia about 1750. *Left:* Portrait of James Rivington, colonial New York newspaper editor. *Right:* Rivington felt he had to apologize to his patriot readers.

On April 16, 1775, Boston printer Isiah Thomas, aware of the difficulties of retaining a free press in Boston, dismantled this press and took it and his type by ferry across the river to Charlestown. There it was loaded in a wagon and carted off to Worcester, where Thomas reestablished his business.

phia, where John Dickinson's *Letters from a Farmer in Pennsylvania* appeared in the *Pennsylvania Chronicle,* 1767–68, and where Thomas Paine wrote fiery articles in the *Pennsylvania Journal* that Provost William Smith of the College of Philadelphia answered in the *Pennsylvania Gazette.* During the struggle, certain editors served only as fronts for organized partisans; perhaps the strongest such group was the Caucus Club in Boston, which used the *Boston Gazette* as its mouthpiece; prominent members included John Hancock, Sam Adams and his cousin John and Dr. Joseph Warren. These men and their like elsewhere contributed hundreds of propaganda articles under assorted pen names, using public journalism as the handiest method of communicating their ideas.

Most editors were also printers. To put the case more clearly, master printers ordinarily put out papers as part of their regular business. The wooden presses, most of them made in England, were limited in capacity and hardly new by 1776, and most of the lead type, which was set by hand, was old and worn; but a greater problem was getting paper enough, even though nine paper mills were in operation by 1765. A familiar advertisement offered good prices for clean rags that could be converted to paper. Good ink was also scarce, doubly so after the English supply was cut off. Circulation was limited, ranging from a hundred copies to a thousand; the *Boston Gazette,* after surviving a libel suit brought by the governor, hit a prewar peak of two thousand. After the war began, circulation shot up, with two papers exceeding thirty-five hundred—partly because the number of newspapers sharply decreased. Distribution was by carrier, locally, and by mail at any distance. Advertisements were varied and interesting—there were notices about theatrical performances, exhibits, runaway wives and apprentices, auctions, ship sailings, quacks and nostrums and merchandise. Local news was neglected; deaths and marriages, for example, were noticed only for prominent individuals. The little real news readers absorbed was supplied by correspondents in other cities, usually other editor-printers who doubled as postmasters.

With few exceptions, newspapers were weekly. Printed as they were on good rag paper, copies that have survived are in better condition than any modern newspaper a year or two old. Small in size, with four pages only, the average issue could easily be read at one sitting. As a rule there were from three to five columns, set in fine print with no bold-type headlines. The only illustrations were crude cuts in advertisements. Subscriptions, costing from six to ten shillings a year, brought in less income than the advertising: three shillings for an original insertion, two shillings for each additional use. The high postage rates, based on distance, made it prohibitive to subscribe to a paper issued in a remote city, but travelers often carried papers along to give to friends or to sell—at inflated prices—to interested strangers along the route.

It tells us something about both the postal system and the infrequency of newspaper publication that news of the Battle of Lexington and Concord was printed in Boston on the day of the battle, April 19, 1775, in Philadelphia on April 25, in New York and Baltimore on April 27, in Williamsburg on April 29, in Charleston on May 9 and in Savannah on May 31. War news thereafter was highly irregular, being printed as it happened to drift in; it was always late, seldom accurate, often wholly untrue, sometimes no more than rumor.

Of the thirty-seven newspapers being printed when the war began, fourteen were in New England, thirteen in the Middle Colonies, including three in German in Pennsylvania and ten in the five Southern colonies. Delaware and New Jersey had none. Most were published in coastal cities; the only inland cities with newspapers were Hartford, Albany and Lancaster. In remote regions, the chances of ever seeing a recent paper were very slim. In the entire colonial area, one white family in twenty took a paper on a regular basis, and even if each copy was passed along to neighbors, a newspaper was as much a curiosity for a sizable fraction of the population as the Franklin armonica or a symphonic concert. The isolation creating this condition has a bearing, no doubt, on the reported indifference toward the war of a good third of the whites. What the forty thousand families served by journalism got, meanwhile, was little actual news but plenty of propaganda.

Contemporary editors might have rejected this judgment with asperity. In their own eyes, they were the preeminent agents of communication and also of popular education, as an anonymous quatrain printed in the *New York Journal* in 1770 neatly put it:

> *'Tis truth (with deference to college)*
> *Newspapers are the spring of knowledge;*
> *The general source throughout the nation*
> *Of every modern conversation.*

Magazines were even scarcer than newspapers and more limited in distribution. The first periodical to use that term was the *Gentleman's Magazine* of London, which began its long run in 1741. Two Philadelphia printers followed suit the same year, Andrew Bradford with his *American Magazine* and Franklin with his *General Magazine*. Neither survived more than a few months, and fourteen others launched before 1775 were all short-lived. Only two were in existence in 1775 and both were ardently patriotic: Isaiah Thomas's *Royal American Magazine*, out of Boston, and the *Pennsylvania Magazine*, which reached a circulation of about fifteen hundred, chiefly because of the contributions by Thomas Paine. But colonials in general preferred the established British magazines, which, like British books, were the mainstay of the many urban booksellers. Philadelphia, with numerous bookshops and master printers, was the capital of the colonial book trade. New York was far behind, showing relatively little interest in either books or magazines.

The Printer As Educator

The master printer was one of the most respected individuals in his community. His newspaper, if he printed one, was only one of several products of his press (or presses, for larger shops had two or three) that made him a major agent of communication and popular education. He was apt to be better known for his almanac, which was consulted daily for its meteorological tables—the times of sunrise and sunset, the tide tables, the phases of the moon and the weather predictions—and for scores of other useful facts like tables of weight and measurement equivalents, recipes and gardening advice, along with good and bad verse, quotable maxims and anecdotes. For the great many families in the land without access to schooling, the almanac provided a basic home-study curriculum, limited but practical and renewed annually. After 1765, colonial almanacs, especially in New England, shifted markedly in emphasis; anyone keeping his almanacs for the next ten years would have had a fairly accurate record of recent public events, the texts of various charters and documents, many lines from the better English poets (especially those praising liberty), biographical sketches of Britons friendly to the patriot cause and of leading colonial patriots, considerable indoctrination in political radicalism, suggestions for reducing economic dependence on Great Britain, encouragement of civil disobedience and even recipes for homemade gunpowder. Like the rebel newspapers, in other words, the almanacs communicated radical politics and educated for armed resistance. Almanacs published by Tory printers lost ground steadily and eventually disappeared.

A good printer was assured a good income. One in each colony was official printer by appointment, but even without such a plum, the expanding economy kept the presses busy to keep up with orders. Commercial forms multiplied, and so did blanks for the notes and drafts that substituted for specie and paper money. Any kind of "useful information"—legal and medical handbooks, business directories, conversion tables for the coins of different countries, maps and navigation charts, illustrated booklets of clothing and furniture design,

THE
Royal *American* Magazine,

OR UNIVERSAL
Repository of *Instruction* and *Amusement*.

For MARCH, 1774.

CONTAINING,

An Oration; delivered March 5th, 1774, at the Request of the Inhabitants of the Town of Boston. By the Hon. John Hancock, Esq.   Page 83
On Human Happiness,   89
Essay on the Origin of Letters,   90
Justice and Generosity; or the remarkable History of Wilbraham Wentworth, concluded,   91
A Counsel to the Ladies,   94
Method of distilling Salt Water,   95
Experiment on Tea,   96
Treatise on the Small-Pox.   98
Dr. Tissot's Method of recovering drowned Persons.   100
The Fortune-Hunter, continued.   101

POETICAL ESSAYS.
Castle Building,   Page 105
Verses addressed to a Young Lady, 106
A Manuscript found among the Writings of the late Benjamin Pratt, Esq; of New-York,   107
Answer to the Rebus in No. II.   ibid
HISTORICAL CHRONICLE.
General History of America.   108
DOMESTIC INTELLIGENCE.
Messages of the Governor, Council and House of Representatives, of the Massachusetts Bay.   110—119
Marriages and Deaths,   120
Meteorological Observations on the Weather.
Governor Hutchinson's History, &c.

With the following EMBELLISHMENTS, viz.
I. The Bust of the Hon. JOHN HANCOCK, Esq; supported by the Goddess of LIBERTY and an Ancient Briton. II. The FORTUNE-HUNTER, a humorous, historical Piece.

A M E R I C A:
BOSTON, Printed by and for I. THOMAS, near the MARKET.
Sold by D. FOWLE, in Portsmouth, New-Hampshire; THOMAS & TINGES, in Newbury-Port; S. and E. HALL, in Salem; J. CARTER, Providence; S. SOUTHWICK, Newport, Rhode-Island; E. WATSON, Hartford; T. and S. GREEN, New-Haven; T. GREEN, New-London; J. HOLT, New-York; T. and W. BRADFORD, Philadelphia; W. GODDARD, Philadelphia and Baltimore; A. GREEN, Maryland; R. WELLS, and C. CROUCH, in South-Carolina.

Left and opposite: Covers of two of the very few magazines issued in American before the Revolution. *Below:* Symbol used by the Boston Weekly Post-Boy.

manuals for specific skilled trades, advice to parents and, as war clouds gathered, the formulas for gunpowder and instructions for making bullets—found ready buyers.

One profitable sideline—in a business that might be called a collection of sidelines—was broadsides. Printed on only one side of the paper, they could be attached to walls, like advertising handbills, for anyone to read. Run off one afternoon and sold by young hawkers the next morning, they often sold out by noon—the fastest return on any investment in the period. Some broadsides, however, had more than ephemeral interest; the *Life and Confessions* of Herman Rosencrantz, who was executed in Philadelphia in 1770, ran through two editions of 2,000 copies each and was in demand for over a month. The low price of broadsides, a penny or two, and the sensational subject matter account for the rapid sale; they reported executions of condemned criminals and their dying remarks, fatal accidents, natural disasters, civil disturbances and scandalous behavior—newsworthy events that seldom appeared in the newspapers. A drawing at the top of the page often gave a visual notion of the event reported. The text was sometimes in ballad form and intended to be sung to a tune indicated below the title, but most survive of those as verse without music because the tunes have long since been forgotten.

In the decade of mounting tension, printers increasingly turned out broadsides of political interest, spreading the word to at least as many people as read Paine's *Common Sense*. Joel Barlow, one of the poets known as "the Connecticut Wits," remarked in 1775 that "one good song is worth a dozen addresses and proclamations." A prime example of the political broadside ballad was "The Rallying Song of the Tea Party"; it was strongly partisan and derisive of the British, and it had the directness and simplicity needed for instant comprehension—for Bostonians, at least, who knew about the raiders' disguise as Indians and where the Green Dragon Tavern was:

> *Rally Mohawks! bring out your axes,*
> *And tell King George we'll pay no taxes*
> > *On his foreign tea;*
> *His threats are vain, and vain to think*
> *To force our girls and wives to drink*
> > *His vile Bohea!*
> *Then rally boys, and hasten on*
> *To meet our chiefs at the Green Dragon.*
>
> *Our Warren's there and bold Revere*
> *With hands to do, and words to cheer*
> > *For Liberty and laws;*
> *Our Country's "braves" and firm defenders*
> *Shall ne'er be left by true North-Enders*
> > *Fighting Freedom's call!*
> *Then rally boys, and hasten on*
> *To meet our chiefs at the Green Dragon.*

As sung to a tune then familiar, the crudity of this ballad would not have been noticeable; but literary excellence was hardly the criterion. Better poetry was being written and some of it was being printed, but for the masses the broadside ballad counted much more. Printers who issued them knew what the public liked and how to reach it.

One writer of hymns reached the patriotic public. William Billings (1746–1800), a lame, one-eyed Boston tanner and composer—a daring composer considering the church music of the day—introduced lively new tunes in his *New England Psalm Singer* in 1770. The most popular was "Chester"; its belligerent words caught on:

Let ty-rants shake their i-ron___ rod, and slav-'ry clank her___ gall-ing chains, We fear them not.___ We trust in___ God, New___En-gland's God___ for-ev-er___ reigns.

By the time the war broke out, it was the closest thing to a national anthem that the Americans had. In 1778, when Billings brought out *The Singing Master's Assistant,* he updated it with added verses:

Howe and Burgoyne and Clinton, too,
  With Prescott and Cornwallis join'd,
Together plot our overthrow,
  In one Infernal league combined.

When God inspired us for the fight,
  Their ranks were broke, their lines were forc'd,
Their ships were Shelter'd in our sight,
  Or swiftly driven from our Coast.

The foe comes on with haughty Stride,
  Our troops advance with martial noise,
Their Vet'rans flee before our Youth,
  And gen'rals yield to beardless boys.

What grateful Off'ring shall we bring,
  What shall we render to the Lord?
Loud Hallelujahs let us Sing,
  And praise his name on ev'ry Chord.

By Word of Mouth

Impossible to document is the oral transmission of news and opinions. Earlier, when colonies were isolated from each other and sections within colonies had little use for each other, the diversity was a barrier to exchange of ideas; but the rapid development of intercolonial business in the 1760s and 1770s and the improved means of travel lowered the barriers. Stagecoaches were classes on wheels, with current events a major subject; and drivers were purveyors of news, telling people in one town what was happening in others. Increasingly, taverns and ordinaries were information centers, where commercial travelers from Portsmouth and Philadelphia and Charleston could talk together over their food and drink.

With each new provocation from England, however, oral communication took on added political overtones. Reports of outrages circulated by word of mouth. Loyalists learned to be discreet as the indignation grew and as news filtered through of angry rebels manhandling friends of Great Britain. The pace accelerated sharply in 1772 with the creation of the Committees of Correspondence, which blanketed the colonies with questions that invited discussion. The dispatch of couriers from one city's rebel group to another's further stimulated the exchange of ideas and the development of plans for integrated action.

The Stamp Act lighted a fuse that was to burn, slowly at first and then more rapidly, toward a bomb of unpredictable dimensions. The British government could have cut the fuse at any time by making a change in policy from repression to conciliation; instead, it fanned the advancing sparks. Communication in all its forms brought the colonials steadily closer together, in mingled dread and exhilaration.

7

The Sizzling Fuse

Until 1765, the people of the thirteen colonies were living in peace, prospering and confident of maintaining their progress, generally contented with their status as British subjects and enjoying broad freedom of action under a permissive administration. They sometimes grumbled about specific conditions, like the scarcity of specie and the curbs on manufacturing; but on the whole they were satisfied. Whatever sense there was of having a separate identity, as Americans, was weak if on the conscious level at all. The English bought what the colonies produced and sold what the colonies could use, in an economic exchange that worked reasonably well. In the long struggle with royal governors for control of internal affairs, elected assemblies had steadily gained ground, but nobody was suggesting eventual self-government.

Then came the Stamp Act. Three acts of Parliament in the two previous years might have alerted the colonists: the Royal Act of 1763, which reserved to the king the disposal of all western lands, and, in 1764, the Sugar Act levying taxes on certain imports and the Currency Act forbidding the issuance of paper money. But the Stamp Act hit harder. It required the purchase of stamps to affix to every legal and business document: contracts, receipts, bills of sale, even the printed banns announcing intent to marry. If the Crown ministers had deliberately tried to annoy and alienate the colonies, they could not have drawn up a more obnoxious law.

The response, immediate and strong, tells us much about colonial character. Men who had never questioned Britain's right to legislate denounced the act and demanded its repeal. Others swore they would not obey it. Patrick Henry gained instant fame with his fiery speech as the House of Burgesses passed the Virginia Resolutions: "If this be treason, make the most of it!" That was in May; by October resentment was so general that nine colonies sent delegates to a Stamp Act congress in New York, which framed other resolutions to forward to London. No earlier British action had prompted such unified action; the colonials realized, for the first time, that separate protests were useless and that only by joining could they hope to influence the authorities in England.

Parliament repealed the Stamp Act early the next year but reaffirmed its right to tax and proceeded with other legislation no less odious. Protests, petitions and resolutions failed. In 1768, inspired by Sam Adams, assemblies began exchanging news and opinions in a circular letter, something like a round robin—one further means of joint action. Ordinary citizens, meanwhile, in neighborhood taverns and on business trips, were exchanging views and building up the spirit of resistance, speaking less and less as colonials, more and more as Americans.

Not all the colonials, however. Many thousands of them saw only chaos and ruin in resistance and looked upon rebellious acts, like the Boston Tea Party, as openly treasonable. The growing tension gave them a label, Loyalists. Most of these people were respected members of their communities until rebel opinion muddied their reputation. They were not the first victims of emotional nonthinking nor were they the last. Tolerance of unpopular opinion, in times of great stress, has never been an American trait.

The Price of Loyalty

Political parties did not exist before the Revolution; they began to form as the war advanced and men looked ahead with hopes of controlling postwar affairs. Earlier, the colonies were too diverse

Cartoon satirizing plight of Bostonians—here being helped by colonials from outside the city—after the British closed the Port of Boston in retaliation and punishment after the Tea Party.

for any such clear division as existed in England between Whigs and Tories, but in the decade between the Stamp Act and the outbreak of fighting, men loyal to Great Britain and advocates of rebellion opposed each other in colonial assemblies and on the streets, in a loosely structured partisan fashion. If they had formed into parties that in any way resembled what developed later, the Loyalist group might not have had to suffer so much.

Allegiance to established government is ordinarily a virtue and disloyalty a crime; but revolutions have a way of upending ordinary values. Where Loyalists were numerous enough, as in New Jersey, which provided six battalions for the British army, or in New York, where housewives cheered Washington's defeat and withdrawal, they could ride out the storm. Where the rebel spirit was dominant and mob action out of control, as in New England cities, no identified Loyalist in the final years of "peace" could be confident of his safety. Many prudently fled before they were forced to, going to England or the West Indies but most commonly to Nova Scotia. Others, less prudent or more optimistic, stayed too long. Some were too stupid or too stubborn to leave and suffered like

M'Fingal in Trumbull's poem. Most lost their civil rights, and the exiles lost their property by confiscation—a rather extreme penalty, when we view it objectively, measuring not the danger that the Loyalists posed but the degree of rebel fury on the eve of the war.

Loyalists, like other people of the period, were a diverse lot. Many were converted to patriots by the "Intolerable Acts" of 1774 that affected all classes; others professed conversion out of simple expediency. Neutrality was useless, for in extremist rebel thinking anyone not *for* rebellion had to be *against* it. Relatively few Loyalists were firm enough in their beliefs and bold enough to defy public opinion by speaking out against the rebels.

One of these was Benjamin Marston, a prosperous Marblehead merchant, a Harvard graduate like his father, a great-great-grandson of Edward Winslow, early governor of Plymouth Colony, and so well regarded, before loyalty became a crime, that he was elected eight times as moderator of the Marblehead town meeting. A biographer describes him as "a man of education and refinement . . . of generous spirit and sanguine disposition; a warm friend, and his resentments not lasting . . . of a vigorous disposition, active mind and habits . . . something of an artist, and something of a poet, equally at home in navigating a ship or laying out a town." But none of this was remembered after he publicly criticized the Continental Congress; Marblehead banished him and confiscated his property, and he fled to Boston. When the British garrison was transferred to Halifax, he went along.

The next summer, homeward bound from a trading voyage to the Caribbean, he was captured by a privateer and taken to Plymouth, where the local Committee of Safety examined him. His account, understandably prejudiced, begins with a list of the committee members:

Opposite: Tavern where plans for the Boston Tea Party were developed. *Right:* British Stamp Act agent being tarred and feathered.

1. *Deacon Tody, Chairman, a true Deacon.*
2. *Captain Weston; he owes his existence to the very people he is now insulting. His wig and head would completely fill a corn basket.*
3. *Deacon Diamond, a pious whining body.*
4. *Mr. Drew, a gentleman with a ragged jacket and, I think, a leather apron.*
5. **** somebody I could not see, he sat in ye dark, and I forget his name.*
6. *Silas Bartlett, a good sort of man, made a fool of to serve the purpose of ye occasion.*
7. *Mr. Mayhew, a simpering how-do-you-do-sorry-for-your-loss kind of body.*
8. *D. Lorthrop, one that has been handsomely and kindly entertained at my home. He can do dirty work.*
9. *Mr. Croswell, a youngish looking kind of a body. These were all met together at Mr. Mayhew's, with one accord, and were all of one mind—so they ordered me to prison.*

In such examinations, Loyalists were denied the benefit of counsel. Old friends arranged Marston's transfer from the local gaol to the home of his brother-in-law, and after three months he was given the liberty of the town; but he was soon asked to leave and returned to Halifax. In 1778, he was again captured at sea by a privateer; this time he was taken to Boston, consigned to a guard ship, but transferred to a friend's house until he was exchanged with a hundred-odd other prisoners. On a visit to the Danish island of St. Croix in 1779, he saw his first cargo of African slaves and was horrified; Massachusetts Loyalists as a group were in the forefront of antislavery sentiment. In 1781, he was captured a third time and taken to Philadelphia, where the Quakers were very kind to him and to other prisoners.

Marston was one of about a hundred Harvard graduates who, as Loyalists, lost their property and citizenship. All told, about two hundred thousand Loyalists fled the colonies or were banished. Few of them were college graduates and people of culture, but most were well above the average in income and social position. It's at least possible that resentment of their success, among the nobodies in the population, had as much to do with their persecution as their identification as Loyalists. An irony here is that men of the caliber of the exiles, rather than the rabble that harassed them, emerged in political control after the war; but in the process America lost many fine people, including some from the oldest, most honored colonial families— Sewalls, Winslows, Saltonstalls and others.

Some Loyalists suffered less than others. One was the Rev. Mather Byles, one of the better poets of the time but more famous as an inveterate punster. When General Knox entered Boston after the British withdrawal in 1776, Byles remarked, "I never saw an ox fatter in my life." The general was not amused. Similar public statements annoyed Byles's congregation at Hollis Street Church, and he was dismissed as pastor. On June 2, 1777, the Boston selectmen tried him, found him guilty of being "an enemy of the United States" and put him under house arrest. When the soldier guarding his front door had to go on an errand, Byles shouldered his musket and marched back and forth in his place. Later, after the guard was removed, Byles said he'd been "guarded, reguarded, and disreguarded." But despite his comic antics, he was as outspoken a Loyalist as any and was particularly contemptuous of rabble-rousers. Watching the thousands of marchers at the funeral of Crispus Attucks in 1770, he spoke bitterly of "that Indian, half negro and altogether rowdy, who should have been strangled before he was born," and he endorsed the sentiment expressed by a friend who

GREEN DRAGON TAVERN

Where we met to plan the Consignment of few Shiploads of Tea.
Dec 16 1773
John Johnson 7 Water Street
Boston Mass. 1773

asked, "Which is better—to be ruled by one tyrant three thousand miles away, or by three thousand tyrants not a mile away?"

Massacre and Tea Party

Compared with other revolutions, ours was relatively bloodless in the first ten years. A good many individual Loyalists were physically assaulted, but few were killed; stripping them, daubing their bodies with tar and covering them with feathers was the usual way of expressing disapproval. The quartering of British troops in Boston gave rise to several incidents; every time there was an altercation, a crowd collected, and tension increased. On the night of March 5, 1770, three or four young men tried to pass through an alley near the Brattle Street barracks, where a sentinel was brandishing his sword and striking with it on the brick walls and stone windowsills. He challenged the young men, but they insisted on passing, and in the ensuing scuffle one of them was slightly wounded in the head. The noise drew thirty or forty people—too many to make a rush up the narrow street. The officer of the day was informed, but meantime bells were ringing and a larger crowd began to gather; some were armed with clubs but mostly they threw pieces of wood, chunks of ice or snowballs at the soldiers, daring them to fire. The soldiers thought they heard the order and fired; three men were killed on the spot, and two died later from wounds. The leader of the mob, Crispus Attucks, was dead.

Well over six feet tall, very strong and known for his reckless courage, Attucks was called a mulatto but was actually more mixed in his racial heritage. His family name went back to John Auttuck, an Indian executed in 1676 for his part in a raid on Medfield, Massachusetts. Black and white strains were introduced later, in what proportions nobody could say. Born near Framingham, Crispus was the property of Deacon William Brown, who lived in that town.

Following the incident, the bodies of Attucks and another out-of-towner lay in state in Faneuil Hall. Three days later separate hearses for four of the victims of what was quickly called the Boston Massacre led the procession to the Granary burying ground, followed by the coaches of distinguished citizens of Boston and a crowd of thousands on foot. The four coffins were put in one grave. All shops were closed, and bells were rung in Boston and neighboring towns. It was said to be the largest gathering of people on this continent up to that time.

Paul Revere, in his engraving of the event (which he sold for "eight pence lawfull money"), exaggerated the horror with copious blood matching the British uniforms and renamed the custom house in the background "Butcher's Hall." No other piece of propaganda had greater effect.

The Boston Tea Party, late in 1773, was more typical of rebel activities. It was well organized and executed, and it was directly related to a specific act of Parliament, the Tea Act that gave a monopoly to the East India Company. Members of several patriotic clubs and numerous outsiders without invitation disguised themselves as Indians, boarded three tea transports in the darkness and systematically dumped their cargo into the harbor. One result was a series of tea parties in other ports, but Boston alone was penalized. Bostonians could easily have raised the money to pay for the tea, but if they had, the propaganda value would have been lost. Defiance had come to mean more, by 1774, than reconciliation.

If the British viewed Boston as the hotbed of rebellion, they were correct. The Committee of Correspondence created there in 1772 was a long-range propaganda machine, skillfully operated. It began by sending letters to New England town meetings. The wording was not inflammatory, but it was strong enough to prompt local discussion of the current situation. After an hour or more of debate, often heated, on the issues suggested by Boston, the town meeting ordinarily elected a committee to draft a reply and set the date for a special meeting to consider the draft and perhaps change its wording before it was posted to Boston. The Committee of Correspondence was less interested in the answers themselves, however, than they were in the expression of opinions that the procedure provoked.

Deacon Brown, who had owned Crispus Attucks, was one of a committee of seven named by the Framingham town meeting to draft its reply; and Deacon Hosmer chaired the comparable committee in Acton. Deacons were numerous in New England, largely because they retained the title, like colonels in Virginia, after their terms in office expired; but a deacon was almost always a man people turned to for important service. Most of the replies drafted by committees and approved for submission were cautious and conciliatory. But once having sent them and then discovering later that even moderate hopes were futile, the townspeople were prepared for stronger stands as the situation worsened.

On the Alert

Franklin's dismissal as deputy postmaster followed an incident related to the colonial tradition of a free press and comparable in modern times to the publication of the Pentagon papers. In his campaign to expose and discredit British officials most hostile to the colonies and to counter their attacks upon himself, Franklin managed to secure a number of official letters written by Governor Hutchinson of Massachusetts. He leaked them through Sam Adams to Boston newspaper editors, who were only too ready to print them. The *Boston Gazette and Country Journal,* for example, began a series of Hutchinson letters on June 5, 1775, with a prefatory excerpt from a note the governor had written in 1773: "I wish you would burn what letters you think may raise a clamor here which I have ever wrote, as we are all mortal, and know not into whose hands they may fall. The world never had more bad men in it; and tho' I have never wrote any thing criminal, yet I have wrote what ought not to be made public."

Nobody would have known that Franklin was responsible for the leak if he had not admitted it in public, to save the reputation of a friend who was charged with the act. How much effect publication of the letters had on colonial readers might be hard to measure, but colonial editors enjoyed a remarkable freedom to print what they pleased. British authorities tried to restrain them but, as in the famous 1735 trial of John Peter Zenger, failed utterly. The war changed the situation, however; Benjamin Edes had to move his *Boston Gazette* out of Boston to Watertown after the Battle of Lexington and Concord, and other newspapers also moved inland, beyond the wrath of British authorities, and kept up their attacks on Great Britain. Printers had been particularly threatened by the Stamp Act, since it specified a halfpenny or penny tax, depending on size, on every copy sold and a shilling tax on every advertisement. Early repeal of the Stamp Act removed this threat, but the editors never forgot it and were alert to every new restriction imposed by Parliament. Several weeklies adopted Franklin's old sketch of a divided snake and the motto Join, or Die, directly under the masthead. William Bradford's *Pennsylvania Journal* devoted the entire first page, the day before the Stamp Act was to take effect, to a tombstone and a tongue-in-cheek farewell to freedom of the press. Other editors adopted a skull and crossbones as a reminder to readers. The opinion editorial had not yet been invented, but pictorial propaganda was no less effective as communication and was perhaps more so at a time of widespread illiteracy.

John Dickinson of Pennsylvania had contributed to the concept of union in his "Liberty Song," issued in 1768:

Then join hands together, brave Americans all!
By uniting we stand, by dividing we fall.

This proved too wordy, however, and was promptly

shortened to the slogan we remember: United We Stand, Divided We Fall. Franklin gave the idea a new twist in 1776, remarking, as he signed the Declaration, "We must all hang together, or assuredly we shall all hang separately."

Twilight of the Governors

On the evening of June 13, 1775, a crowd gathered outside the home of John Wentworth, New Hampshire's last royal governor, demanding the surrender of a dinner guest named John Fenton. Such lack of courtesy, or of respect for authority, was by then not uncommon; governors in other colonies were no less well acquainted with threats and insults and with the rapid waning of their former prestige. Fenton's crime was a speech he had made that morning in the colonial assembly, urging acceptance of the latest British proposals for reducing tension. What he said was mild enough, but things had reached such a stage that any open opposition to the popular will could rouse resentment and invite personal attack.

Fenton at first refused to leave, but when the men outside wheeled a cannon into position and began beating the walls with clubs, he gave himself up. The governor, fearing for his own safety, fled later that night with his wife and five-year-old child to Fort William and Mary in Portsmouth Harbor, where the guns of H.M.S. *Scarborough* provided a reliable cover. It was the end of a thirty-four year family rule in New Hampshire.

Before 1741, the colony had been administered by the royal governor of Massachusetts, but in that year the Crown officials decided to give it a governor of its own and chose a native son, Benning Wentworth. Deep in debt at the time of his appointment, he at once began using his office to gain wealth and power, and he proved so adroit a politician that he held the post for a full quarter-century, longer than any other colonial governor. His portrait by Joseph Blackburn suggests a corpulent Roman emperor. When he resigned in 1767, he was succeeded by his nephew John, who, though quite different in attitude and behavior, in his eight years in office could never untie the knot of family rule that Benning had tied. He tried, for example, to broaden the base of representation in the assembly, but the system defeated him. A major handicap was the makeup of his council; all its members in 1771 were relatives—his own father, four uncles, a cousin and the cousin's father and a more distant relative. All eight, moreover, belonged to the merchant group in Portsmouth that could maintain its economic dominance only by preserving the status quo.

Most New Hampshiremen accepted the situation as long as they shared the profits. In addition to both being governors, Benning and John both served as Deputy Surveyor of the King's Woods; but instead of protecting the forest, Benning was its worst enemy. To oblige his friends and relatives in the Portsmouth oligarchy, he developed a vast timber operation. Contracts with the Royal Navy for masts and spars were lucrative, but in his greed Benning wanted more profit and sold to other customers, in high-handed disregard of British laws. The money rolled in, making New Hampshire prosperous year after year and giving steady work, at good wages, to thousands of lumberjacks, sawyers, teamsters, warehousemen, longshoremen and seamen. Benning won other friends by his lavish grants of public lands, some to English noblemen, and by handing out numerous commissions. He had enemies, especially in the assembly, who hated him but were too few in number to be a threat; he allowed no hostile town to elect a member to the assembly.

Any colonial governor, shrewd enough and unscrupulous enough, might have done as well. The privilege every governor had of making land grants provided an easy method of self-enrichment, for he could grant land to himself or to members of his family. Much more important, in terms of governing, was control of the assembly. In two colonies, Connecticut and Rhode Island, the governors were elected, a signal victory for assembly and citizens. Every governor, however, was expected to abide by both his royal commission, which was read aloud at his elaborate public installation, and his secret instructions, much more detailed; it was seldom easy to heed these conscientiously and at the same time consider local interests. The best governors found ways to satisfy both the London hierarchy and the people; the least competent were quickly replaced. Most governors, even the political hacks and retired generals and admirals, were reasonably competent and conscientious; but what was merely difficult before 1765 became impossible ten years later.

Governors did not always cooperate, or bungled the attempt. When, in 1775, Boston carpenters refused to build barracks for the British garrison, General Gage asked Wentworth to recruit a few. But the man chosen as recruiter was caught by a mob in Rochester and forced to reveal the facts; the alternative would have been demolition of the mansion recently built for the governor near Lake Winnipesaukee. Later, when the militia ignored Wentworth's order to mobilize and disperse the riotous mobs, the governor urgently asked for troops, but Gage had none to spare.

By then the economic picture had greatly changed. In 1764, a mast twenty-four inches in diameter at the base cost a Portsmouth contractor six pounds but could be sold for thirty-five while a thirty-inch mast cost twenty-five pounds and brought seventy-five. Such profits encouraged rivals, especially in Maine, where the forest was virtually unbounded. Canny purchasing agents for the Royal Navy began awarding contracts to men willing to accept a profit of only 100 percent or even less, and, in 1772, the Casco Bay port of Falmouth for the first time shipped out more lumber than Portsmouth. The British government, moreover, had begun enforcing the inspection of lumbering practices, to the indignation of workmen; in 1772, angry lumberjacks and sawyers manhandled a sheriff who struck them as a little too inquisitive. A governor who could not ward off such interference or keep daily wages from slipping, as they did when the profit margin narrowed, no longer deserved support; and John Wentworth, though he was hardly to blame, paid the penalty.

In 1774, several town meetings in New Hampshire—at Dover, Exeter, Greenland, Newcastle and Portsmouth itself—adopted radical resolutions. The chief issue there as elsewhere was being taxed by Great Britain without being given any voice in the matter, but the underlying reason was unquestionably the decline in personal income from the lumber trade—which employed far more men in New Hampshire than agriculture. Disaffection showed up also in the assembly. When Wentworth, in desperation, ordered the assembly to dissolve for refusing to act on his recommendations, it disobeyed the order and met on its own authority in Exeter. Thereafter, until the June night in 1775 when the governor fled, New Hampshire had a dual government—royal rule about to collapse and the illegal assembly seizing the initiative.

Government in Transition

It's one thing to overthrow an established government, and something else again to replace it. In the rebels' favor, the government to be overthrown was an ocean away, with relatively weak means of control, although these were strengthened as resistance mounted by the dispatch of a considerable military force. But the rebels were divided, thirteen ways, while Great Britain was a single power with all the advantages of unitary planning and coordinated effort. The Continental Congress, organized hurriedly and with a bare two years to establish even the semblance of unity, did a remarkable job considering all the odds. No civil service employees stationed throughout the colonies could be instructed to prepare for new conditions; there simply was no intercolonial government before 1774 or any bureaucracy. Instead, there were thirteen distinct jurisdictions, no two organized in exactly the same way and none quite ready to surrender its autonomy to a centralized government.

Yet the transition from colonies to independent states was relatively smooth. The worst troubles —apart from the war itself—came in the final months of royal rule, when governors could no longer demand and get obedience and when lawless mobs roamed city streets to the dismay of governors and substantial citizens alike. Disruption of the courts was particularly serious: Wills could not be probated or property distributed among heirs, debtors had a welcome reprieve while their creditors could not collect what was owed them and indicted men could not be brought to trial. In some colonies the whole system of law enforcement was momentarily at a standstill and civil peace in jeopardy.

With royal government powerless, the only remaining agencies for governmental continuity were the assemblies. Theoretically they could not act independently of the governors, but somebody had to, and they did. The New Hampshire assembly, in order to establish an operative base

227

that would win public support and compliance, declared itself a House of Representatives and adopted a state constitution in January, 1776, six months before the Declaration of Independence. Pennsylvania's assembly followed much the same course, declaring Pennsylvania a commonwealth and repudiating the hereditary proprietorship of the Penn family. After the British seized Philadelphia in 1777, the assembly moved to Lancaster. In New York, where the British controlled only the city and its immediate vicinity, patriot leaders organized a state government in 1777, with George Clinton as first governor and John Jay as first chief justice; the temporary capital was Kingston, up the Hudson River. Massachusetts did not adopt a state constitution until 1780, but the provincial congress governed independently.

Some colonies could not achieve home rule so quickly. In Georgia, Maryland and New Jersey, Loyalists and patriots were too evenly divided, although patriot sentiment was strong enough to elect delegates to the Continental Congress. South Carolina, under the leadership of great merchants and planters including Christopher Gadsden, Henry Laurens and Arthur Middleton, simply converted its assembly into an independent body in March, 1776; it could continue meeting in Charleston because the British were unable to take that city until 1780. North Carolina was politically too chaotic to organize as a state until after the war. Virginia didn't have to make any significant change; its House of Burgesses carried on as usual but with a liberal majority and increased representation from the yeoman farmer class. Delaware, which had never been a completely separate colony, seized the opportunity to cut the remaining ties with Pennsylvania and declared itself a state in 1776.

Especially in outlaw assemblies that defied orders to disband, conservative members insisted on asking how much authority they really had, and how far they could go in passing legislation. The same question was asked in the Continental Congress, and the answer agreed upon there proved acceptable to the assemblies as well; since all were illegal anyway, as long as the British government refused to acknowledge independence, there was no limit to what they could do. That technical point settled, the assemblies, by whatever new names some of them adopted, turned quickly to the really important matter of averting anarchy by restoring the normal functions of government.

Where courts had been suspended, reopening them was among the first needed steps. The former royal judges were empowered to continue if they renounced their ties with Great Britain. Most assemblies acted also to reduce the property qualifications for political rights. New Hampshire, for example, abolished the twenty-pound valuation for voting and extended the vote to every legal inhabitant who paid taxes. Similar reductions elsewhere multiplied the electorate. Other legislation provided for levying and collecting taxes, extending representation to new districts, reapportioning more closely to population, affirming the continuance of the militia, appropriating money for the Continental army and electing delegates to the Continental Congress. No less important were measures to control the growing lawlessness; counties and local communities were authorized to establish Committees of Safety. Where state constitutions were not created, assemblies assumed executive as well as legislative authority.

Much that the assemblies did at this crucial period was only what they had long been doing under the royal governors. If now they were without the guidance of governors, they were also free of their opposition and interference. Long experience in the legislative process eased the transition, and so did the support of responsible citizens. Colonials, accustomed to orderly government, were even readier to accept what their representatives decided than earlier, when decision-making had to be shared with appointed governors. One further help was the elimination of the governor's councils; these had never been too significant, but their very existence, as handpicked advisers of the governors, had been a general irritant. Some assemblies replaced the councils with their own members meeting separately as an upper chamber, producing an early form of our bicameral legislatures.

Among other reforms adopted by most of the assemblies was repudiation of religious preference. Established churches varied in their power, colony by colony, and in effect meant little where there was sectarian multiplicity; but the struggle to disestablish was not always easy; antidisestablishmentarianism was a formidable enemy to religious freedom Anglicans had traditionally enjoyed.

Where local autonomy was strong, as in the towns of New England and eastern Pennsylvania, the transition was hardly noticeable. Since royal government had never reached down to local levels, no change was needed in the political structure; the citizens kept on governing themselves as they always had. Communities had more to do, however. To care for families displaced from the closed port cities, they had to create Committees of Ways and Means; and because some of the strangers were lawless vagrants, a night watch often seemed advisable to protect life and property. With general war a certainty in the immediate future, special tax levies were needed to equip and maintain the quotas for the Continental army. One duty not always appreciated was controlling animosity toward local Loyalists, who, if they hadn't already left town, were usually kept under house arrest.

Men with long experience in self-government had the group ability to handle all emergencies. Good citizens were no more unanimous than they have ever been about how things should be done, but they knew how to settle their differences. Their most immediate concern was neither independence from Great Britain nor emerging nationalism but the preservation of law and order. Mob violence and British reaction had brought urban progress to a virtual standstill; economic life in the small communities could not be allowed to fall apart. Slogans of freedom were fine in their place, and so were civil disturbances aimed at royal governors and tax collectors; but for responsible local leaders, unruly mobs were a greater threat to progress than any number of British troops.

Which carried more weight in the Revolution, ideology or basic economic considerations, is a continuing question among historians; but nobody needs to settle it. Both operated to make the Revolution a success. Ideology or simple ardor or emerging awareness of being American—or all three in combination—made the free agents willing to support the Continental army until the British gave up, while simple prudence encouraged the orderly transition from royal to independent government at all levels. Assuming and enlarging self-government, out of necessity, completed the Revolution in "the minds of the people," nullifying the British notion that Americans could not govern themselves. It wasn't easy, but it was accomplished.

There was still unfinished business, for even with self-government the Americans were not yet independent. The fuse that was lighted in 1765 and sizzling by 1774 had detonated the first bomb at Concord and was burning on toward the greatest explosion in our history, the Declaration of Independence. The Revolution was over, in the minds of the people, but the war to confirm it had to run its long course.

8

The People's War

Right: Franklin's symbolic device from the May 9, 1754, issue of his *Pennsylvania Gazette*—he had used it during the French and Indian Wars to call for union of the colonies. *Opposite:* Title page from a militia manual published in Boston in 1772. The three sketches are from an English book on warfare, widely used and adjusted to their needs by colonials.

It was an odd sort of battle, that April day in 1775, beginning, on the part of the British, as a search-and-destroy expedition and ending as a rout. Its turning point was the formal confrontation at Concord's North Bridge and a single exchange of volleys. But most of the combat that day, on the British march through Lexington to Concord and in the disastrous retreat back to Boston, had been in the "backwoods" method and had succeeded, in the British view, only because the rebels greatly outnumbered the force Gage had assigned. Forays into the countryside were obviously a mistake; henceforth all contacts with the rebels had to be in the open, where British experience would be a distinct advantage.

Gage realized his errors after the battle, but clung to assumptions we can now see were faulty; but so did his superiors in London. The armed rebels in eastern Massachusetts had not fled in panic at first sight of Regulars, as the earl of Sandwich had been positive they would, yet contempt for the colonials as fighters held firm.

On more serious levels, responsible British opinion held that even with numerical superiority, the armed Americans would lack the essentials for military success. The supply of muskets and bayonets, bullets and powder, would soon be exhausted, and the naval blockade of all the ports would prevent their replenishment from abroad. Whatever command structure could be hastily formed would be no match for the British war command, with its long experience. Will to fight, moreover, would dissolve after a few defeats. The Battle of Lexington and Concord was no indication, in British thinking, of military probabilities. Call this fatal overconfidence or put it down to the flaws in military logic that are always abundantly evident, after the event, in every war.

Militia and Minute Men

One costly British error was deprecating the militia tradition that was as old as the colonies themselves. Civilians in Europe were no longer on call for military service, but all able-bodied males in the colonies, from the age of sixteen, were required by law to own a gun and to be enrolled in the militia, a vast citizen army.

All members of the militia had once been "Minute Men," trained to assemble instantly at a given signal, either the beating of a drum or several musket shots. But as the danger of Indian attack receded in the older settlements, the companies gradually lost their battle readiness. About 1740, several colonies set apart a few handpicked units for special training; these were most numerous in Middlesex and other Massachusetts counties close to Boston. They were not officially known as "Minute Men," but the term began appearing in records in 1756, and by 1775, everybody knew what it stood for. The older militia companies continued their decline, while the selected companies, about a quarter of the total, steadily gained in skill and prestige. They comprised the core of armed rebellion until the Continental army could be organized under George Washington. In a real sense they were a military elite, attracting as volunteers the ablest young men in the country.

One of the new Middlesex companies had been authorized by the Acton town meeting in November, 1774; it numbered forty young recruits. Choosing a captain had been easy: the one logical candidate was Isaac Davis, a thirty-year-old gunsmith whose land, a mile west of the Acton meetinghouse, was excellent for drilling and target practice. Most of the youths had never seen a British Regular, but the hope that they soon would counted more than

the eight pence per drill the town had voted to pay them. The drills were held twice a week for three hours. Any member more than half an hour late forfeited his eight pence for the day.

For the young recruits, the enemy was not a government three thousand miles away but General Gage and his redcoats in Boston, twenty miles away, who at any time might act to rob them, as they put it, of even more of their freedoms. Hours of drill in the strange maneuvers that Captain Davis found in war manuals—the parallel ranks alternating their volleys, the lockstep advance, the concerted thrust of sword or bayonet—could become tedious, but they built up confidence. There wasn't much time—a few months only—to bring the company from initial clumsiness to an acceptable level of competence. The people in Acton had no way of knowing that General Gage, in those same months, was trying without much success to train his bored troops in the backwoods method of fighting. Nor were they necessarily aware that throughout the colonies other gawky recruits were preparing for war; the one concern of Abner Hosmer and his friends was the welfare of family and neighbors in Acton and in Middlesex County. The risks, and the possibility of dying, only sharpened the cutting edge of excitement; such worries were for older people, like sober Deacon Hosmer or Captain Davis—or mothers everywhere.

Two Ways of Waging War

The heroics of April 19, some well documented, others in the realm of local and family legend, are cherished in the collective memories of hundreds of old communities. What they tend to obscure is an important fact, one General Gage could not believe possible, that the rebels were well organized. They assembled swiftly, under an effective command structure, and with adequate discipline. The battle was hardly one for the textbooks, but it succeeded. There was even proof, at the North Bridge, that the rustics understood the European method of fighting, while the Regulars could not cope with the backwoods method they had held in contempt.

The first Continental Congress, assembling in Philadelphia in September, 1774, had spent most of its time debating issues and passing resolutions. Before it adjourned in October, it provided for a second Congress the next May if the situation should require it. The events of April 19 removed all doubts on that score.

The delegates were as divided as they had been the preceding fall, with moderates, between the red-hot rebels and the cautious conservatives, in the majority. They reiterated their hope that Great Britain would moderate its course, but at the same time they prepared for the worst. In a few short weeks they performed almost a miracle of improvisation; they created a Continental army, enrolled thirty-five thousand men, appointed one of their own members as commander-in-chief, established a Board of War to direct military operations, contracted with colonial merchants for munitions and supplies, issued paper money to meet the costs, opened negotiations with foreign governments for aid and recognition and began a propaganda campaign to rouse martial enthusiasm in all the colonies. Most of the delegates had served in colonial assemblies and were familiar with parliamentary procedures, but none of them had had any experience in planning for war.

In sharp contrast with the learn-by-doing Congress, the British government was long established, and its military branches, the army and navy, were by 1775 experienced and efficient instruments of national policy. By the early eighteenth century, war had come to be recognized in Europe as a spe-

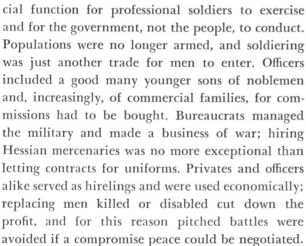

cial function for professional soldiers to exercise and for the government, not the people, to conduct. Populations were no longer armed, and soldiering was just another trade for men to enter. Officers included a good many younger sons of noblemen and, increasingly, of commercial families, for commissions had to be bought. Bureaucrats managed the military and made a business of war; hiring Hessian mercenaries was no more exceptional than letting contracts for uniforms. Privates and officers alike served as hirelings and were used economically; replacing men killed or disabled cut down the profit, and for this reason pitched battles were avoided if a compromise peace could be negotiated.

This pattern was wholly foreign to all colonials except those who had served under British officers in the French and Indian Wars that ended in 1763 and veterans of the Royal American Regiment, formed in 1755 after Braddock's defeat but disbanded by 1775. What remained was the militia tradition, the grass-roots army, maintained for local defense and trained, until war became imminent, in what we now call guerrilla warfare. The British gave it the backwoods label and dismissed it as reliable for repelling Indians or for battles in dense woods but utterly useless for massed frontal assaults, in the

open, that were currently standard in Europe. Such tactics required absolute discipline and long drilling to weld companies and battalions into efficient units. The colonials did not have much chance during the Revolution to use their own traditional method, with individuals acting pretty much on their own initiative, because the British avoided battles with cover. Since the American war aim was to drive the British out, there was no choice but to adopt the European system. Manuals of war described that system and American officers had to study them carefully. One manual published in 1768 had this to say: "No recruit to be dismissed from drill, till he is so expert with his firelock, as to load and fire fifteen times in three minutes and three quarters."

In the months before Lexington–Concord, the Minute Man drilling had been in this kind of fighting. Whether the British Regulars could have adapted themselves to the backwoods style in the same brief period is improbable, but apparently no British general except Gage even considered it. The ability of the Americans to learn the European method suggests a high degree of adaptability and determination. They took open pride, in fact, in beating the foreign professionals at their own game.

In the European battle system, armies faced each other on open terrain, about two hundred yards apart. One might have the advantage of higher ground or of shallow trenches or breastworks and thus be clearly on the defensive; but engagements were just as likely to be without such aids for either side. For a charge, the regiment or battalion formed in two or sometimes three close ranks, shoulder to shoulder, with reserves about six feet to the rear, ready to replace men who fell and left gaps. Each rank in turn fired a volley and had a few precious seconds for reloading. Muskets were hardly lethal at more than seventy or eighty yards, but with so many of them fired at once, and with the volleys five seconds apart, some of the lead balls were certain to hit their targets. The shooting was only a preliminary, however, to the deadlier hand-to-hand combat with edged weapons.

Weapons and Defenses

The chief firearm of the Revolution, used by both sides, was the musket, a sturdy smoothbore shoulder gun weighing about ten pounds, relatively inexpensive to make and easy to fire, if not very accurate. One shortcoming was its tendency to recoil, as John Trumbull observed in *M'Fingal:*

> *But as some muskets so contrive it*
> *As oft to miss the mark they drive at,*
> *And though well aimed at duck or plover,*
> *Bear wide, and kick their owners over.*

The standard musket of the British army was the "Brown Bess," introduced in 1702 and so named

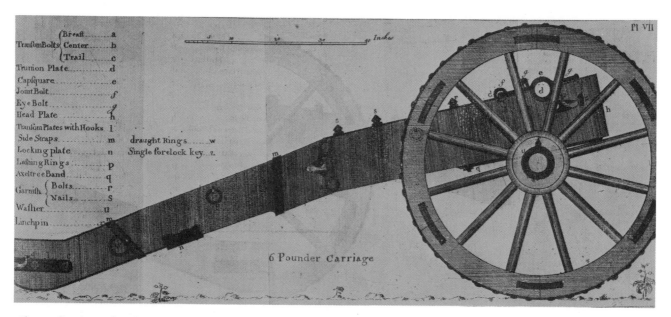

Above: Carriage of a six-pound artillery piece.
Opposite: Canister shot (left) and grape shot (right) of Revolutionary times. Canister works on much the same principle as a shotgun. Grape can go through rows of men.

because the barrel was colored brown by immersion in an acid pickle. The stock was walnut, the mountings were brass and the ramrod, by 1775, was steel rather than wood as earlier. About an inch of gunpowder and then a varying number of lead balls—usually one of the gun's caliber, about three-quarters of an inch, and several of buckshot size—were put in the barrel at the muzzle end and packed down by the ramrod. Pressure on the trigger released the steel hammer with its imbedded bit of flint; the resulting spark ignited the powder, expelling the charge. The flint (which had to be imported from Europe) made the musket a flintlock, much superior to the older matchlock, which required ignition by applying the burning end of a fuse to the powder at the base of the barrel. Both terms, *flintlock* and *matchlock,* though used for the guns themselves, refer more specifically to the firing apparatus, known as the gunlock. An old matchlock gun could be converted into a flintlock gun by changing gunlocks.

The average colonial could afford to own only one gun and ordinarily chose a musket he could use both for hunting and on muster day. The caliber varied from .70 to .75 of an inch, but what troubled officialdom more was the fact that few of them had studs on the barrel to hold bayonets, as British muskets all did. As a result, privates in the Continental army had to be given their choice of a bayonet or a sword, which most of them preferred anyway. Officers favored sabers, curved and with only one cutting edge. Pole arms, about as old as any weapon in the history of warfare, were also quite common in both armies. Sergeants were expected to carry halberds, with a sharp point at the top and, just beneath it, a flat edge in front and a hooked edge in back. Platoon leaders, at the firm insistence of General Washington, entered battle with spontoons, somewhat like halberds but closer to spears. A few infantrymen carried tomahawks, which could just as

well be called light battle-axes except for their Indian origin. Mounted troops, whose heads were vulnerable in close combat, wore metal helmets, hollow hemispheres of brass or iron that were known as skull caps, or the picturesque jockey caps made of heavy boiled leather with metal mountings and topped by a foxtail or a crest of horsehair.

Only a few colonial units corresponded with the romantic image of a ragtag army individually attired and equipped, hostile to discipline but able, by their very independence of spirit and fierce hatred of King George, to outfight the British professionals. In prosaic fact, the chief difference between the armies was the color of their uniforms, blue or almost any other color for the colonies, regiment by regiment, except the bright red of His Majesty's Regulars. Even when a frontier company insisted on buckskin, it was of a uniform cut and color.

Colonial industry was much better prepared than London officials supposed it could be to meet the sudden demands of wartime logistics, turning out uniforms and insignia, boots and spurs, saddles and bridles, knapsacks and saddlebags and cartridge cases, tents and blankets and other camp supplies, as well as weapons and munitions. Not everything was available at once or of good quality; some of it was poor to the point of shoddiness, for there were profiteers in the Revolutionary period as there always have been in wartime. There was only one serious logistical problem, procuring a sufficient number of muskets.

Although every adult male was required to own a gun, not every gun was in good condition. Many were heirlooms, passed along from fathers to sons and in poor shape from long use as hunting pieces. Most were of British make, but the outbreak of fighting cut off the supply from England; the Continental Congress and the Board of War had

Above: Close-up of lock on Towne of Boston musket—"AR" and crown indicate British manufactured during reign of Queen Anne. *Opposite, left to right:* Towne of Boston, Committee of Safety and British "Brown Bess" muskets.

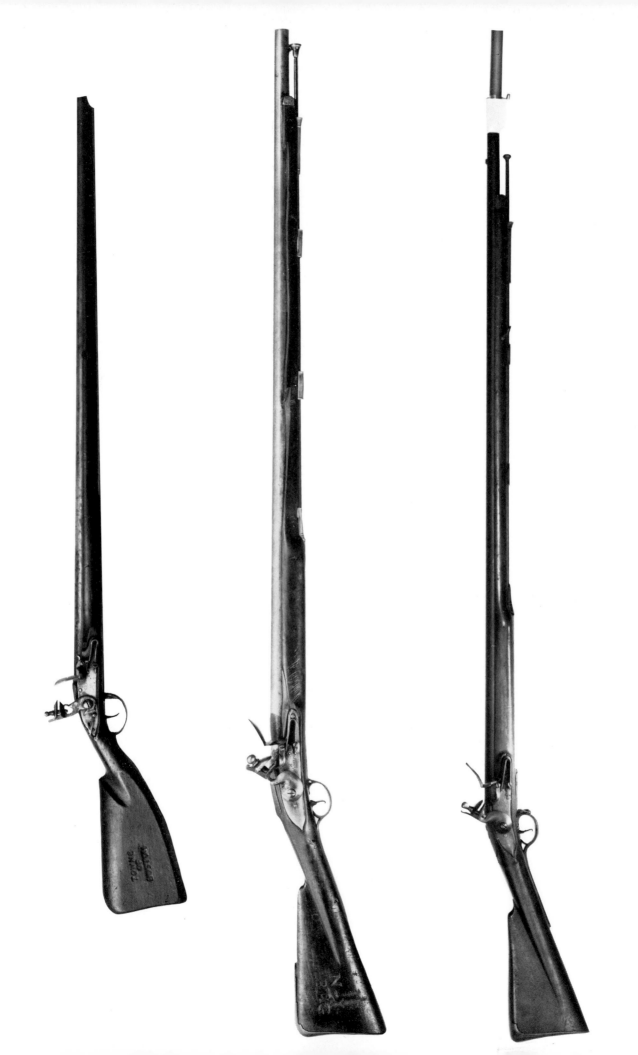

the choice of seeking guns in other countries or expanding domestic gun-making. They did both. They also added to the stockpile by confiscating the contents of British arsenals and by encouraging privateers to waylay and capture British supply ships—the particular ambition of men like John Paul Jones.

Most new muskets, however, came from France. In 1776, Congress sent several agents to Europe to solicit loans and military aid, and some of them were able to secure muskets. Because shipping them direct to American ports was very risky, if possible at all, most of them were sent to Bermuda and West Indian ports for subsequent reshipment to the rebels. The most successful emissary was Silas Deane of Connecticut, who worked out with the French an elaborate method of supplying arms through a dummy corporation known as *Roderique Hortalez et cie*. This ruse was necessary because France, while sympathetic, was not yet ready to enter the war openly.

The Congress, taking no chances of failure in such missions, acted swiftly to speed up local gun production. A resolution adopted November 4, 1775, recommended that each colony contract with gunsmiths for flintlock muskets with a three-quarter-inch bore, a barrel three feet eight inches long, a steel ramrod, a bayonet eighteen inches in the blade and, to discourage profiteering, a fixed price. Massachusetts, the day before, had issued these exact specifications and set the price at three pounds; and most of the other colonies, sooner or later, did what the Congress urged. Guns produced according to specification were called "Committee of Safety muskets," but some of them differed slightly—in barrel length, for example.

Colonies adopted different methods of securing muskets. Connecticut, after May, 1776, resorted to impressing guns from private owners. Rhode Island and New Hampshire, with few gunsmiths of their own to turn to, sent agents to buy muskets where they could; the Salem–Marblehead region of Massachusetts was their favorite hunting ground. New York gave Brown Bess muskets to gunsmiths to serve as models. So did Pennsylvania, but because outsiders bought up most that were for sale in that colony, the assembly was forced to establish its own gunlock factory. Maryland appointed, as inspector at Baltimore, one Thomas Ewing, who proved each gun with an ounce of powder and two balls. If he was satisfied, he stamped his initials on the lock. But he was so exacting, on one occasion rejecting nineteen of a batch of thirty-two from the factory at Frederick, that the Maryland Committee of Safety had to relax its standards or risk running short of guns.

Virginia, one of the first colonies to act, created a gun-repair shop at Fredericksburg in the fall of 1775 and early the next spring expanded its capacity to the making of guns. The Committee of Safety also contracted with private firms, such as the Rappahannock Forge at Falmouth, just north of Fredericksburg. The three colonies south of Virginia, relatively late in joining the war effort and with limited industrial facilities, relied chiefly on privateers bringing in the French guns from Bermuda and the West Indies. But however they were secured, all the muskets used by the colonials in the Revolution, whether old or new or reconditioned, were much alike, closely resembling the dependable Brown Bess of the British army.

"Don't One of You Fire . . ."

The idea of rifling the bore of a gun was not new with the gunsmiths in the Lancaster area of Pennsylvania; it was first tried in fifteenth-century Italy, and by the late seventeenth century it was a widely

adopted practice in mountainous sections of Germany. What the Lancastrians added, in producing the famous "Pennsylvania rifle" in the early 1700s, was a lengthened barrel, better balance and a handsomely decorated stock. Rifling means adding a spiral groove on the inner surface of the barrel to turn the missile in its flight and, like a properly thrown forward pass in football, to give precise direction. The Pennsylvania rifle, known also at a later date as the Kentucky rifle, won world fame for its accuracy at considerable distances. Rifles were harder to make than muskets, less sturdy and more expensive, their chief handicaps being their tendency to foul and the difficulty of forcing bullets down the barrel without damaging the spiral groove. American hunters solved this problem by using balls smaller than the barrel's caliber but wrapped in a greased patch of linen or thin buckskin, thus cleaning the surface with each firing and also checking the escape of gas that reduced the speed and accuracy of the missile. If hard pressed, a rifleman could forgo the patches and fire five or six times in a minute, but at the risk of damaging the rifle.

Most people living along the coast in 1775 had never even seen a rifle. When the war began, frontiersmen were among the first to offer their services, so many of them that the Continental Congress, in its act of June 14, 1775, creating the Continental army, authorized ten rifle companies, two each from Maryland and Virginia and six from Pennsylvania. The fixed quota was 800, but 1,460 men responded to the call and marched from four hundred to seven hundred miles to join the forces assembling at Cambridge under General Washington. En route some of them gave exhibitions at Frederick and Lancaster, and at Cambridge they amazed civilian onlookers with their skill. The repulse at Bunker Hill was attributed,

in official British reports, to the American use of rifles, but this was hardly the case; if the rebel troops had been armed with rifles, there would have been no point in the famous order, "Don't one of you fire until you see the whites of their eyes." Such an order could apply only to men armed with muskets.

In no major engagement of the war except the first, at Concord and Lexington, and the Battle of King's Mountain, North Carolina, in October, 1780, were rifles of prime importance in deciding the outcome; on both occasions the Americans enjoyed the cover of walls and trees. Riflemen were sometimes deployed against Indian allies of the British or as snipers and scouts flanking columns on the march; but most Continental officers shared the British contempt for them, chiefly because loading and aiming took too much time. Gen. Anthony Wayne, called "Mad Anthony" for his hotheaded impetuosity, once remarked that he never wanted to see another rifle, especially one without a bayonet. And a Maryland offer to send a new rifle regiment to Philadelphia was politely declined because of "a superabundance of riflemen in the Army."

Any assertion that rifles won the Revolution is pure fantasy. The military establishment proved too conservative to consider changing the basic pattern of warfare in order to exploit the rifle, and besides, not only were muskets cheaper to make and repair, less complicated for infantrymen to handle and less subject to damage, but the longer barrel of the average rifle could not easily support a bayonet for the close-in combat that climaxed the conventional battle. Benjamin Franklin, acquainted with the rifle but aware that the military mind was stubbornly committed to the musket, urged, tongue in cheek, that the Continental army use bows and arrows instead.

The Quality of Generalship

If the rifle did not win the Revolution, neither did superior generalship. Some generals were more effective than others, or luckier, but none on either side was an outstanding tactician. A good many battles were not so much won by a general as lost by the blunders of his opponent; and some of the generals, Horatio Gates among them, gained honor in one campaign only to forfeit it by a miserable performance in a later one. George Washington was hardly a military genius; he owed his success as commander-in-chief to personal qualities that inspired respect.

Luckily for the Americans the British officers, despite their professionalism, were generally not superior, for the selection process encouraged mediocrity. A man without a nobleman's title or family affluence or powerful friends might hope to become a major or a lieutenant colonel, but command of a regiment was beyond his reach. General Gage was better than the British average, but he let his concern for the politics of preferment blind him to the immediate welfare of his troops in Boston; poorly housed, insufficiently drilled and bored by inaction, they had only scorn for their commander and little interest in their assignment to the colonies.

The colonials, meanwhile, had no professional army and no opportunity prior to 1775 for anyone to gain experience at the top command level. The militia was decentralized; county regiments existed but the effective unit was the local company. This had a certain advantage, however, for there was no general staff to shelter incompetence when the war began or to block the path of promotion. As in subsequent wars, some men with no military experience whatsoever were able to prove their latent capacity for command.

There were no demigods in the Continental army; it only seems so to later generations with their need for national heroes. Men were men as they are today, with traits of strength and weakness and the normal range of ability. No one officer can be singled out as average or typical, but it may help illumine American character, Revolutionary model, to trace the war career of a minor officer, John Trumbull, no relation to the poet of the same name.

With war imminent, Trumbull set about recruiting and drilling an infantry company in his native Lebanon, Connecticut. His credentials were his graduation from Harvard, youngest in his class of 1773, and the fact that his father was governor. Recruiting was no problem; almost everywhere in the colonies there were more volunteers than places for them in new companies. Not until later, when the early enthusiasm wore off, did anyone balk at the low pay. The army that assembled outside Boston in the summer of 1775, eager for action, was a mixture of militia companies and brand new units like Trumbull's, led by captains with no more military experience than the privates.

The Lebanon company, now merged into the First Connecticut Regiment, marched toward Boston and was assigned to high ground from which the young captain, not yet twenty, could sketch the countryside. It was hardly a dangerous location, but when a reward was offered for enemy cannon balls, several recruits lost one or both feet in the attempt to stop them while they were still rolling. Some of Trumbull's drawings were shown to General Washington, who asked for a pictorial plan of the whole area; and Trumbull prepared one. The upshot was an invitation to serve as an aide-de-camp. But instead of making more maps, he had to help entertain visitors, and after nineteen days of socializing and more luxury than he cared for, he requested transfer. Late in life he enjoyed being known as Washington's aide-de-camp, but at the time he found more satisfaction in being promoted to brigade major. His new superior, Horatio Gates, took a liking to him and, within weeks, nominated him for a colonelcy. Majors were paid thirty-three dollars a month, colonels fifty dollars, but the difference in prestige was enormous.

After Gage abandoned Boston in March, 1776, transferring his base to Nova Scotia, Gates and his staff were ordered to the Northern Division anchored at Albany. Trumbull could now observe a new face of war, the abject misery of defeated troops. Memories of the courtly elegance at Washington's headquarters receded fast as survivors of the Quebec defeat straggled into Crown Point and Ticonderoga, hungry, ragged, exhausted, disheartened. Given the job of reporting their condition, Trumbull estimated that of the fifty-two hundred men who got that far, twenty-eight hundred needed immediate hospital care—which the army's medical branch could hardly begin to provide.

Rejection of his proposal to fortify Mount Defiance, just across the Lake George outlet from Ticonderoga, and pique over the delay in confirmation of his promotion led Trumbull to resign from the army in an angry letter to Congress, early in 1777. But in the summer of 1778, he repented and became a volunteer aide-de-camp to Gen. John Sullivan in the Rhode Island war theater. Dreams of glory replaced his desire for promotion; he took needless risks, like galloping past enemy lines within easy musket range, to prove his courage under fire, and before long so overtaxed his strength that he was invalided out of service.

Many officers in the Continental army, to be frank about the matter, owed their appointments more to ambition or prominence than to any military talent. Paul Revere became a lieutenant-colonel in coast artillery because of his prominence in rebel politics. Richard Montgomery, a graduate of Trinity College in his native Dublin, migrated to New York, married the daughter of Robert Livingston and was commissioned a general. The general he replaced, Philip Schuyler, belonged to one of Albany's wealthiest families; he resigned after acquittal by a courtmartial. At the outset, if less so later, social standing was an excellent springboard for top-level command in that people's war for democracy. The planter aristocracy of Virginia produced two generals, George Washington and Henry ("Light-horse Harry") Lee. Benedict Arnold, in contrast, had been a druggist in New Haven; his marriage in 1778 to Peggy Shippen, of a staunchly Loyalist family in Philadelphia, hardly endeared him to the Board of War.

As the war progressed, social prominence counted less than performance. Nathanael Greene, a Rhode Island ironmaster, proved a remarkably competent organizer in his role of quartermaster-general. John Sullivan, famous for his 1779 punitive expedition against Indian allies of the British in the Chemung Valley, left a law practice in Somersworth, New Hampshire, to become an officer. George Rogers Clark of Virginia, commander in Kentucky and other far western regions, had been a surveyor, and the three prominent partisan leaders in the South—Francis Marion (the "Swamp Fox"), Andrew Pickens and Thomas Sumter—were small-scale farmers with a limited experience in Indian warfare.

What solid prior experience and professional competence existed in the upper echelons came chiefly from abroad, in the persons of Lafayette, a marquis who had entered the French army early in life, Kosciusko and Count Pulaski from Poland and, from Germany, Baron von Steuben, Washington's drillmaster and inspector-general, and

Johann Kalb, a self-styled baron who was second in command in the Carolina campaign until he was fatally wounded at Camden. The Continental Congress, it may be noted, dragged its heels before granting commissions to these patriots by adoption. The simple fact is that the Revolution might have failed without substantial help from abroad.

Call to Arms

One question in Massachusetts minds just after the initial battle as to whether men in other colonies would come to their support was promptly answered: from Virginia a commanding general, from the frontier more riflemen than were needed, from almost everywhere new companies and regiments, eager for action. A second question, related to the first, concerned particular groups that lived apart and had the reputation of preferring to be left alone, like the Germans in Pennsylvania. Again, anxiety was unnecessary, for more German-Americans served in the Continental army, in proportion to their numbers, than members of any other group by national origin. Their response may best be illustrated by an incident one Sunday in Woodstock, Virginia.

John Peter Gabriel Muhlenberg, born in Trappe, Pennsylvania, and trained for the Lutheran ministry, became a nominal Episcopalian, as the only way to keep his legal status as a clergyman, when he took the church at Woodstock. But it was Lutheranism that he preached, and his flock was solidly German. On the Sunday in question, shortly after the war began, he turned his sermon into an ardent plea for men to join the rebellion. At the emotional climax, he threw aside his clerical gown to reveal his uniform as a Continental officer, and his listeners rose of their own accord and thundered out the old Lutheran hymn *"Ein feste Burg ist unser Gott."* Within half an hour, 162 members of the congregation were enrolled in the army.

No sector of the population failed to contribute soldiers. Some Quakers defied the dogmatic pacifism of their sect. Jews rivaled the Germans in proportion to their numbers. French and Dutch and Swiss, Scots and Irish, even recent immigrants from England, forgot their mutual suspicions and enlisted. For many it was a chance to work off old hatreds of England; for others it was the means of removing the taint of social inferiority. But whatever the motives, it was a people's army and a people's war.

Life in Time of Crisis

Men in even larger numbers avoided army service, for a different assortment of motives—indifference, cowardice, moral repudiation of violence or unwillingness to interrupt the drive toward success. Tradesmen on the make were particularly opposed to fighting. The economy was dislocated, as in every war, but if some trades were suspended, as they were in the closed port cities, others expanded rapidly, especially those producing military supplies. One for which the war was a welcome stimulus was the making of textiles, which had to be converted rapidly from a very localized operation, in homes or in the shops of custom tailors, to an industry substantial enough to turn out military textiles of many sorts. As part of the determination to forgo imports, just before the war, American collegians wore at commencement clothing of domestic make, most of it handmade; after the war, and because of it, much more clothing was made in factories and sold at retail.

British laws and regulations that had earlier restricted production could now be ignored, a boon to hat-makers and ironmasters and others who had suffered from specific acts of Parliament. Loss of the major foreign market was particularly hard on exporters of raw materials—tobacco, rice, indigo—who could not, like the skilled tradesmen, turn readily to other sources of income. Another obvious casualty was shipping, but an alternate course was possible. The war produced a massive conversion: Skippers became fleet captains, merchant ships turned into floating arsenals and peaceful fishermen assumed the traits of seaborne warriors. The British blockade did not foil the privateers—a dignified term for licensed pirates—but it encouraged the use of small harbors and gave them an importance unknown earlier. Their remoteness created no problem of finding crews, for most experienced sailors lived on farms near the coast and some were always available wherever a privateer might drop anchor. There wasn't much profit in privateering, but it was better than sitting out the war.

It was hardest at the outset, but easier after the French became allies and provided the support of their navy. The numerous Englishmen who persisted in disparaging everything and everyone in the colonies later refused to believe that American sailors could defy the Royal Navy as they did; the crews manning the privateers, they stoutly maintained, must have been Europeans. Some may have been, but colonial seamen were numerous enough by the outbreak of the war, and solidly enough grounded in seamanship, to man the hundreds of privateers that harassed British shipping.

Ocean commerce declined during the war but never halted; the only total loss was trade between the colonies and England. Some of the wealthiest merchants were ruined, not so much because their trading activities were reduced as from their reputation as Tories. A new breed of traders, rebel in sympathy, took their place, and seaborne trade was back close to normal within a year after the Declaration, especially with France and the West Indies.

Rural Americans, except in single-crop Southern areas, were little affected by the war. Loss of income from sales to city markets was not serious for families used to homestead self-sufficiency. For once these people had no reason to envy the urbanites or to begrudge them their cultural advantages. The depopulation of the occupied ports, most drastic in Boston, left most of the largest cities not quite empty shells but places without their familiar noise and bustle and easy profits. Charleston alone lost no population. Newport, in sharp contrast, never regained its commercial importance.

Life in New York was not greatly affected. The British blockade did not force a mass exodus of workmen to the interior, partly because there wasn't a developed interior, like that near Boston, for the unemployed to fall back on. The few patriotic families cut down on entertainment, but the more numerous Loyalists saw no reason to retrench. Rebel hotheads dumped some tea in the harbor, burned the house of the last royal governor, William Tryon, forcing him to retire to a man-of-war at anchor, and exulted when Washington, fresh from his victory in Boston, entered New York in the spring of 1776. He didn't stay long, however; by August, his inexperienced troops, badly mauled by Regulars under Lord Howe, retreated to Westchester County, and the Sons of Liberty watched morosely as Tyron returned to dry land to continue royal government for the rest of the war. When the fighting began, entertainment in New York did not come to a standstill as in other cities, for the occupying British forces and their local Tory friends organized concerts and theatricals. Regimental bands welcomed any opportunity to play for an audience, and English operas and musical farces were staged, indoors or outdoors depending on the season. The mall in front of burned-out Trinity Church became a favorite place for promenading beaus and belles while a military band played amid the gravestones.

British officers and their friends turned out plays that lampooned the rebels. One, the anonymous *Battle of Brooklyn,* delighted Loyalists on Long Island in the summer of 1776. Another was *The Blockade,* written by General Burgoyne during the siege of Boston. The British, of course, could disregard the congressional ban on theatricals. But if patriotic plays could not be acted, they could be published, and two by Mercy Warren, sister of James Otis and wife of the president of the Provincial Congress of Massachusetts, were widely read and did much to sustain morale.

The characters of her first play, *The Adulateur* (1773), were thinly disguised public figures. The bashaw of "Upper Servia" was clearly Governor Hutchinson, and his chief lieutenants were local Tories easily recognized at the time. The "good guys," in revolt against the bashaw's tyranny, can even today be recognized as John Hancock, Sam and John Adams and James Otis. The play reaches its climax when the janizary (General Gage) is ordered to open fire on the citizens, an obvious parallel to the Boston Massacre; and the closing speech, by Brutus (Otis), prophesies civil war and eventual rebel victory. Mrs. Warren's second play, *The Group,* was put on sale the day before the Battle of Lexington and Concord; it has little dramatic action until the point at which the British officials comprising "the group" import a general to act as their hatchet man.

After the British pulled out of Boston, two more plays, of unknown authorship, were printed and sold: *The Blockheads* in 1776, a parody of Burgoyne's *Blockade,* and later *The Motley Assembly,* aimed at Boston's Loyalist families. The ban on plays, imposed to avert trouble at large gatherings, had eliminated one useful instrument of propaganda; but printed plays were a reasonably effective substitute.

The better poets were undeterred by any ban and did much to keep rebel enthusiasm strong. Philip Freneau's reputation, hitherto based on romantic lyrics, was suddenly broadened by two savage satires he wrote in 1775, "General Gage's Soliloquy" and "General Gage's Confession," and by "Emancipation from British Dependence" in which he called the British scoundrels, pirates, banditti and butchers. He described King George as having "a mighty soft place in his head" and as being "the Third of his name and by far the worst fool."

John Trumbull also gained in popular esteem with the first cantos of *M'Fingal,* published in 1776. In one passage he reported the raising of a liberty pole, a common event in rural communities:

And on its top, the flag unfurl'd
Wav'd triumph o'er the prostrate world;
Inscribed with inconsistent types
Of Liberty and thirteen stripes.

The flag thus described was the one General Washington first adopted, known as the Grand Union flag, with the crosses of St. George and St. Andrew where the stars now are. The present design was adopted by Congress on June 14, 1777, the original Flag Day.

Trumbull's weakness, if he hoped to appeal to the masses, was his satiric restraint; he did not lash out violently or stoop to the scurrilous. But Francis Hopkinson, like Freneau, both could and did, in his "Battle of the Kegs." This ballad rose out of an actual event: David Bushnell, famous for designing a submarine to blow up British warships (which it never did), loaded several kegs with explosives and floated them down the Delaware toward a British anchorage. The plan failed, but the furious cannonade from the men-of-war invited derision as a sign of pure panic. Hopkinson's ballad is as fresh today as it was in 1777. The most memorable quatrain was no doubt shocking to a few readers at the time but welcomed by more of them:

Sir William he, snug as a flea,
Lay all this while a snoring,
Nor dreamed of harm as he lay warm
In bed with Mrs. Loring.

The only verses rivaling "The Battle of the Kegs" in popularity were those set to music in the anonymous "Yankee Doodle."

The war was fought over a wide area, yet the life of most communities went on much as usual. Schools functioned normally, but colleges had difficulties. Harvard had to move its operations to Concord for six months but returned in time to give General Washington an honorary LL.D. in May, 1776. Its chief loss was the half ton of lead roofing on Harvard Hall, which was removed by the army and cast into bullets. Princeton suffered far greater damage; located on the main highway between New York and Philadelphia, the campus was alternately occupied by redcoats and rebels, and on one occasion Nassau Hall, serving as a British fortress, was heavily shelled by attacking Americans. Kings College remained in the hands of New York's Loyalists and was renamed Columbia only after the war. Most colleges, however, were strongly patriotic, with the students forming military companies. The drill of the Harvard company was very popular because, when it ended for the day, three or four buckets of rum were passed around. At William and Mary the young president, James Monroe, showed his colors by assuming personal command of the student company. But the great wartime event at William and Mary was not military but academic—the founding

of Phi Beta Kappa on December 5, 1776, the first Greek-letter college society and by all odds the most significant of them all.

"When Peace Yielded to War"

On April 19, 1776, few Americans took time out to recall what had happened just a year before. As a date, its significance would grow only gradually, in retrospect, as the point in time when peace yielded to war. A most uneasy peace it had been, full of hardly bearable tension; and the war was one that began almost by accident, in a large-scale skirmish, with no formal declaration ahead of time and no acknowledgment afterward. But after a year there could be no doubt that the war was real.

For the Hosmers in Acton, for Widow Davis with her four young children, for the families and friends of others killed in that first battle, the anniversary was a day for quiet remembering. But other days of death had come and gone, in an ever-widening circle, and more were certain to follow. One grim day of defiance had spawned a far-flung grimness, with more defeats than victories and no certainty of how it would all end, or when.

The prospects were not good for Washington's army, inadequately trained, not yet hardened by experience and plagued by desertions and unwillingness to reenlist. The conquest of Montreal late in 1775 had been exhilarating, but the joy and hope it raised had been dashed by the debacle at Quebec and by the news that General Montgomery had been killed on the final day of the year. Then in January came Thomas Paine's *Common Sense* with its glowing words about "the seed-time of Continental union, faith, and honor" and its solid argument for independence, so convincing that no one could dismiss it as the aim of the war. About union there could no longer be any question; the people

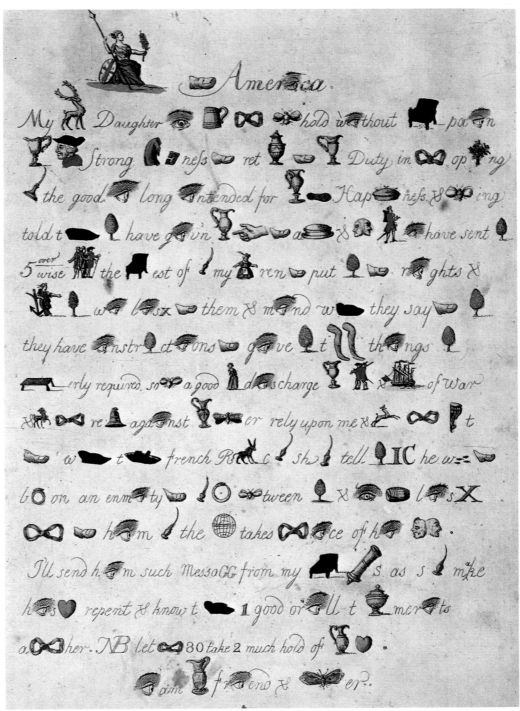

Rebus, "Britannica to America," 1778. For those who do not care to puzzle it out, it reads: "I cannot behold without great pain your headstrong backwardness to return to your duty in not opposing all the good I long intended for your sole happiness and being told that you have given your hand to a . . . and two-faced man I have sent you five over wise men the greatest of all my children to put you to rights and hope you listen to them and mind what they say to you   They have instructions to give you those things you formerly required   So be a good girl   Discharge your soldiers and ships of war and do not rebel against your mother   Rely upon me and do not consult to what that French rascal shall tell you   I see he wants to bring an enmity to all unity between you and I   But listen not to him   All the world takes notice of his two faces   I'll send him such messages from my great cannons as shall make his heart repent and know that one good or ill turn merits another   Note well   Let not . . . take too much hold of your heart

I am your Friend and Mother

were all in this together now, whatever their views or behavior. Honor was an abstraction, hardly worth the loss of years of labor, something of value for gentlemen, perhaps, but not for ordinary people. As for faith, there was little, so far, to give it firm support. George III was a stubborn king, bent on punishing rebels he considered criminals; he would keep the pressure on.

Yet in the year just ended much had happened. It was reassuring to civilians that they could maintain their accustomed way of life with minimal adjustment and sacrifice. Workmen forced from their jobs found employment in new locations. Some trades languished, but others flourished as never before. Institutions, religious and educational, were little affected. The transition of government at all levels from royal to local control was advancing steadily, and irresponsible mob action was subsiding. The port cities were closed, but the country was functioning without them. If independence meant a continuance and expansion of life as it was, for most people, after a year without dictation from London, even the neutrals had to hope for a military victory to cut forever the ties with England.

It was not so easy for the citizen soldiers. Sufficient numbers of them proved their commitment to rebellion by reenlisting, despite the setbacks and the sometimes horrible conditions of unheated camps, wretched food and clothing, dismal field hospitals and martinet officers who meted out punishments for minor infractions—whippings at the stake in a hollow square of troops, running the gauntlet, riding the "wooden horse" with a musket tied to each foot or picketing, which was suspension by thumbs or one arm with a foot just reaching a stake sharp enough to hurt but not so sharp that it pierced the skin. Even worse was the whirligig, a cage that could be revolved so rapidly that its occu-

pant often emerged with mind deranged; but this was usually reserved for notorious camp-followers. To discourage desertion, moreover, a good many sunshine patriots were convicted at drum-head trials and summarily shot.

As for combat, the Continentals disliked the pitched battles in the open but caught on rapidly under the patient guidance of Baron von Steuben, the drillmaster. More important, their behavior under fire totally belied the gross charges that they were cowards, lacking in manliness. They never forgot, those men who stayed loyal and endured so very much, that they were civilians fighting only because somebody had to if the land that was theirs was to continue free. Professionals they were not, but they proved they could stand up to the experienced redcoats and the Hessian mercenaries, and even outfight them.

By 1776, the self-image was far removed from what it had been before the Stamp Act. Dependent colonialism was forgotten; it no longer seemed novel to speak of oneself as an American or to think of far-off people, of many backgrounds and with obvious differences, as Americans too. One final act remained, to announce to mankind the determination to *be* American and no longer dependent on a distant power. That act took place that summer, well into the second year of fighting, when delegates of the thirteen former colonies settled their differences, set aside their remaining doubts and unanimously adopted, on the fourth day of July, 1776, the Declaration of Independence.

The people's war remained to be won, to justify the Declaration and confirm the Revolution, ours to remember and to honor always on the greatest of our anniversaries. None of it was easy, but the Revolutionary generation did it. What later generation has done more?

Index

Acadia (Nova Scotia), 24
Acton (Mass.), 12–13, 224, 232–33
Actresses, 156
Adams, Abigail, 174, 175
Adams, John, 14, 64, 95, 97, 174, 198, 212, 244
Adams, Samuel, 152, 197, 212, 220, 224, 244
Adulateur (Warren play), 244
Advertisements, 212
Agriculture, *see* Rural life
Albany (N.Y.), 21, 145–46
Alcohol, 66–68
Alexandria (Va.), 70
Allen, Jolley, 84
Allspice, 64
Almanacs, 181, 214
American Company, 193–95
American Magazine, 213
American Philosophical Society, 200
American Revolution, events preceding,
    220–47
  Boston Massacre and Tea Party, 223–24
  colonial government and, 225–27
  Franklin and, 224–25
  generalship and, 240–42
  loyalists during, 220–23
  militia and Minute Men preparedness,
    233–35
  outbreak of war, 245–47
  rebel government and, 227–29
  weapons and arms, 235–39
Ames, Levi, 76–79, 97, 103
Amish, 27, 126
Amusements, 68–79
Anabaptists, 162
Anderson, Joseph Horatio, 192
Anglicans, 21, 47, 65, 79–80, 162, 174
Annapolis (Md.), 145, 147, 177
Antes, John, 197
Apothecaries, 88–89, 150
Apple-picking, 82
Apprentices, 46, 129
Architecture and building, 182–85
*Arithmetic: or, that Necessary Art Made
    Most Easy* (Hodder), 54
Armonica, 196, 197, 198
Arms, 235–39
Arnold, Benedict, 80, 241
Artists, 186–93
Attucks, Crispus, 222–23

Bache, Richard, 210
Bachelors, 59
"Baiting," 75–76
Baker, John, 93
Bakers, 150
Baking, 111–12
Baltimore (Md.), 145, 147
Bank drafts, 83
Bankruptcy, 100
Banns, reading of, 60
Barbers, 150
Barker, Francis, 12
Barlow, Joel, 216
Barnes, John, 192
Barns, 127
Barrett, Colonel, 12–13
Bartram, John and William, 200
Bathing, 84, 92
Battle of Brooklyn (play), 244
Bayonets, 236
Beacon Hill (Boston), 57, 182
Bears, 76
Bed-coat, 87
Beds, 40
Beecher, Henry Ward, 65
Beecher, Lyman, 65
Beekman family, 23
Beer, 66
Beggar's Opera (Gay), 195
Bembridge, Henry, 192
Benezet, Anthony, 67
Bernard, Governor, 137
Berrying parties, 82
"Bespoke work," 150
Bethesda Orphan Home (Ga.), 56
Bethlehem (Pa.), 196–97
Bibles, 181
Bickerstaffe, Isaac, 195
Biessel, Conrad, 196
Bigelow, Jacob, 200
Billings, William, 217
Bill of exchange, 83
Births, 40–44
Black stem rust, 124
Blackburn, Joseph, 226
Blacks, 20, 28–32, 162
  See also Slavery
Blacksmiths, 109, 130–35, 148
Blackstone, William, 35
Blanchard, Calvin, 12

Blanchard, Luther, 12
Bleeding, 89
Blockade (Burgoyne play), 244
Blockheads (play), 244
"Bloomery," 131
Body odor, 92
Boiling, 111
Bond, Thomas, 200–201
Bondage, 32–36
  See also Indentured servitude
Book of Architecture (Gibbs), 184
Books, 178–82, 199
Bookstores, 181
"Borning-room," 40–44
Boston, 21, 46, 144–46, 157–61
Boston Chronicle, 211
Boston Evening Post, 75, 211
Boston Gazette, 212, 224–25
Boston Latin School, 47, 57
Boston Massacre (1770), 97, 223–24
Boston Newsletter, 156, 211
Boston Post Road, 204
Boston Tea Party (1773), 204, 223–24
Bowery (N.Y.), 23
Bowling Green (N.Y.), 161
Boy with a Squirrel (Copley), 189
Bradford, Andrew, 213
Bradford, William, 225
Branding, 99
Brandy, 67
Brass, 152
Breakfast, 65
Bremmer, James, 197–98
Brewing, 152
Brewton, Miles, 178
Brick, 157, 160, 184
Brick ovens, 112
Brick Market (Newport), 158
Bridenbaugh, Carl, 185
Bridgeport (Conn.), 146
Brimmer, John, 170
British army, 233–35
British East India Company, 224
British navy, 226–27, 243
Broadsides, 216
Bronson, Oliver, 135
Bronx (N.Y.), 23
Brooklyn (N.Y.), 23
Brooks, Thomas, 56
Brown, Martha, 80

Brown, William, 223–24
"Brown Bess" (British musket), 235–36
Bubonic plague, 92
Buckland, William, 184
Building and architecture, 182–85
Bundling, 59–60
Bunker Hill, Battle of (1775), 239
Burgoyne, John, 244
Burials, 101–105
Burke, Edmund, 16
Burwell family, 128
"Burying rings," 104
Bushnell, David, 244
Button (game), 70
Buttrick, Major, 13
Byles, Mather, 222
Byrd, William, 129
Byrd family, 128

Cabinetmakers, 152, 185
Calinda (dance), 70
Calvert family, 25
Calvinists, 162
Candlemakers (chandlers), 148, 153
Canes, 83
Cape Cod (Mass.), 21
Capes, 83
Carding, 112
Cards, 68
Carpenters, 150–52
Carter, John, 60
Carter, Robert, 31, 56–57, 65, 70
Carter, William, 60
Carter family, 128
Catholics, 21, 162
Cattle breeding, 120, 125–26
Caucus Club (Boston), 212
Caudle, 64
Chaise (carriage), 205
Chariots, 205
Charleston (S.C.), 21, 24, 27, 37, 85, 144–
    45, 147, 160, 161, 228
  schools in, 56
  urban life in, 177–78, 197
Cheese, Marcy, 156
Chesapeake Bay, 147
Chesterfield, Lord, 181
Chew, Justice, 64
Childhood, 44, 88
Children, 40–44, 97 See also Schooling

Chimneys, 111
Chocolate, 153
Christening blanket, 40
Christmas, 79
Churning, 116
Cider, 65, 66, 120
Cities, see Urban life
Clark, George Rogers, 241
Clark, J. Newington, 99
Clinton, George, 228
Cliveden, 185
Clocks, 152
Cloth, 113–16
Clothes, 83–87, 113–16
Clubs, 75
Coach travel, 205–209
Coal, 160
Cocked hats, 83
Cod, 136
Coinage, 82–83
Colden, Jane, 156
Collins, Richard, 192
Colonial governors, 225–27
Comfortier, 66
Commencements, 80–82
Commentaries on the Laws of England
    (Blackstone), 35
Commercial shipping, 137, 148, 243
Committees of Correspondence, 144, 204,
    224
Committees of Safety, 228
Committees of Ways and Means, 229
Common Sense (Paine), 17, 181, 216, 245
Communication and transportation, 204–
    17
  coach and passenger travel, 205–209
  freedom of press and, 210–13
  mail service and, 209–10
  printing and, 213–17
  roads and, 204–205
  word of mouth and, 217
Concerts, 197–98
"Concord Hymn" (Emerson), 108, 140
Conestoga horse, 120, 205
Congregationalists, 23
Connecticut, 21, 37, 46, 146, 226
Continental army, 232, 239
Continental Congress, 16, 227–28, 233
Contraception, 88
Convicts, 35

Cook, Tom, 100–101
Cookbooks, 64
Cooking, 63–66, 111–12
Coopers, 137, 148, 150
Copley, John Singleton, 57, 146, 188–90
Coppersmiths, 135
Corbin family, 128
Corn, 111–12, 124
Cornmeal, 112, 124
Cotton, 116
"Country work," 148
Courts, 97–101, 227–28
Cradles, 40
Craigie House, 184
Cresswell, Nicholas, 70, 128, 172, 208
Crèvecœur, Michel Guillaume
    Jean de, 20, 23, 24, 27
Crime, 96–101, 162–64
Crop rotation, 126
Currency Act (1764), 220
Curricle (carriage), 205
Curriers, 148
Cutlers, 135, 150

Dana family, 24
Dancing, 68–72
Dangerfield, William, 56, 101
Dartmouth College, 58
Davis, Isaac, 12–13, 232–33
Day, Thomas, 30–31
Deane, Silas, 238
Death, 101–105
Death rate, 88
Declaration of Independence (1776), 247
Delancey family, 24
Delano family, 24
Delaware, 21, 146, 157
Delaware River, 21, 24, 228
Dengue (breakbone fever), 92
Dentistry, 93–94
Dickinson, John, 180–81, 212, 225
Dilworth, Thomas, 54
"Disorderly marriages," 60
Divorce, 63
Doctors, 88
Dolls, 68
Douglass, David, 193–95
Draper, Margaret, 156
Dress, 83–87
Drinking, 66–68

"Drinking Song" (Franklin), 67–68
Drugs, 89
Ducking stool, 99
Dummer Academy (Mass.), 57, 68, 82
Duneau, Elizabeth, 56
"Dung-hill fowl," 63
Dunkards, 27
Du Pont family, 24
Durand, 192
Dutch, 23–24, 64, 121, 161–62, 242
Dutch apple cake, 64
Dutch oven, 111
Dutch Reformed Church, 162
Duychinck, Gerardus, II, 192
"Dying Groans of Levi Ames," 76

Earle, Alice Morse, 60
Easter, 80
Eddis, William, 32, 177
Edes, Benjamin, 225
Education, 46–58
Edwards, Jonathan, 59
Election Day, 80
Eliot, Andrew, 103–104
Ellyson, Sarah, 60
Emerson, Ralph Waldo, 108
English, 23, 242
Entail laws, 121, 123–24
Entertainment, 68–79
Ethnic origins of colonial population,
    21–27
Ewing, Thomas, 238

Fairfax, Thomas, 123
Family size, 87–88
Faneuil Hall (Boston), 72, 157, 223
Farming, see Rural life
Farriers, 135
Fashion, 83–87
Father's Legacy to His Daughters (Gregory), 181
Fay, Martin, 198
Feke, Robert, 188
Fenton, John, 225
Festivals, holidays and, 79–82
Finlay, Hugh, 210
Finns, 23–24
Fire departments, 166
Fires, 95–96, 111, 166
Fishing, 116, 136–38

Fithian, Philip, 31, 56–58, 65, 70
Fitzhugh family, 128
Flax, 116, 152
Food, 44, 63–66, 111–12, 166
Four Books of Architecture (Palladio), 182
Fourth of July, 80
Framingham (Mass.), 80, 224
Franklin, Benjamin, 17, 47, 67–68, 75, 85,
    108, 152, 182, 197, 200, 209–10, 224–
    25
Free School Act (1712), 56
Freemasons, 75
Freemen, 36–37
French, 24, 242
French and Indian Wars (1689–1763), 17
Freneau, Philip, 180, 244
Frontiersmen, 85
"Frugal housewife," 63
Fruit, 63, 124
Funerals, 101–105
Fur trade, 152
Furniture, 152, 170, 185–86
"Fustian," 116

Gadsden, Christopher, 228
Gage, Thomas, 14, 226, 233, 240
Gaine, John, 211
Galloway, Joseph, 180
Galwin, Peter, 97
Gambling, 72
Games, 68
Garden, Alexander, 200
Gates, Horatio, 240–41
Gay, John, 195
George III (King of England), 16, 247
Georgia, 21, 125, 147, 228
Georgian architecture, 182–84
Germans (Penn. Dutch), 27, 36, 48, 64,
    80, 120–21, 174, 196, 242
Gibbs, James, 184
Gillingham, James, 185
Ginger, 64
Glass, 152–53
Gloves, 83, 103, 152
Goddard, John, 185
Goddard, Mary Katherine, 156
Godfrey, Thomas, 193
Goldsmith, Oliver, 181
Goldsmiths, 130, 153
Government, takeover of colonial, 227–29

Governors, colonial, 225–27
Gravestones, 104–105
Great Britain, 16, 17, 35–36
Greene, Nathanael, 241
Greenwood, Isaac, 94
Gregory, John, 181
Group, The (play), 244
Guns, 235–39
Gunston Hall, 184
Guy Fawkes Day, 80

Hair styles, 85
Halberds, 236
Hale, Nathan, 55
Hancock, John, 75, 84, 205, 212, 244
Hancock house, 185
Hangings, 68, 76–79, 97, 99
Harbors, 145–48
Harrison, Peter, 157–58, 182–84
Harrison family, 128
Harrower, John, 33, 56–57, 60, 101
Hartford (Conn.), 145
Harvard University, 57–58, 72, 245
Harvey, William, 89
Hat Act (1732), 152
Hatters, 150, 242
Hayward, Deacon, 14
Haywood, James, 14
Health, 87–94
Heating, 111
Henry, Patrick, 220
Heselius, Gustavas, 188
Highway robbers, 208
Hillegas, Michael, 198
History of Sandford and Merton (Day),
    30–31
Hodder, J., 54
Hodges, Richard, 99
Holidays, festivals and, 79–82
Homespun, 116
Honyman, Robert, 204, 208
Hookworms, 92
Hopkinson, Francis, 192, 197–98, 244–45
Hornsmith, 150
Horse breeding, 120, 205
Hosmer, Abner, 12–13, 14, 224, 233, 245
House of Burgesses, 37, 128
House raising, 109
Housewright, 148
Housing shortages, 160

Howe, William, 157–58, 243
Hudson River, 21, 24, 121, 146
Huguenots, 24
Hutchinson, Thomas, 97, 182, 184, 224–25, 244
Hygiene, 84–85, 92

Illness, 87–94
Indentured servitude, 32–36, 79
  children and, 60
  marriage and, 63
Independence Hall (Philadelphia), 172
Indians, 20, 32, 112
Indigo, 125, 243
Ink, 48, 212
Inoculation, 92–93
"Intolerable Act" (1774), 221
Irish, 25–27, 36, 75, 242
Iron Act (1750), 132
"Ironclads," 85
Ironworking, 130–35, 152, 242

Jack, John, 105
Jay, John, 228
Jefferson, Thomas, 57, 180
Jews, 24–25, 162, 242
Johnson, Samuel, 16, 100
Joiners, 148, 152, 185

Kalb, Johann, 242
Kalm, Peter, 25, 93
King's Mountain, Battle of (1780), 239
Kings University (N.Y.), 58, 245
Kittery, 21
"Knippers," 85
Knox, Henry, 222
Kosciusko, Thaddeus, 241

Lamar family, 24
Lancaster (Pa.), 145–46
Land grants, 34
Landau (carriage), 205
Laurens, Henry, 228
Laurens family, 24
Lawrence, William, 99–100
Leaching, 116
Lebanon School (Conn.), 57
Lee, Ann, 156
Lee, Arthur, 200
Lee, Francis Lightfoot, 40

Lee, Henry, 241
Lee, Philip, 70
Lee, Richard Henry, 40
Lee family, 128
Lent, 80
Leprosy, 92
Letter from an American Farmer (Crève-cœur), 20
Letters from a Farmer in Pennsylvania (Dickinson), 181, 212
Letters to His Son (Chesterfield), 181
Lewis Hallam and Company, 193–94
Lexington–Concord, Battle of (1775), 12–14, 232, 239
"Liberty Song" (Dickinson), 225
Libraries, 181–82
Life and Confessions (Rosencrantz), 216
Life expectancy, 88
Light opera, 195–96
Liquor, 66–68
Literature, 178–82
Livingston, Robert, 241
Locke, John, 43
Locksmiths, 152
"Loggerhead," 66
Longfellow, Henry Wadsworth, 206
Lopez, Aaron, 25
Lotteries, 72
Love, marriage and, 58–63
Loyalists, 14–16, 66, 144, 220–23
"Lubbers," 128–29
Lucena, James, 25
Ludeman, John, 61
Ludwell family, 128
Lutherans, 162

Magazines, 213
Mail service, 168, 209–10
Maine, 21
Manhattan, 21, 23, 161
Manors, 121
Marion, Francis, 241
Maritime commerce, 137, 148, 243
Marriage, 58–63, 87
Marston, Benjamin, 221–22
Martin, Alexander, 90–92
Maryland, 21, 23, 25–27, 33, 35, 228
Maryland Gazette, 156
Masons, 148
Massachusetts, 21, 46, 97, 121

Massachusetts Spy, 211
Medicine, 87–94, 200–201
Meng, John, 192
Mennonites, 27, 87
Metal workers, 130–36
M'Fingal (Trumbull), 181, 221, 235, 244
Middleton, Arthur, 228
Midwives, 40, 156
Mifflin, Thomas, 174
Mighty Destroyer Displayed (Benezet), 67
Militia, 232–35
Millers, 148
Miniature paintings, 192
Minute Men, 12–14, 232–35
Mode, Magnus, 99
Monies, 82–83
Monroe, James, 245
Montgomery, Richard, 241, 245
Moravians, 27, 32, 48, 162, 196–97
Morgan, John, 201
Mortality rates, 88
Motley Assembly (play), 244
Mount Vernon, 184
Muhlenberg, John Peter, 242
Music, 196–99
Muskets, 235–39

Names, 40
Narragansett trotters, 120, 205
"Natural children," 60
Nelson family, 128
New Bedford (Mass.), 146
New England Primer, 52–54
New England Psalm Singer (Billings), 217
New Guide to the English Tongue (Dilworth), 54
New Hampshire, 16, 21, 46, 146, 225–27
New Haven (Conn.), 21, 145, 146
New Jersey, 21, 23, 97–99, 146, 152, 228
  ironworking in, 132–33
New Jersey College, 58
New London (Conn.), 145, 146
New Rochelle (N.Y.), 24
New Sweden, 23–24
New York, 16, 21, 95–96, 121, 144–46, 228, 243
  urban life in, 160–70
New York Gazetteer, 211
New York Mercury, 211

Newport (R. I.), 24–25, 144–45, 157–58, 243
Newspapers, 210–13
"Night-watch," 164
"Nooning house," 65
Norfolk (Conn.), 145, 147
North Carolina, 21, 24, 123, 125, 147, 157
Norwalk (Conn.), 146
Norwich (Conn.), 145, 146
Nova Scotia, 24
Nutmeg, 64, 67
Nutmeg holder, 67

Octaroons, 32
Ordinaries, 206
"Ordination beer," 67
Orphans, 55, 100
Orrery, 196, 199, 200
Otis, James, 103, 244

Padlock, The (Bickerstaffe), 195
Page family, 128
Paine, Robert Treat, 40
Paine, Thomas, 17, 181, 199, 212, 213, 216, 243
Painting, 186–93
Palladio, Andres, 182–84
Pamela, 181
Pamphleteering, 180
Paper, 48, 152–53, 212
"Party walls," 161
Pattison, Edward, 136
Paupers, 100
Peale, Charles Wilson, 146, 190
Peel, 112
Pencils, 48
Pennsylvania, 21, 23, 24, 47–48, 83, 228
  German farming in, 120–21, 126–27
Pennsylvania Dutch, see Germans
Pennsylvania Journal, 225
Pennsylvania rifle, 239
Perfume, 84
Perkins, Elizabeth, 154
Peter, John Frederick, 196
Pewter, 135, 153, 170
Phi Beta Kappa, 245
Philadelphia, 21, 24, 48, 85, 92, 144–46
  urban life in, 160, 170–77
Philadelphia College, 58, 201
Philipses, 23

Pickens, Andrew, 241
Pillory, 99
Plague, 92
Plantation system, 121–24, 127–29
Plantation tutor, 56
Plays, 243–44
Plows, 126
Poems on Various Subjects (Wheatley), 180
Poetry, 178–80
Political writing, 180–81
Pope's Day, 80
Population of the colonies, 20–37, 87–88
  of cities, 145
  freemen, 36–37
  indentured servitude, 32–36
  origins of, 23–27
  slaves, 28–32
  statistics on, 21
Porter, Andrew, 48
Portrait painting, 186–90
Ports, 145–48
Portsmouth (N.H.), 21, 144–47
Post office and mail service, 168, 209–10
Poultry, 63
Powder puffs, 85
Powel, Samuel, 182
Prayer books, 181
Preparatory schools, 56–57
Presbyterians, 25, 162
Press, freedom of, 210–13
"Pressed cloth," 116
Pretty Little Pocket Book, 68
Primogeniture laws, 121, 123–24
Prince of Parthia (play), 193
Princeton University, 57–58, 199, 245
Printing, 152, 156, 213–17
Prints, 192
Privateers, 243
Progress of Dullness (Trumbull), 180
Promissory notes, 83
Propertied freemen, 37
Protestants, 25, 80
Providence (R.I.), 145–46
Public hangings, 68, 76–79, 99
Public services, 92
Pulaski, Casimir, 241
Puritanism, 23

Quadroons, 32

Quakers, 21, 47, 48, 85, 144, 162, 196, 242
Quartering of troops, 223
Queens College (N.J.), 58
Quincy, Josiah, 16, 75, 85, 97, 177–78, 197, 208
Quitrent, 123

Rail (rayle), 87
"Rallying Song of the Tea Party," 216
Randolph, Benjamin, 185
Randolph family, 128
Rapalje Children (Durand), 192
Ravenel family, 24
Redemptioners, 32–33
Redwood Library (Newport), 158, 182
Regulators, 178
Religious holidays, 80
Rensalaers family, 23
Revere, Paul, 12, 75, 93–94, 135, 204, 223, 241
Revere family, 24
Rhode Island, 25, 37, 79, 226
Rhode Island College, 58
Rich, John, 195
Richardson, Ebenezer, 97
Rickets, 89–90
Rifles, 238–39
Rifling, 238–39
Rittenhouse, David, 200
Rivera, Jacob, 25
Rivington, James, 211
Roads, 204–205
Robbins, John, 12
Robbins, Joseph, 12
Rogers, John, 60
Roosevelt, John, 170
Rope makers, 137
Rosencrantz, Herman, 216
Royal Act (1763), 220
Royall, Isaac, 188, 189
Royall house, 184
Rum, 65, 66, 152
Rural life, 108–40, 243
  farming competency, 120–27
  fishermen, 136–38
  self-sufficiency of, 108–20
  smiths, 130–36
  spinners and weavers, 138–40
  tobacco farming, 127–29
  tradesmen, 129–30

Rusbatch, Samuel, 192
Rush, Benjamin, 201

Sage, Letitia, 192
St. Andrew's Lodge, 75
St. Cecilia Society, 197
Salting meat, 63
Saltonstall family, 222
Savannah (Ga.), 24, 145, 147
Savannah River, 21
Savery, William, 185
Sawyers, 148
Scabies, 92
Schooling, 46–50, 55–58
Schuyler, Philip, 241
Schuyler family, 23
Schwenkfelders, 27, 48
Scots, 25, 35–36, 55, 57, 242
Scrapple, 64
Scurvy, 92
Sea travel, 208
Seabury, Samuel, 180
Self-sufficiency, 108–20
Serle, Ambrose, 96, 158, 170, 208
Sewalls family, 222
Sewers, 92
Sewing, 84
Shakers, 156
Shaving, 85
Shellfish, 136
Shipbuilding, 130, 152
Shippen, Peggy, 241
Shippen, William, 201
Shippen family, 160, 226–27
Shipping, 137, 148, 243
Shipwrights, 137
Shoemakers (cat whipper), 148
Shoes, 83, 152
"Shoot," 75–76
"Shorter Catechism," 52
Sickness, 87–94
Silversmiths, 130, 153
Simitière, Pierre, Eugène du, 166, 182, 192
Simmons, William, 138–40
Singing Master's Assistant (Billings), 217
Slander, 99
Slavery, 28–32, 63, 70, 79, 105, 125
    indentured servitude, 32–36
    maritime commerce and, 137–38
Sleeping, 40–43, 87

"Small drink," 67
Smallpox, 92–93
Smearcase, 64
Smelteries, 132
Smibert, John, 188
Smith, Sarah, 61
Smith, Sydney, 180
Smith, William, 212
Smith family, 130–36
"Smock marriages," 60–61
Snuff, 153
Soap, 84, 111, 116
Some Thoughts Concerning Education
    (Locke), 43
Songs, 216–17
Sons of Liberty, 75, 144
Sons of St. Patrick, 75, 197
Sora rail, 65
"Soul-drivers," 33
"Sourings," 67
South, 55–57, 123–24, 127–29, 177–78
South Carolina, 21, 24, 27, 34, 37, 125,
    147, 178, 228
Spas, 94–95
"Speech of Death to Levi Ames," 76–79
Spinning, 112–13, 138–40
Spinsters, 59
Spontoons, 236
Stafford Springs, 95
Stagecoach, 205–209
Stamford (Conn.), 146
Stamp Act (1765), 60, 103, 220, 225
State governments, 227–29
Steel, 132
Sterne, Laurence, 181
Steuben, Frederick William von, 241
Stiegel, Baron, 153
Stockings, 83, 99
"Stone-wall," 67
Stowe, Harriet Beecher, 65
Street cleaning, 92
Street lights, 161, 164
"Strenuous medicine," 89
Stuart, Gilbert, 190
Stuyvesant family, 23
Sugar, 63
Sugar Act (1764), 36, 220
Sullivan, John, 241
Sumter, Thomas, 241
"Sunday clothes," 85

Surgeons, 88–89
Swedes, 23–24, 48
Swiss, 24, 242
Swords, 236
Syms-Eaton School (Va.), 56

Tailors, 148
Tanners, 116, 148
Taverns, 66–68, 154, 206–208
Taxation, issue of, 17, 220
Taylor, John, 99
Tea Act (1773), 224
Teachers, 55, 156
Teeth, 93–94
Temple, Sally, 104
Tennant, William, 100
Textile industry, 138–40, 152
Thanksgiving, 79–80
Theater, 193–96, 244
Thomas, Isaiah, 156, 211, 213
Timber, 129–30
Tinkers, 148
Tinsmiths, 135–36, 153
Tobacco, 125, 127–29, 243
Toilet-training, 43
Town development, 121
Towne, Benjamin, 211
Tradesmen, 129–30, 148–53, 242–43
Transportation, see Communication and
    Transportation
Truck farming, 120
Trumbull, John, 57, 180–81. 189, 221,
    235, 244
Trumbull, John, 240–41
Trumbull, Jonathan, 57–58
Tryon, William, 144, 243
Tufts, Henry, 100–101
Tufts, Thomas, 185
Turkey shoots, 68, 75

Unkity Hall, 182
Urban life, 144–201
    of Boston and Newport, 157–58
    building and, 182–85
    furniture of, 185–86
    learned professions in, 199–201
    music in, 196–99
    of New York, 161–70
    painters and artists in, 186–93
    of Philadelphia, 170–77

port cities and, 145–48
problems of, 158–61
of South, 177–78
theater and, 193–96
trades of, 148–54
women in, 154–56
writing and literature of, 178–82

Van Courtlandt family, 23
Venereal disease, 89, 92
Vermont, 16, 21
Verplanck, Daniel Crommelin (Copley), 192
Virginia, 21, 23, 33, 35, 37, 57, 70–72, 123, 125, 228
Virginia Gazette, 60
Voting qualifications, 37

"Walkabouts," 32
Warm Springs, 94
Warren, Joseph, 212
Warren, Mercy, 244
Washington, George, 75, 79, 85, 138, 174, 185, 195, 196–97, 208, 232, 240–41, 243, 245

Water supply, 92, 166
Wayne, Anthony, 239
Weapons, 235–39
Weavers, 113, 138–40, 148
Wentworth, Benning, 225–26
Wentworth, John, 225–27
West, Benjamin, 188
Whaling, 136–37
Wharton family, 160
Wheat, 124
Wheat cradle, 124
Wheatley, Phillis, 156, 180
Wheelrights, 135
Whippings, 99
"Whistle-belly-vengeance," 67
White, George, 208
Whitworth, Abraham, 61
Wigs, 85, 150
William and Mary College (Va.), 56, 57–58, 177, 245
Williamsburg (Va.), 65, 177
Wilmington (Del.), 146
Wine, 63
Winslow, Anna Green, 46–47, 68, 85

Winslow family, 222
Winter, 109
Winterthur Museum, 186
Winthrop, John, IV, 200
Wistar, Caspar, 153
"Wolf rout," 75–76
Wolfe Tavern (Newburyport), 67
Women, 48, 55, 87, 99, 154–56
Wood supply, 109–11, 129–30, 160–61
Wool, 112–13, 138
Word of mouth communication, 217
Work ethic, 44, 92
Wren, Christopher, 184
Writing, 48, 156, 176–82

Yale, 57–58
Yellow fever, 92
Yeoman farmers, 128–29

Zenger, John Peter, 225

Photo Credits

The following photographs were taken by George Fistrovich. Materials used in these photographs were loaned by individuals and organizations whose names appear following the page numbers. Mr. Fistrovich wishes to thank Susan B. Swan for her expert technical assistance in the preparation of the photographs.

Jacket
2–3: William Baldwin, Philip H. Bradley, Inc., Historical Society of Delaware
10–11: The Henry Francis du Pont Winterthur Museum
18–19: William Baldwin, Philip H. Bradley, Inc., Dale E. Hunt, James C, Sorber
26: Mr. and Mrs. Joseph A. McFalls
30: James C. Sorber
31:(top) Historical Society of Delaware

33: Historical Society of Delaware
38–39: The Henry Francis du Pont Winterthur Museum
41: Chester County Historical Society
42: Chester County Historical Society
43:(left) Chester County Historical Society; (right) Historical Society of Delaware
44–45: Chester County Historical Society
50–51: Chester County Historical Society
54: Chester County Historical Society
66: Chester County Historical Society
69: Mr. and Mrs. Joseph A. McFalls
70–71: Chester County Historical Society
71: James C. Sorber
73:(bottom) Mr. and Mrs. Joseph A. McFalls
74: Mr. and Mrs. Joseph A. McFalls
78: Chester County Historical Society
79:(top right) Chester County Historical

Society; (bottom) James C. Sorber
82: Private collection
83:(top) Chester County Historical Society; (bottom) Mr. and Mrs. Joseph A. McFalls
86: Mr. and Mrs. Joseph A. McFalls
87:(both) Mr. and Mrs. Joseph A. McFalls
90: Chester County Historical Society
106–107: Chester County Historical Society
108:(both) Chester County Historical Society
110:(all)
111: Chester County Historical Society
113: James C. Sorber
114:(left) James C. Sorber; (right) Chester County Historical Society
115–19:(all) Chester County Historical Society

131: Private collection
132:(both)
134:(left) James C. Sorber; (right) private collection
135: James C. Sorber
142–43: The Henry Francis du Pont Winterthur Museum
145: Bostonian Society, Old State House
150: Chester County Historical Society
151:(top) The Henry Francis du Pont Winterthur Museum; (bottom) Chester County Historical Society
153: Mr. and Mrs. Joseph A. McFalls
154–55: Private collection
155:(both) Private collection
185: Mr. and Mrs. Joseph A. McFalls
186:(both) Chester County Historical Society
187:(left) Chester County Historical Society; (right) James C. Sorber
199:(top) Mr. and Mrs. Joseph A. McFalls
202–203: The Henry Francis du Pont Winterthur Museum
218–19: M. R. Conner, Richard McCabe Murray
230–31: Historical Society of Delaware
234:(both) Historical Society of Delaware

ALL OTHER ILLUSTRATIONS:
12–13: The John Carter Brown Library, Brown University
15:(top) The John Carter Brown Library, Brown University; (bottom) The Connecticut Historical Society
23: The Henry Francis du Pont Winterthur Museum
24–25: Library Company of Philadelphia
27:(top, both) Bostonian Society, Old State House (photo by Richard Merrill); (center) courtesy Smithsonian Institution; (bottom) Library Company of Philadelphia
28–29: Library of Congress
31:(center) The Baltimore Museum of Art; (bottom) Library Company of Philadelphia
35:(top) Newport Historical Society; (bottom) The New-York Historical Society
36: The Henry Francis du Pont Winterthur Museum
37:(both) Library Company of Philadelphia
46–47: Colonial Williamsburg
49: The New-York Historical Society
52: The New-York Historical Society
53:(top, both) Yale University Art Gallery, Mabel Brady Garvan Collection; (bottom) Rare Book Division, The New York Public Library
58–59: Firestone Library, Princeton University
59:(top) Library Company of Philadelphia; (bottom) American Antiquarian Society
62: American Antiquarian Society
72: The Connecticut Historical Society, Morgan B. Bräinard Collection
73:(top) Library Company of Philadelphia
75: Index of American Design, National Gallery of Art, Washington, D.C.
76:(both) Library Company of Philadelphia
77: The John Work Garrett Library of The Johns Hopkins University
79:(top left) Bostonian Society, Old State House (photo by Barney Burstein)
81: The Historical Society of Pennsylvania
91:(top) Ohio Historical Society, Campus Martius Museum; (bottom) Colonial Williamsburg
92: Bostonian Society, Old State House
94: The Connecticut Historical Society
95: Museum of the City of New York
96:(top) Library Company of Philadelphia; bottom) I. N. Phelps Stokes Collection, Prints Division, The New York Public Library
98: The Historical Society of Pennsylvania
102: Photo by Ann Parker
103:(both) Photos by Ann Parker
120–21: New York State Historical Association, Cooperstown
122–23: Prints Division, The New York Public Library
123: Copy by C. R. Jones from the original in The Concord Antiquarian Society

125: Charleston Library Society
126: Colonial Williamsburg
127: Carolina Art Association, Charleston, S.C.
130: Courtesy Smithsonian Institution
133:(top, bottom left) Courtesy Smithsonian Institution: (bottom right) Bostonian Society, Old State House (photo by Richard Merrill)
138:(top) Peabody Museum (photo by Mark Sexton); (bottom) Courtesy Smithsonian Institution
139:(both) Marblehead Historical Society
140: Courtesy Smithsonian Institution
141: Library Company of Philadelphia
146–47: The New-York Historical Society
148:(both) Library Company of Philadelphia
149:(top right, bottom left) Library Company of Philadelphia; (bottom right) courtesy Smithsonian Institution
158–59: Bostonian Society, Old State House (photo by Richard Merrill)
159: Bostonian Society, Old State House (photo by Richard Merrill)
161: Bostonian Society, Old State House (photo by Richard Merrill)
162–63 Reproduced by permission of The John Street United Methodist Church (photo by Museum of the City of New York)
164–65: Museum of the City of New York
165: The New-York Historical Society
166: The Historical Society of Pennsylvania
167: Museum of the City of New York
168–69: I. N. Phelps Stokes Collection, Prints Division, The New York Public Library
170–71: The Edward W. C. Arnold Collection, loaned by The Metropolitan Museum of Art (photo by Museum of the City of New York)
170: Courtesy Smithsonian Institution
171:(bottom) The Edward W. C. Arnold Collection, loaned by The Metropolitan Museum of Art (photo by Museum of the City of New York)
172–73: The Historical Society of Pennsylvania